Fashioning Celebrity

Eighteenth-Century British Actresses and Strategies for Image Making

Laura Engel

THE OHIO STATE UNIVERSITY PRESS • COLUMBUS

Copyright © 2011 by The Ohio State University.
All rights reserved.

Library of Congress Cataloging-in-Publication Data

Engel, Laura.
  Fashioning celebrity : eighteenth-century British actresses and strategies for image making / Laura Engel.
        p. cm.
  Includes bibliographical references and index.
  ISBN-13: 978-0-8142-1148-9 (cloth : alk. paper)
  ISBN-10: 0-8142-1148-8 (cloth : alk. paper)
  ISBN-13: 978-0-8142-9247-1 (cd)
  1. Actresses—Great Britain—Biography. 2. Celebrities—Great Britain—Biography. 3. Theater—Great Britain—History—18th century. 4. Siddons, Sarah, 1755–1831. 5. Robinson, Mary, 1758–1800. 6. Wells, Mary, b. ca. 1759. 7. Kemble, Fanny, 1809–1893. I. Title.
  PN2597.E54 2011
  792.0'28092241—dc22
                                           2010038010

This book is available in the following editions
Cloth (ISBN 978-0-8142-1148-9)
CD-ROM (ISBN 978-0-8142-9247-1)

Cover design by Mia Risberg
Text design by Juliet Williams

∞ The paper used in this publication meets the minimum requirements of the American National Standard for Information Sciences—Permanence of Paper for Printed Library Materials. ANSI Z39.48–1992.

9 8 7 6 5 4 3 2 1

Contents

List of Illustrations   v
Acknowledgments   vii

Introduction   1
Chapter One   Sarah Siddons's Diva Celebrity   26
Chapter Two   Mary Robinson's Gothic Celebrity   59
Chapter Three   Mary Wells's Notorious Celebrity   98
Epilogue   Fanny Kemble's Inherited Celebrity   135

Notes   149
Bibliography   171
Index   178

Illustrations

Figure 1	Thomas Gainsborough. *Sarah Siddons*, 1785	37
Figure 2	Thomas Gainsborough. *Queen Charlotte*, 1781	39
Figure 3	Benjamin West. *Queen Charlotte*, c. 1779	41
Figure 4	William Hamilton. *Mrs. Siddons and Her Son in the Tragedy of Isabella*, 1785	42
Figure 5	William Beechey. *Mrs. Siddons with the Emblems of Tragedy*, 1793	52
Figure 6	Sir Joshua Reynolds. *Sarah Siddons as the Tragic Muse*, 1784	55
Figure 7	George Romney. *Mrs. Mary Robinson*, 1781	68
Figure 8	John Hazlitt. *Mrs. "Perdita" Robinson after Reynolds*, 1782	70
Figure 9	T. Colley. *Perdito and Perdita—or—the Man & Woman of the People*, engraving published 17 December 1782	73
Figure 10	Anonymous. *Scrub and Archer*, print published 25 April 1783	74
Figure 11	Anonymous. *Florizel and Perdita*, print published 18 October 1783	75
Figure 12	Thomas Gainsborough. *Mrs. Mary Robinson (Perdita)*, 1781	77
Figure 13	Sir Joshua Reynolds. *Mrs. Mary Robinson*, 1784	79

Figure 14	Thomas James Northcote. *Mrs. Wells as Hebe*, 1805	100
Figure 15	John Downman. *Mrs. Wells*, 1792	111
Figure 16	John Downman. *Mrs. Siddons*, 1787	112
Figure 17	Sir Joshua Reynolds. *Selina, Lady Skipwith*, 1787	114
Figure 18	Henry Perronet Briggs. *Fanny Kemble and Her Aunt, Mrs. Siddons*, c. 1830–31	136
Figure 19	Anonymous. *Fanny Kemble, 1809–1893*, from *Harpers's Weekly*, 1893	141
Figure 20	Thomas Sully. *Queen Victoria*, 1838	143
Figure 21	*Fanny Kemble in Old Age* (undated)	144
Figure 22	*Victoria, Queen of England* (undated)	145

Acknowledgments

Fashioning Celebrity originally began as my dissertation at Columbia University. I want to thank my advisors Julie Stone Peters, Jean Howard, and Michael Seidel who encouraged me to go forth with what must have seemed then to be a slightly eccentric undertaking. In the years that followed I gained a tremendous amount of guidance and support from friends and colleagues. I am particularly grateful to the former dean of the McAnulty College of Liberal Arts at Duquesne University, Francesco Cesereo, and the former acting dean, the late Albert C. Labriola, for granting me a pre-tenure sabbatical, and several internal college grants from the Wimmer Family Foundation, the National Endowment for the Humanities, and the Faculty Development Fund, which were all essential to finishing the book. I am also indebted to Christopher Duncan, our current dean, for providing the funds necessary to print the illustrations in the book. Thanks as well to Jim Phillips of the Duquesne University Office for Research for awarding me a Presidential Scholarship Grant to complete revisions on the manuscript.

I am very fortunate to have excellent colleagues in the Duquesne University English department. I want to thank Linda Kinnahan, Anne Brannen, Dan Watkins, and Magali Michael, in particular, for being such exceptional mentors and for believing in this project in its various stages. My students at Duquesne, both undergraduate and graduate, have been a source of great inspiration for me, and I thank them for their energy, enthusiasm, and insight. Thank you as well to Jessica Jost-Costanzo for copyediting the original manuscript and Suzanne Cook for her help with the index. Many thanks to my *superb* readers at The Ohio State University Press, Kristina Straub and Lisa Freeman; their suggestions for revision made the book even better than I imagined it could be. Sandy Crooms and the staff at The Ohio University Press have been a joy to work with from the beginning. Librarians at the Folger Shakespeare Library, the New York Public Library, and The Houghton Theatre Collection at Harvard University were extremely helpful, often going above and beyond to track things down for me.

I am grateful to friends who have lived with this project for many years, particularly, Kari Jensen, Mike Seaman, Allison Colbert, Greg Barnhisel, Corinne Branquet, Dave Guillou, Aimee Curtright, Newell Washburn, Jennifer Defoe, Paul Silver, Julia Laurin, Mary Trull, Adrian Slobin, Jared Smith, Elisa Mantel, Laura Miller, Steve Burt, and Carol Howard. Very special thanks to Marilyn Francus, whose advice, friendship, and shared love of caffeine kept me on track. And to my wonderful family: Elaine Reichek, James Engel, Margery Engel, John Engel, Diana Engel, Maria Engel, Luisa Engel, Barbara Fried, the late Sheldon Fried, and my *boyz,* John Fried, Henry Fried, and Emmett Fried, none of this would be possible without you. Finally, to my father, George Clark Engel Jr. I wish he had lived to see this book become a reality.

A SECTION of chapter 1 originally appeared in my article "'The Personating of Queens': Lady Macbeth, Sarah Siddons, and the Creation of Female Celebrity in the Late Eighteenth Century," in *Macbeth: New Critical Studies*, edited by Nicholas Moschovakis (New York: Routledge Press, 2008), 240–49 and is reprinted here with permission from Routledge Press.

An earlier version of chapter 3 was originally published as "Notorious Celebrity: Mary Wells, Madness and Theatricality" in *Eighteenth-Century Women: Studies in Their Lives, Work, and Culture*, vol. 5 (New York: AMS Press, 2008), 181–205, and is reprinted here with permission from Linda Troost, the senior editor of *Eighteenth-Century Women*.

Introduction

IN THE MIDDLE of Fanny Burney's debut novel *Evelina,* the heroine gets separated from her party at an outdoor concert and is accosted by a group of gentlemen. Hearing her protestations one of the men exclaims, "Heaven on earth! What voice is that?" Another replies, "The voice of the prettiest little actress I have seen this age!"[1] Evelina retorts with horror "'No—No—no—' I panted out, 'I am no actress—pray let me go—pray let me pass.'" Her potential suitor, Sir Clement Willoughby, immediately arrives to rescue her. Assuring the gentlemen that they are "mistaken" about Evelina's identity, he leads her away to safety. Part of Evelina's education in Burney's novel is to learn how to appear to be a respectable lady in polite society. What is interesting about this moment is Burney's idea that for young attractive women the alternative to being viewed as respectable is to be seen as an actress. Although one could read this episode as another example of Evelina's vulnerability and lack of sophistication, it also seems to be equally about the potential threat of the figure of the actress at an historical moment when shifting ideas about femininity contributed to an atmosphere of anxiety about female propriety, circulation, recognition, and representation. Burney poses significant questions in this scene that are central to this study: who is the lady, who is the actress, and how can one tell them apart?

In an era when acting was usually regarded as a suspicious profession for women, late-eighteenth-century actresses were the featured players in a society obsessed with fashion, rumor, and intrigue. Gossip about actresses' affairs and liaisons filled the papers. Scandalous memoirs and biographies circulated in coffeehouses. Caricatures of their extravagant behaviors lined the print shops. Yet, at the same moment, certain actresses had achieved more legitimacy than ever before. They enjoyed a stable income, mingled with royalty and aristocrats, and posed for portraits by the leading artists of the day. *Fashioning Celebrity* considers the lives and careers of four actresses: Sarah Siddons (1758–1839), Mary Robinson (1758–1800), and Mary Wells (1762–1829), with an epilogue on Fanny Kemble (1809–1893). I argue that these actresses used conventions of eighteenth-century painting, fashion, literature, and the theater in their attempts to manipulate the fluctuating tide of public opinion by casting themselves as captivating heroines both on stage and off. By writing memoirs and posing for portraits, they redefined the status of theatrical women, providing a series of techniques for achieving celebrity. While Siddons and Kemble enjoyed enormous success, Robinson and Wells were best known for their notorious attachments, stints in and out of debtor's prisons, and bouts of madness.

In the eighteenth century, as in contemporary culture, the idea of celebrity was tied to narrative possibilities. In other words, celebrity, and particularly female celebrity, materialized through projections of idealized representations of femininity specific to particular historical moments. Eighteenth-century audiences' fascination with actresses suggests that female celebrities had the potential to disrupt, revise, and reinvent traditional models of female identities by calling into question the relationship between authenticity and theatricality central to ideas about desirable femininity both on- and off stage. The public's wish to see female celebrities as both authentic (as "real" women) and theatrical (as seductive stars) maintained an almost impossible standard for female fame. Celebrity culture celebrated actresses' power at the same time that it exposed actresses' vulnerability by positing models of female normality, value, and virtue that female performers could never truly adopt. Thus, the ironic nature of female celebrity in the late eighteenth century was inextricably linked to the production and reproduction of cultural illusions about femininity, ideas that are still operating in the twenty-first century. *Fashioning Celebrity* suggests that eighteenth-century practices of self-representation, created through visual, textual, and theatrical codes, mirror contemporary ideas about marketing, framing, and selling the elusive self. Examining early modes of visual, narrative, and theatrical self-promotion provides a way to chart a history of our contemporary obsession with fame and, more specifically, our preoccupation with the rise and fall of famous women.

The title *Fashioning Celebrity* descends from Stephen Greenblatt's famous phrase, but it also refers directly to the relationship between celebrity and fashion. Both fashion and celebrity can be understood as a series of surface relations where meaning is read through exterior visual codes. This emphasis on exteriority calls into question models of subjectivity that focus on the division between a "theatrical" or surface identity and an "authentic" or real self underneath. For actresses, these two states or "bodies" operate simultaneously at all times. *Fashioning Celebrity* also suggests that actresses had some agency in the shaping of their public images while at the same time their personas were fashioned in many ways already for them by the tastes, desires, and anxieties of eighteenth-century audiences. I use Siddons, Robinson, and Wells as particular case studies of actresses who employed narrative, theatrical, and visual forms of self-representation to design their public images.[2] With a particular emphasis on these actresses' memoirs, I propose an expanded definition of autobiography that highlights the complex relations between theatrical, visual, and textual representations. Actresses' strategies for self-representation in their autobiographical narratives are directly related to the impact of their portraits and their theatrical roles. So much of the actresses' techniques for creating their personas relies on audiences' knowledge of these images and performances as well as their own sense of their self-image as primarily visual.

Fashioning Celebrity explores a significant moment in the history of women and fame, which is a history that until recently has not received enough scholarly attention. Since the publication of Kristina Straub's groundbreaking work *Sexual Suspects: Eighteenth-Century Players and Sexual Ideology*, along with Elizabeth Howe's *The First English Actresses: Women and Drama, 1660–1700*, Shearer West's *The Image of the Actor: Verbal and Visual Representation in the Age of Garrick and Kemble*, and Sandra Richards's *The Rise of the English Actress*, a growing number of literary critics, historians, theater theorists, and feminist scholars have recognized the vital role of theatrical performers in investigations of eighteenth-century culture. Judith Pascoe's *Romantic Theatricality*, Catherine Burroughs's *Women in British Romantic Theatre*, and Betsy Bolton's *Women, Nationalism and the Romantic Stage* established the significance of actresses, female dramatists, and theater critics to the formerly male-dominated realm of Romantic studies. In addition to literary scholarship, studies focusing on portraits of late-eighteenth-century actresses have heightened interest in images of early female celebrities. Gill Perry's *Spectacular Flirtations*, in particular, provides a fascinating analysis of portraits of actresses and the celebrity culture that flourished around their images. Cheryl Wanko's *Roles of Authority: Thespian Biography and Celebrity in Eighteenth-Century Britain* and Mary Luckhurst and Jane Moody's collection, *Theatre and Celebrity in Britain, 1660–2000*, offer frameworks for ongoing research on celebrity culture in the eighteenth century. Both books firmly establish the origins of celebrity culture in the eighteenth century, providing much-needed documentation on the social and economic conditions that made it possible for celebrity culture to flourish. Wanko's discussion of Lavinia Fenton's *Life of Lavinia Beswick, Alias Fenton, Alias Polly Peachum* (1728) and Charlotte Charke's *A Narrative of the Life of Mrs. Charlotte Charke* (1755) focuses on the first half of the century and establishes a compelling background for the later actresses discussed in *Fashioning Celebrity*.[3]

Drawing on these and other important works, *Fashioning Celebrity* takes a new approach to the study of late-eighteenth-century actresses by examining the significance of reading actresses' memoirs (written by themselves), portraits, and theatrical roles *together* as significant strategies for shaping their public images. By emphasizing the importance of reading narratives through visual and theatrical frameworks and visual and theatrical representations through narrative models, I demonstrate the ways in which actresses' identities were imagined through a variety of discourses that worked dialectically to construct their public personas. The book is neither a complete overview of actresses over the course of the eighteenth century nor is it a comprehensive look at the performance history or visual history of each of the actresses represented. Instead, I focus on significant elements of the actresses' lives that relate to the context, creation, and impact of their memoirs, portraits, and particular theatrical roles in order to understand the ways in which certain types of female celebrity materialize and alternatively vanish in late-eighteenth-century culture.

For late-eighteenth-century actresses, fashioning celebrity was based on copying, manipulating, and reinterpreting models of idealized female identities. Audiences expected actresses to be both genuine and extraordinary, a paradox that was directly related to anxieties and fantasies about women in the public sphere. Actresses signified the cultural fantasy still prevalent in contemporary society that women are objects of desire to be possessed, copied, watched, and seduced. The flip side of this fantasy was the anxiety that actresses could use their seductive talents to acquire too much power through their professional achievements and personal liaisons. The threat of women acting outside of traditional roles and codes of behavior was particularly relevant at the end of the eighteenth century when shifting ideas about individual agency were reflected in a tumultuous atmosphere of inevitable social change. Revolutions, an expanding economy at home and abroad, royal instability (George III's madness and his son's transgressions), the rise of print culture, and the unprecedented growth of the theater were just some of the factors that placed actresses, as distinctly public individuals, at the center of shifting ideas about the role of women.

Historically, audiences have been attracted to celebrities for their "real" factor, the idea that the celebrity on stage or on screen is the same person in real life. Felicity Nussbaum has argued: "The highest praise for a star actress in eighteenth-century commentaries was that she consistently became the person she impersonated, alleviating the strain between public and private identity but more significantly between uncertain rank and recognizable status."[4] Borrowing Joseph Roach's concept of "public intimacy," Nussbaum suggests that actresses actively constructed private personas in order to "allow patrons to feel that they 'knew' the actress," which in turn fueled sales of tickets, memoirs, portraits, and the production of celebrity culture.[5] Shearer West, Heather McPherson, and Laura Rosenthal have argued that the appearance of authenticity, the notion that that the actress's persona off stage was linked to her persona on stage, particularly in relation to the remarkable career of Sarah Siddons, is at the heart of what makes a startlingly successful female celebrity. Yet despite the appearance of power in the idea of authenticity, the concept of authenticity is an illusion that masks female agency and the power associated with female performances. When actresses are considered to be "just like us," the skill, professionalism, and power associated with women acting and performing often remains unrecognized.

Actresses, by the very nature of their profession and position in the public realm, can never truly be seen as authentic. Authenticity is more about the audiences' reaction to the actress, in other words their understanding of her celebrity persona, than it is about the actress herself. As Roach argues, "the real disappears" for audiences in favor of the illusion of what they would like the celebrity to be.[6] The actresses in this study manipulate the concept of authenticity in their strategies for fashioning celebrity in several ways. Siddons uses the idea of authenticity to disguise her ambition and to veil the carefully crafted nature of her personas. Robinson uses the concept of authenticity as a seductive tactic and as a ploy for sympathy. By making her "real" persona appear available and elusive, she manages to fashion herself as both seductive and vulnerable. Wells's continuous satire of authenticity, demonstrated by her excessive theatricality, reveals some of the mechanisms behind fashioning celebrity and the paradoxes associated with women, fame, and power. The varying degree to which each actress was able to sustain her celebrity points to the significance of the illusion of authenticity in producing an ideal feminine persona in the late eighteenth century. Actresses' awareness of the significance and ambiguity of authenticity is clear in their strategies for fashioning celebrity in their memoirs and portraits. Memoirs are self-authored and portraits are self-authorized documents of image making, which are interestingly materials that are inextricably linked to claims of truth and memory.

CELEBRITY GHOSTS

Memoirs and portraits are material objects that are particularly connected to the phenomenon of ghosts. In their narrative and visual depictions of specific subjects memoirs and portraits conjure both the presence and absence of individuals who are no longer with us. Marvin Carlson has described the experience of the theater as similarly tied to a haunting sensibility:

> The retelling of stories already told, the reenactment of events already acted, the re-experience of emotions already experienced, these are and have always been central concerns of the theatre in all times and places, but closely allied to these concerns are the particular production dynamics of the theatre: the stories it chooses to tell, the bodies and physical materials it utilizes to tell them, and the places in which they are told. Each of these production elements are also, to a striking degree, composed of material "that we have seen before," and the memory of that recycled material as it moves through new and different productions contributes in no small measure to the richness and density of the operations of the theatre in general as a site of memory, both personal and cultural.[7]

This sense of déja vu, of having been seen and experienced before, is also particularly connected to the actor's body. As Carlson explains, "The recycled body of an actor, already a complex bearer of semiotic messages, will almost inevitably in a new role evoke the ghost or ghosts of previous roles if they have made any impression whatever on the audience, a phenomenon that often colors and indeed may dominate the reception process."[8] Joseph Roach has argued that the aura surrounding a famous actor's body even after his or her death is a significant marker of the effects of celebrity on the culture at large. Discussing the various narratives surrounding the life and death of the eighteenth-century actor Thomas Betterton, Roach writes: "A fiction like 'Betterton' defines a cultural trend in which the body of an actor serves as a medium—an effigy, as I have defined the word—in the secular rituals through which a modernizing society communicates with its past."[9] Celebrity is tied to this notion of the actor's ghostliness. Celebrity can in fact be defined as the degree of impact of the actor's haunting aftereffect on his or her audiences.

Carlson's and Roach's arguments are particularly relevant to my study of fashioning celebrity. For an actress, fashioning celebrity involves calculating the effect of her own performances and appearances on people's memories. In crafting her public image she must strategically imagine how traces of particular versions of herself will haunt the minds and imaginations of spectators. Siddons's, Robinson's, and Wells's strategies for shaping their public images, their projections of how they wished to be remembered, can be found in their memoirs and portraits, which are also connected to the idea of ghostliness. Siddons's and Robinson's memoirs, both published posthumously, can be read as specific musings on how each actress wanted to be remembered after her death, and as detailed records of how they ideally imagined themselves during their lifetime. Just as the theater is a ghostly experience, reading memoirs and viewing portraits are similarly ghostly activities. Reading memoirs conjures the ghost of the subject who is also the author. Portraiture invokes the ghost of the subject, the ghost of the artist, and the haunted traces of the theatrical scene of the portrait being painted.

Carlson's emphasis on the impact of recycling and repetition in the theater; the reuse of theatrical elements, actors, sets, costumes, performance; and the juxtaposition of the familiar with the new also happens in the genres of autobiography and portraiture. Readers of actresses' autobiographies would have expected to find certain generic patterns and tropes in each memoir: a recounting of the actress's discovery, her greatest roles and love affairs, plus information about her most famous triumphs and infamous disappointments. Perhaps even more importantly readers would have expected particularly notable events to appear in specific texts given the reputation of the actress both on and off stage. In order to be successful Mary Robinson's memoirs, for example, need to provide a sympathetic narrative of her scandalous relationship with the Prince of Wales. Sarah Siddons would have been expected to include a version of her triumphant return to Drury Lane after Garrick's initial rejection of her several years earlier. Mary Wells had to account for her lover, Edward Topham's accusation that she was mad and unfit to care for her children. Viewers of portraits of actresses would also have had certain ideas about how the actress should look. These expectations were based on both familiar conventions of eighteenth-century portraiture and on the actress's appearances on and off stage.

In addition, actresses' performances were judged according to comparisons with other actresses in similar roles. This ghosting phenomenon could either work positively or negatively for fashioning celebrity. Siddons's performance of Lady Macbeth, for example, was the standard against which all other Lady Macbeths were evaluated. Mary Wells's deliberate imitations of Siddons in her most famous roles, represents a subversive adoption of the phenomenon of celebrity ghosting. Wells's act of mimicking and parodying Siddons's signature performances exposes the constructed mechanisms behind Siddons's claims to authenticity. Mary Robinson employs yet another ghosting strategy. By relying on her audiences' memories of the visual characters she portrays in her portraits to fashion her varied personas in her memoirs, Robinson, in effect, ghosts herself. For each actress in this study, then, fashioning celebrity involved a negotiation between the familiar and the new. These strategies for fashioning celebrity depended on narratives of desirable and acceptable femininity specific to the late eighteenth century. Actresses' portraits, memoirs, and theatrical roles helped to reinforce these narratives, to build on them and to depart from them. Tracing these actresses' strategies for fashioning celebrity suggests a way of thinking about a performance history of gendered identities both conventional and unconventional.

The actresses in this study capitalized on the shifting nature of representations of femininity in their strategies for fashioning celebrity by employing discourses specific to late-eighteenth-century culture. Siddons's diva celebrity connected her public persona to royalty and maternity, legitimate forms of feminine display. Robinson's Gothic celebrity emphasized the ambiguous boundaries between reality and illusion, embodiment and ghostliness, the past and the present. Wells's notorious celebrity tied her persona to madness, mimicry, and deviance. These discourses surrounding celebrity are about confirming and questioning categories associated with defining the individual subject. Thus, fashioning celebrity highlights the process of formulating individual identities.

Actresses as highly visible and highly constructed subjects can help us to consider aspects of our own relationship to female celebrities and to celebrity culture in general. We are a culture still uneasy about the relationship between women and power, and we are also a culture still obsessed with celebrities. Many of the paradoxes that these actresses faced in fashioning their celebrity still exist today. Taking a closer look at the mechanisms involved in image making can tell us something about our own relationship to celebrity culture and, more specifically, to the haunting and lasting connections among women, fame and power.

LATE-EIGHTEENTH-CENTURY ACTRESSES AND CELEBRITY

In his study of the history of fame in western culture, Leo Braudy suggests that contemporary ideas about celebrity originated in the eighteenth century. Eighteenth-century society's emphasis on the individual, along with the emergence of modern image-making technology, allowed for a degree of self-fashioning that was impossible in earlier periods. He writes: "Eighteenth-century culture introduced the individual to an awareness that his life could be contemplated, shaped and sold. . . . In this world acting and self-promotion abounded. The proliferation of new modes of communication, the breakdown of hierarchy, and the careers now open to talents made it easier to author oneself."[10]

Cheryl Wanko adds to Braudy's definition of celebrity in her study of eighteenth-century thespian biography, *Roles of Authority*. She writes "Celebrity is a form of large scale public attention, customarily labeled 'fame' in previous times. . . . Celebrities differ from the traditionally 'famous' in that they have rarely executed any heroic actions, nor have they been born into a noble or royal class in which such regard naturally accompanies station."[11] The notion that talent could be the reason for success and that one could achieve fame regardless of one's original family status are particularly significant factors in the study of eighteenth-century actresses. For the first time, actresses had the chance to participate in active campaigns of self-promotion. Two primary tools for self-authorship were writing memoirs and posing for portraits. Actresses used these methods to frame and stage their identities and to sell these idealized images of themselves to a wide range of spectators.[12] But with this new access to celebrity a question emerged: Who deserved to be famous and why? In a world of shifting ideals and alliances the dilemma of how one should "appear" was ever present.

The question of how to market oneself effectively was a particularly difficult one for actresses. Actresses could never be regarded as paragons of eighteenth-century femininity because they participated in a profession defined by display and impropriety. Although female performers had been on the British stage since Charles II reopened the London theaters in 1660, acting was still considered to be a questionable profession for women over one hundred years later. In the late eighteenth century, actresses' reputations were still influenced by the same social pressures as the first British female performers. Theater historian Elizabeth Howe's introduction to her study of English actresses during the Restoration echoes many of the ideas in Kristina Straub's study of later eighteenth-century players. Howe explains: "Although the working actress was an exception to the typical domestic female, she was subject to the same ideological constraints and her gender difference was emphasized (and enjoyed) by constant reference to her sexuality both onstage and off."[13] Furthermore, Straub contends, "whereas the discourse of professionalism helped to legitimate actors' 'feminine excesses,' it intensified the contradiction between femininity as a public spectacle and emergent definitions of the middle class woman as domestic and private, veiled from the public eye."[14]

Historically, an actress's "legitimate" reputation was built on the idea of faithfulness to her husband and devotion to her children. Audiences, however, consistently saw actresses as extreme representations of femininity—they were good or bad, comic or tragic, prostitutes or virgins, mistresses or mothers. Spectators consistently blurred the distinctions between an actress's life on stage and her activities in the "real" world, a phenomenon that both helped and hindered the process of fashioning their celebrity. As Deborah Payne has astutely argued, "The fascination with the lives and skills of actresses can be situated at the intersection of civic prominence, virtuoso display, and professional anxiety. Stories about 'stars' are always contradictory, both celebrating upward mobility (the little girl who made it big) and debunking that same mobility (if someone like that could make it . . .)."[15] Interest in actresses' activities off stage was tied to anxieties about the prominent men they were associated with. By the late eighteenth century, some actresses had established themselves as professional mistresses and even wives for royalty and aristocrats. Dorothy Jordan—a well-known comic actress—shared ten children with the Duke of Clarence (only later to be abandoned and left destitute). Harriet Mellon became the Duchess of Albans, and Elizabeth Farren married Lord Derby. Shifting attitudes toward the theater and the role of the actress made this kind of class mobility possible.

In the latter half of the eighteenth century, roles for actresses shifted from the raucous tastes of the Restoration to a more sentimental, moral vein. A new emphasis on Shakespeare, moral tragedies, and sentimental comedies gave actresses the opportunity to appear both desirable and admirable. Actresses became barometers of fashion and style; their portraits were painted by leading artists of the day, including Thomas Gainsborough, Joshua Reynolds, and Thomas Lawrence. Their dresses, hairstyles, and accessories were reviewed, praised, and parodied in the gossip columns. It was suddenly possible to celebrate the actress in legitimate ways that had never previously been permitted.

The latter half of the eighteenth century was known as the age of the actor. Due largely to the Licensing Act of 1737, which allowed only Covent Garden and Drury Lane to put on plays in London, audiences became accustomed to seeing the same actors and actresses perform the same plays again and again. Audiences became familiar with the careers and starring roles of particular actors and actresses, a phenomenon that established a foundation for the celebrity worship that flourished during this period. In order to accommodate the demand for tickets, Covent Garden and Drury Lane expanded substantially during this period. Covent Garden was able to accommodate 2,500 spectators in 1791 while Drury Lane seated 2,300. The

Haymarket Theatre, which was granted special permission after 1767 to show plays during the summer, could seat 1,500.[16]

Actresses became part of an emerging trend. Eighteenth-century players and audiences began to represent a microcosm of a changing society. The growth of commerce and industry produced a class of newly wealthy individuals who mixed with aristocrats, proving that it was possible to move up in the world without the privilege of birth or rank. Actresses like Siddons, Robinson, and Wells were swept up in this tide of class movement. Unfortunately, as quickly as they acclimated to lives of leisure, they could be thrust aside and left with nothing.

The threatening notion that actresses could effortlessly imitate the styles, behaviors, and liaisons of aristocratic women gave rise to disturbing questions about the identity and value of a true gentlewoman. As the nineteenth century grew closer, the influence of a culture of sentiment and sensibility made it increasingly difficult for theatrical women to appear worthy. Novels, plays, and poetry emphasized the importance of a heroine's inner qualities rather than the splendor of her outward appearance. Actresses were caught in a representational dilemma: how could they present themselves as respectable and sympathetic at the same time that their livelihoods were based on theatrical display? Using their access to the public, actresses developed strategies to promote positive images of themselves by employing the tools available to them. They concentrated on three main publicity techniques: print (writing memoirs, novels, poetry, articles), pictures (posing for fashionable portraits by leading artists), and the stage (promoting themselves whenever possible in specific roles that they would be identified with).

As Robyn Asleson has noted, actresses in the late eighteenth century, specifically the period between 1776 and 1812, when Siddons, Robinson, and Wells were at the height of their careers, witnessed an "unprecedented conspicuousness in the public eye."[17] Gill Perry explains that actresses' portraits were a vital part of the "growth of exhibition culture in Britain during the second half of the eighteenth century. . . . The theatrical or 'celebrity' portrait featured prominently in public exhibitions and critical commentaries of the period, especially those which surrounded the Royal Academy shows from 1769 onwards."[18] According to Perry "portraits of well-known figures in Royal Academy exhibitions were viewed by an animated and sometimes unruly public, which compared anecdotal and observed knowledge with the images presented on the walls."[19]

Audiences adored actresses. They clamored for information about their private lives and relished the scandals and intrigues fed by the growth of newspapers, prints, and memoirs. Actors and actresses were the main box office draws, and they became associated with specific roles in which they excelled.[20] Often these parts were inextricably linked to the actors' personas off stage. In his essay, "On the Tragedies of Shakespeare, considered with reference to their fitness for stage representation" (1811), Charles Lamb considers the difference between a reader's identification with a character in a novel and a playgoer's understanding of character, which is formed by the gestures and the expressions of the actor:

> such is the instantaneous nature of the impressions which we take in at the eye and ear at a playhouse, compared with the slow apprehension oftentimes of the understanding in reading, that we are apt not only to sink the play-writer in the consideration which we pay to the actor, but even to identify in our minds in a perverse manner, the actor with the character he represents. It is difficult for the frequent playgoer to disembarrass the idea of Hamlet from the person and voice of Mr. K. We speak of Lady Macbeth, while we are in reality thinking of Mrs. S.[21]

As Lisa Freeman, in her excellent study, *Character's Theater: Genre and Identity on the Eighteenth-Century English Stage,* explains, "Suffice it to say here that in the eighteenth century—the age of the actor—the fictional persona created by the playwright often had to compete with the persona or public reputation of the actor or actress taking that part. In this very basic sense the 'character' presented to an audience was neither singular nor unitary, but rather manifold and incongruous."[22] Audiences' confusion over actresses' private and public personas was fed by a growing print culture that capitalized on the public's fascination with the behind-the-scenes lives of actresses. Newspapers, pamphlets, treatises, memoirs, biographies, portraits, prints, engravings, illustrations, sculpture, and porcelain were some of the ways that actors' images were circulated, bought, sold, and discarded by eager audiences.[23] Public monitoring of actresses focused primarily on their "performances" behind the scenes. Such unflattering portrayals suggested that women making their living on display were at odds with notions of domesticity and privacy central to respectable eighteenth-century ladies. Nonetheless, the theater was a central form of entertainment among the elite, and actors and actresses became a fixture in many aristocratic circles.[24] As fashion plates, objects of desire, and collective fantasy, actresses were at the center of a society where people were judged by the way that they appeared. Eighteenth-century actresses were in charge of selling and marketing their images, a process that involved dangerous negotiations between their private and public personas.

SIDDONS, ROBINSON, AND WELLS

For Siddons, Robinson, and Wells, calculated and misguided visual, narrative, and theatrical public relations strategies helped to both further and destroy their careers. Although these women had very different lives, there are several factors that qualify them as subjects for this study. All three actresses lived at the same time and knew each other. They acted in the same repertoire of plays (although never together). The same audiences saw them. They were critiqued and applauded by the same reviewers and held to the same standards of feminine style and decorum as the aristocratic ladies who alternately admired and despised them.

All three actresses attempted to craft their images through writing memoirs that varied in length and content. At the end of her life, Siddons wrote a thirty-five-page manuscript for her authorized biographer, Thomas Campbell. This handwritten text is an abbreviated autobiography. Mary Robinson wrote four-volumes of memoirs that were published in 1801, a year after her death. Her daughter, Mary, was also a writer and edited the narrative. Unlike Siddons's memoirs, which were in many ways a necessary addendum to her fame, Robinson's story was a last-ditch attempt to gain financial support and literary legitimacy. Robinson had fallen out of favor after her very public affair with the Prince of Wales. Even though she achieved some success as a poet and novelist, her reputation as Perdita ("the lost one") would follow her to her grave. Wells's three-volume memoirs, published in 1811, were similarly a ploy to make money after her lover, Major Edward Topham, accused her of madness. Despite her attempts to restart her acting career, she, like Robinson, died impoverished and alone.

Robinson and Wells wrote their memoirs as final attempts to rescue their already damaged reputations; these texts were meant to explain how and why the actresses lived the way they did. Siddons, however, was an enormously popular celebrity at the time she wrote her memoirs. At the end of her career she was in many ways expected to chronicle the notable aspects of her life in order to signify her position as a famous person.[25] Thus, unlike Robinson and Wells, who had to incorporate aspects of their private lives in order to represent themselves as sympathetic characters, Siddons includes primarily details of her career successes without recording the sadness and disappointments of her domestic life. Despite her emphasis on her professional accomplishments, Siddons still manages skillfully to present herself as a devoted mother. She is aware throughout the memoirs that she must highlight her maternal qualities in order to de-emphasize her power as a performer. Siddons also wrote extensive comments about her understanding of the character of Lady Macbeth, her signature role. These notes are included in her authorized biography by Thomas Campbell, the same text that features her memoirs. Although Siddons does not frame her "Remarks on the character of Lady Macbeth" as a memoir, I argue that the text is directly related to Siddons's creation of her own celebrity and the careful construction of her public and private selves. While both Robinson and Wells tried to present themselves as similarly sympathetic heroines, their scandalous and often bizarre stories overwhelm their attempts to characterize themselves as "ordinary" eighteenth-century women.

In addition to their memoirs, Siddons, Robinson, and Wells were painted by some of the leading artists of the period. These portraits suggest ways of considering how audiences "saw" these actresses and how actresses worked in conjunction with artists to manipulate conventions of eighteenth-century fashion and painting in order to elevate their personas. At the height of their careers, Sir Joshua Reynolds and Thomas Gainsborough completed portraits of Sarah Siddons and Mary Robinson featured in exhibitions at the Royal Academy. A full-length portrait of Mary Wells was the work of Reynolds's assistant and biographer, James Northcote. Numerous prints and cartoons of these actresses by unknown artists also survive. These images depict the actresses in various ways: as ladies, goddesses, theatrical heroines, society belles, and coquettes. Read alongside the actresses' memoirs, the portraits add additional insight into the process of fashioning celebrity using a range of acceptable visual roles played by eighteenth-century women.

Memoirs and portraits are materials that provide direct evidence of these actresses' strategies for fashioning celebrity. They are self-authored and authorized documents, which does not mean that they tell the real story of the actress; rather they suggest some of the ways in which these actresses took charge of shaping their public images. These texts are informed by the materials surrounding them and by the prevailing notions already circulating about the actresses' celebrity status. I am interested in how Siddons, Robinson, and Wells responded to these prevailing ideas and how they promoted particular versions of themselves while also emphasizing the more desirable aspects of their public personas. I am also interested in how the actresses' strategies for self-representation in their memoirs are informed by the identities represented in their portraits and how both genres reflect questions about authenticity that are also crucial to representations of female celebrity.

ACTRESSES' MEMOIRS

The actor's memoir, a genre established by the actor and writer Colley Cibber with his *Apology for the Life of Colley Cibber* (1740), was a perfect forum for the player to justify his/her theatrical career and to introduce the character of his/her "private" self.[26] These memoirs usually began with a section on the actor's childhood, followed by his "discovery" by someone in the theater. A recounting of his greatest roles or moments on stage followed, along with various anecdotes about people of the theater, gossip, and relevant events in the actor's life. Kristina Straub argues that the appearance of actors' memoirs in the eighteenth century was an example of "larger cultural shifts in the social construction of the subject; historians of eighteenth-century culture have often noted the growth of a concern for, and a fascination with, individual character, as evidenced particularly by the rise of the novel with its focus on individual psychology."[27]

Cheryl Wanko proposes, "thespian biographies reflect and participate in the efforts to place performers within unstable hierarchies of cultural, literary, scientific and financial order."[28] This is particularly true for actresses' memoirs. These texts represent a unique contribution to the expanding theatrical market. Women's ability to create and publish their own words became a common practice in the eighteenth century, marking a shift in ideologies about gender; at the same moment that women became increasingly associated with the private and the domestic, they were also more public than ever before.[29] Actresses were a part of this trend but were ultimately trapped by their inability to be true heroines in an ideal eighteenth-century sense.[30] For an actress, writing a memoir that promises to be the true story of her life implies that she is providing evidence of a coherent private identity. One of the elements that characterize the actress's memoir is this attempt to provide the reader with an individual character that is separate from the roles she has performed on stage. Inherent in such a project is the complicated fact that the actress is going public with what she promises to be private information. From the outset, then, actresses' memoirs are a complex project of self-fashioning that changed according to the literary, theatrical, and visual trends of the moment.

Several years ago Thomas Postlewait described the difficulties in categorizing actresses' autobiographies:

> Individually the autobiographies can be quite unreliable. As historical documents, they often fail to describe accurately what happened to the public career and private life of an actress; as narratives, they fail to articulate fully the social significance and personal consciousness of a professional woman in the theater. Accordingly, theater historians are regularly frustrated and misled by what is reported; literary critics are disappointed by the apparent lack of self-examination. Yet collectively—in their literary, rhetorical, and social formulations of identity—these autobiographies may indeed be

profoundly valuable documents, expressing, however obliquely, complex truths about actresses' lives on and off stage.[31]

Since the publication of Postlewait's essay scholars have written primarily about the significance of Charlotte Charke's and Mary Robinson's memoirs from an interdisciplinary perspective.[32] Yet questions about how to categorize actresses' memoirs in general as literary or scandalous, as less or more important than the commentary surrounding the actress, or as similar or distinct from biography or memoirs written by another author still persist.[33] Linda Peterson has argued that eighteenth-century actresses' memoirs or "*chroniques scandaleuses,*" a category typified by the memoirs of actress/authors Mary Robinson and Charlotte Charke, had by the nineteenth century "quietly disappeared or had been transformed into the respectable artist's life."[34] She explains: "With a few notable exceptions. Most memoirs by women authors and artists turn away from the chroniques scandaleuses, with its association of women's self-writing with indecorous self-display, even prostitution, and embrace instead the genre of the domestic memoir."[35] While it may be the case that nineteenth-century female professionals employed domestic tropes and strategies to characterize their private and public lives, it is problematic to characterize eighteenth-century actresses' memoirs as primarily defined by the generic conventions of the *chroniques scandaleuses.* In fact, as my analysis will demonstrate, writing that is associated with "indecorous self-display" (a notion ascribed to almost all the women who made their living on stage in the eighteenth century) can also be inextricably tied to issues of domesticity and professionalism, the same concerns that dominate later memoirs by notable Victorian women. Rather than dismissing eighteenth-century actresses' memoirs under the category of "scandalous," I contend that it is important to go back and reexamine at the specifics of these texts so that we can begin to re-imagine and reassess eighteenth-century actresses' memoirs as a genre that includes a variety of approaches and literary strategies. Indeed as Jacky Bratton has powerfully suggested about theatrical memoirs in her study of the discipline of theatre history, "There is, I would suggest, a world of historical meaning in what they say about themselves, whether or not we have tangible proof of its truth. This does not mean, of course, that such statements should be taken at face value; rather that the testing and probing to which we should subject them should always be aimed at understanding who said what and why, within the context of their own perception of their world."[36]

Theoretical analyses deriving from the study of actresses' memoirs have suggested that the actress as writer is the ideal representative of postmodern female subjectivity.[37] The actress as writer and subject of her own writings is always performing, masquerading, and enacting her gendered self—proof that there is no such thing as an essential or authentic subject. What becomes doubly complicated in the study of actresses' writings is how to account for the "real"—the historical beings who created these unusual documents often under terrible conditions, while their bodies were ill and fading. I do not want to suggest that reading actresses' memoirs can uncover or reveal the "true" self of the actress in any way, but I do think it is important to acknowledge that the fragments or traces of the many selves that the actresses leave behind in attempting to fashion their celebrity were at some point part of living, breathing beings. Part of our access to the historical trace of their "actual" bodies is in the idealized representations of them in their portraits.

POSING IN STYLE: FASHION AND PORTRAITURE

At the time that Charlotte Charke published the first memoirs by an actress in 1755, journalistic criticism, the print trade, and the market for oil paintings substantially increased. These forms of public image making, easily accessible to audiences, coincided with efforts by the actor/theater manager, David Garrick, to elevate the professional and social status of the actor. It was Garrick who demonstrated that one could be both a gentleman and a theatrical performer. Garrick set a precedent for the fashioning of celebrity and the association between actors and aristocrats, particularly in the area of portraiture. He accomplished this feat through brilliant marketing strategies, one of which was the practice of having his portrait painted by well-known artists.[38]

As the popularity of actors and actresses grew, so did the demand for images of them. Artists and actors mutually benefited from these portraits; the actor gained exposure, and the artist profited from the audience's desire to own images of their favorite performers.[39] By the late eighteenth century, the same artists using similar iconography were painting actors and gentry. These similarities promoted the idea that aristocrats and actors, in effect, shared the same stage. When Siddons reached the height of her career, she did not have to commission portraits of herself; a willing viewer assumed the expense.[40] This was not the case for other actresses, such as Mary Robinson, who were less successful. As we will see, Robinson commissioned several portraits of herself to promote her image.

What emerges in the latter half of the eighteenth century are the effects of portraiture in promoting comparisons between aristocracy and actors. Both aristocrats and actors were having their portraits painted by the same artists, often striking the same poses in similar costumes. Most theatrical portraits did not include theatrical elements. Instead the artist depicted just the actor him/herself, at times including specific visual indicators of his/her career on the stage. West writes: "The relative dearth of images which show the stage itself, or rarer still, the audience, should be balanced against the glut of single and double figure actor portraits."[41]

For all sitters, having one's portrait painted was a kind of theatrical event. A visit to the artist's studio involved settling on a particular costume and pose that would flatter the subject and promote the goal of the portrait. Participating in the visual sign system of the upper class through portraits and fashions gave actresses a chance to engage in acceptable forms of display and spectacle off stage. Actresses used signifiers of clothing, both in and out of the theater, to assume different personas. Because of their high visibility in eighteenth-century life, actresses became arbiters of style and dress, often wearing the latest trends and accessories popular among ladies of higher classes. Leading artists of the day, such as Sir Joshua Reynolds, Thomas Lawrence, Thomas Gainsborough and George Romney, painted portraits of actresses using staging and costumes that also appeared in their portraits of aristocratic women.

In the eighteenth century, having one's portrait painted by a well-known artist was both a form of self-aggrandizement and self-advertisement. The message that a portrait conveyed to the viewer depended on certain symbolic and iconographic visual clues that made up a vocabulary of portraiture specific to the time period.[42] In his *Discourses on Art,* Sir Joshua Reynolds established many of the conventions of eighteenth-century portraiture that other artists would later copy, refashion, and manipulate. According to Reynolds, female subjects should not be painted in contemporary dress. He writes: "He therefore who in his practice of portrait painting wishes to dignify his subject, which we will suppose to be a lady, will not paint her in the modern dress, the familiarity of which alone is sufficient to destroy all dignity."[43] In the subsequent paragraph, however, he explains that one should not forget to preserve some of the modern for "the sake of likeness."[44] In other words, a portrait of a lady should flatter the sitter by dressing her in a costume that signifies dignity: while at the same time, the picture should somehow reflect the actual features of the subject. The lady is then masquerading at the same time that she is herself, mimicking for a moment the daily life of an actress. Portraiture, then, is by its nature theatrical. The sitter is always engaged in a kind of visual masquerade.

For female aristocrats, disguising themselves in portraits was a way of participating in a legitimate form of theatrical display. For actresses, disguising themselves as "ladies" by being painted in aristocratic costumes gave them a powerful visual self-fashioning technique. In an essay on Reynolds and his female subjects, art historian Gill Perry explains that for aristocrats the goal of a portrait was often a degree of anonymity. She writes: "Portraits of women with noble breeding were usually hung and listed in the catalogue without their names in Royal Academy Shows."[45] Furthermore, the fact that aristocratic ladies wished to be painted in costume, usually modeled after dresses in seventeenth-century paintings or signifying allegorical roles such as Hebe or Juno, suggests that for a moment they wished to be somebody else, transforming their lofty status into a fantasy of identity.[46]

In *The Art of Dress: Fashion in England and France, 1750–1820*, Art Historian Aileen Ribeiro suggests that elements of masquerade were an essential part of British portraiture in the eighteenth century. She describes how a "romance of the historical past" was reflected in portraits by artists, such as Gainsborough, Reynolds, and Romney, who created costumes for their sitters that were a mix of current styles and fashions from other eras. She quotes Horace Walpole, who when writing to a friend about a masquerade, remarked, "There were five hundred persons, in the greatest variety of handsome and rich dresses I ever saw. . . . There were dozens of ugly Queens of Scots. . . . There were quantities of pretty Vandykes and all kinds of old pictures walked out of their frames."[47]

As aristocrats used costumes to signify their status and connection to royal figures of the past, eighteenth-century actresses similarly relied on the idea that fashion can be read as a code that provides information about wealth, position, and taste in order to signify the various roles they played both on stage and off. Actresses were uniquely qualified to create characters using elements of disguise because part of their job was to transform themselves visually on stage. Unlike contemporary actors, eighteenth-century actresses had no designated wardrobe consultants or makeup artists.[48] Furthermore, as demonstrated by Garrick, acting theory of the late eighteenth century emphasized a "natural" performance style.[49] Creating the effect of specific identities using visual clues and theatrical signifiers on stage could be translated (on a smaller scale) to life off stage. An actress's ability to pick out and wear the latest styles meant that she could assimilate herself into upper-class society.

While actors were being painted as aristocrats and aristocrats were being painted in theatrical costumes, trends in late-eighteenth-century fashion moved toward an emphasis on less formal dress. The increased availability of inexpensive, simple fabrics allowed actresses to wear the outfits of aristocrats and promote themselves as respectable ladies. Due to the popularity of plain white dresses and neoclassical styles, fashions became easier to buy and to wear.⁵⁰ Even the Queen herself was painted in everyday dress to signify her link with her subjects and her ordinary role as a wife and mother.⁵¹ The de-emphasis on court dress and elaborate styles allowed actresses to blend in more successfully with aristocrats and to look the part of a respected eighteenth-century lady.

The assumption that fashion can be read as a signifier of image making and that fashion conventions are inextricably linked to trends in painting underlies my understanding of the ways in which these actresses adopted a range of easily read personas for eighteenth-century audiences.⁵² It is impossible to consider how and why these actresses marketed themselves in the ways that they did without addressing the importance of visual images and of their signature theatrical roles. Gill Perry uses the idea of flirtation to describe how actresses were able to effectively negotiate their public personas through visual media. She explains, "Although the actress was continually struggling with public perceptions of her ambiguous sexuality, there were forms of flirtatious behavior, which, when defined and developed through dramatic and artistic conventions, could enable the female performer to achieve social mobility, artistic status, and symbolic potential both on stage and in paint."⁵³ While I agree that flirtation is a powerful visual strategy for fashioning celebrity, considering actresses' own writings in terms of flirtation is a more vexed project. Since actresses' careers and celebrity status were based on the way that they appeared on stage, their personas would always be linked to their costumes, gestures, and behaviors. These visual strategies are crucial to understanding the ways in which these actresses characterize themselves in their memoirs. In their memoirs, however, actresses relied on their audience's *memories* of their visual and theatrical selves, which is a different process than the immediacy of viewing a portrait or a theatrical performance. Contained within their authorial strategies are both flirtatious and subversive gestures toward their reading public.

METHODOLOGIES

In the introduction to their collection of essays *Interfaces: Women/Autobiography/Image/Performance*, editors Sidonie Smith and Julia Watson propose some models for thinking about subjectivity and women's autobiography that are useful in framing the ways in which I suggest reading these actresses' memoirs in conjunction with visual narratives of their identities represented in their portraits and in specific signature roles that they played on stage. Smith and Watson propose:

The autobiographical subject is also inescapably in dialogue with the culturally marked differences that inflect models of identity and underwrite the formation of autobiographical subjectivity. And she is in dialogue with multiple and disparate addressees or audiences. . . . We need to consider how narrators negotiate cultural strictures about telling certain kinds of stories, visualizing kinds of embodiment.[54]

In this study I look at the ways in which actresses as narrators (literally, visually, and theatrically) "negotiate cultural strictures about telling certain kinds of stories" and how they "visualize kinds of embodiment" in order to entice and involve readers in their stories. In writing their memoirs and posing for portraits (and in the case of Siddons and Wells choosing and crafting particular theatrical roles), these actresses attempted to secure a legitimate position for themselves in eighteenth-century society. These strategies for fashioning celebrity reveal anxieties about actresses achieving agency through celebrity in a world that was tremendously uneasy about the notion of powerful women in the public sphere.

Furthermore, Smith and Watson stress that narrative and visual representations should be read as inextricably linked: "Visual modes encode histories of representation and invite viewers to read stories within them. Textual modes make their meanings through imagery."[55] Reading the visual in narrative and the narrative in visual is a key element for deciphering actresses' memoirs, which rely on the reader's visual imagination and at times their memory of the actress in specific theatrical roles, to create desire and sympathy, and in analyzing actresses' portraits, which are carefully constructed narratives of their identity designed to entice audiences and to stimulate consumption. It is significant here that the actress does not paint her own portrait; what we have is the male artist's view of her, but the image is a representation based on what he thinks will be popular and marketable for contemporary audiences. Portraits are then a valuable indicator of the ways in which the public might have wished to see actresses, and actresses capitalized on these images in constructing their self-representations in their memoirs.

Current work on the link between performance and gender identity informs my reading of these actresses' self-fashioning strategies. In particular, the idea that gender can be seen as a series of socially constructed and repeated acts influences my thinking about how identities can be manipulated and formulated according to specific societal codes.[56] As Judith Butler has argued, "There is no gender identity behind the expression of gender."[57] For the actresses in this study, performing, posing, and narrating versions of themselves only resulted in success if they could somehow link their personas to available models of desirable femininity. Siddons, for example, enjoyed unprecedented fame because she was able to associate her image with royalty and maternity, two already established and adored female roles. Robinson tried to present herself as a simultaneously tragic and seductive heroine using conventions of the Gothic novel, but she was ultimately unable to disassociate herself from her theatrical self-fashioning and her scandalous affair with the Prince. Wells's representations of herself deviated so far from the "norms" of eighteenth-century femininity that she was characterized as mad and out of control. Her varied roles as a professional actress, journalist, author, and comedienne (as well as her many romantic liaisons) challenged notions of acceptable female behavior. By the time that Fanny Kemble made her debut on the stage it was clear that effective self-fashioning strategies needed to follow the feminine trends of the moment. Kemble's portrayal of herself as a theatrical heroine relied on images of her as a nineteenth-century beauty and as a direct descendant of her famous aunt, Sarah Siddons.

THE CHAPTERS

Chapter 1, "Sarah Siddons's Diva Celebrity," explores how Sarah Siddons successfully styled herself as a true representation of British femininity by highlighting the connection between royalty and maternity in her visual, narrative, and theatrical performances. I use the notion of the "diva," a persona originally associated with female opera stars, to describe a particular way of reading Siddons's strategies for fashioning her celebrity. Siddons's diva celebrity involved constructing performance that generated an enormous degree of power. So much power, in fact, that at the height of her fame she produced an effect on the public similar to that of female royalty. Comparing portraits of Siddons to images of Queen Charlotte, I argue that Siddons projected similar visions of herself as divine and ordinary, domestic and authoritative, fantastic and real. I examine how Siddons invokes images of royalty and maternity to redefine the character of Lady Macbeth in her "Remarks on the Character of Lady Macbeth" and her own character in her rarely read memoirs, *The Reminiscences of Sarah Kemble Siddons, 1773–1785*. Reading Siddons's "Remarks" and her *Reminiscences* in relation to her affiliation with a variety of "Queens"—real Queens (Queen Charlotte) staged Queens (Lady Macbeth), and projected Queens (her own status as a Celebrity Diva)—provides evidence of Siddons's involvement in manipulating and fashioning her own celebrity. By positing Lady Macbeth's character, and by extension her own celebrity, as authentic and natural performances, Siddons effectively casts herself as a legitimate female star rather than an ambitious, power-seeking woman.

Siddons's "personation" of queens allowed her to enjoy an unprecedented legitimate form of female celebrity, but her writings about queens, real, performed, and imagined, reveal her own anxieties and justifications about being a powerful woman in the public sphere. Ultimately Siddons's celebrity, which may have appeared effortless and natural, emerges as a highly constructed process, which left her at times exhausted, at times triumphant, but always aware of the ultimate power of her audiences to approve of her or destroy her. Siddons's writings expose the paradoxical relationship between divas (or supreme female stars) and queens, or put more specifically, the ambivalent and often dangerous relationship between the actress's assumption of power and her actual social status. Reading Siddons's celebrity through the persona of the diva is a reminder that even at her most "authentic" moments Siddons was always putting on a performance.

Chapter 2, "Mary Robinson's Gothic Celebrity," traces the motif of Robinson's Gothic celebrity in two sets of materials that clearly represent Robinson's strategies for self-fashioning: a series of portraits of her painted right after the end of her affair with the Prince of Wales ended badly, and her *Memoirs of the Late Mrs. Robinson,* written in the last months of her life and published posthumously by her daughter Mary. In considering these particular portraits and the memoirs together I pay specific attention to the ways in which Robinson's use of fashion and costume in conjunction with Gothic tropes allow her to foreground the seductive desirable qualities of her persona and to subsequently disappear when those qualities signify the possibility of immorality or deceptiveness. Robinson creates her own celebrity allure by juxtaposing "real" and "imagined" identities in her portraits, and by highlighting and obscuring her "real" body through references to dress and costume in her memoirs. In doing so, she participates in "embodying," acting out, and signifying fantasies and anxieties about female sexuality in late-eighteenth-century culture. Robinson's Gothic celebrity thus emphasizes the dialectic relationship between her varied and often contradictory visual, narrative and theatrical identities.

Chapter 3, "Mary Wells's Notorious Celebrity," focuses on the relationship between celebrity, performance, and madness in Mary Wells's *Memoirs of the Life of Mrs. Sumbel, Late Wells* (1811). While Siddons and Robinson fashioned their images according to convention, Wells's repeated resistance to conventional norms led to public suspicions of her madness and instability. Wells's notorious celebrity, or what I will call her deliberate subversiveness, particularly evident in her imitations of Sarah Siddons, reveals the constructed nature of both the dominant norms of femininity and the parameters for fashioning celebrity in the late eighteenth century. Wells's memoirs, a three-volume narrative, include details of her career in the British theater as an actress, singer, and comedienne (she was famous for her imitations of Sarah Siddons and Dorothy Jordan), her liaisons with famous men, episodes of her alleged madness, her treatment by Dr. Willis (the same doctor who "cured" George III), and her exotic marriage in debtors prison to Mr. Sumbel (who divorced her because she would not abide by the laws of Judaism). Reading Wells's memoirs along with visual images of her, characterizations of her theatrical personas on stage, and accounts of her strange behavior off stage written by her contemporaries, I propose that in the late eighteenth century the possibilities for female celebrity are linked to idealized narratives of female identity in the same way that madness is defined in opposition to constructions of "normal" feminine behavior. Just as Siddons's celebrity became linked to models of femininity based on royalty and maternity, and Robinson's celebrity can be seen as characterized by Gothic strategies, Wells's celebrity became associated with madness and notoriety. Wells's peculiar theatricality on stage was initially read by her audiences and contemporaries as comedic, eccentric, and amusing, while her odd behavior off stage became increasingly labeled as "infamous," "outrageous," and "mad." Her risky performances led to her initial success as a talented mimic and fearless comedienne, but her attempts to translate those performances off stage in order to promote her celebrity eventually led to her demise.

The public reaction to Wells's performances, on stage, off stage, and in print, points once again to a significant set of cultural anxieties surrounding the ambiguous status of actresses at the turn of the nineteenth century, anxieties that centered around actresses' potential ability to rise in class through their liaisons with prominent men and their ability to support themselves individually through their profession. Public characterizations of Wells as "deviant" point to a growing separation between celebrated actresses, such as Sarah Siddons and Fanny Kemble, and lesser known actresses, who struggled as the nineteenth-century theater became focused on a star system. Wells's excessive theatricality also previews depictions of madwomen in nineteenth-century literature whose performative outbursts are juxtaposed with the authentic and docile demeanor of more proper English heroines.

The Epilogue, "Fanny Kemble's Inherited Celebrity," highlights the early career of the actress, writer, and social historian Fanny Kemble. As Sarah Siddons's grandniece and the daughter of the successful actor Charles Kemble, Fanny Kemble inherited a legacy of celebrity. The epilogue opens with a discussion of a portrait of Kemble with her aging Aunt Siddons, an image that emphasizes the transference of the role of theatrical diva from Siddons to Kemble. Throughout her long career, Kemble understood that the key to success was to continue to present herself as available to the public while disassociating herself from the "inauthentic" qualities of actresses. She was wary of the seductions and pitfalls of celebrity. Kemble's early success was largely due to flattering portraits of her painted by Thomas Lawrence and Thomas Sully. Kemble's image was so popular that Sully used a portrait of the actress as a model for his famous image of the young Queen Victoria completed in the year of her coronation. The case of Kemble and the Queen demonstrates the continued association between royalty and celebrities that was promoted by Siddons decades earlier. The epilogue then turns briefly to photographs of the aging Queen and an elderly Kemble in order to illustrate how fashioning celebrity becomes a different task with the invention of photography.

Ending with photographs of Kemble emphasizes how the eighteenth-century practice of self-fashioning through visual, textual, and theatrical codes mirrors contemporary ideas about marketing, framing, and selling the illusory, elusive self. Just as actresses' memoirs continue to intrigue contemporary audiences, the trend of portraits of actresses as "themselves" that originated in the eighteenth century would become a mainstay of every successful actress's career. Marketing oneself through text and image proves to be the most enduring legacy of these early women performers.

One

Sarah Siddons's Diva Celebrity

> Her Majesty had express'd herself surprised to find me so collected in so new a position, and that I had conducted myself as if I had been used to a court. At any rate, I had frequently personated Queens.
>
> —Sarah Siddons, *Reminiscences of Sarah Kemble Siddons*

> It is difficult for the frequent playgoer to disembarrass the idea of Hamlet from the person and voice of Mr. K. We speak of Lady Macbeth, while we are in reality thinking of Mrs. S.
>
> —Charles Lamb, quoted in Bate, ed., *The Romantics on Shakespeare*

> The diva overturns the world's gendered ground by making femaleness seem at once powerful and artificial.
>
> —Wayne Koestenbaum, *The Queen's Throat*

IN 1957, at the thirty-fifth annual Pageant of the Masters in Irvine, California, the actress Bette Davis posed as Sarah Siddons in a recreation of Sir Joshua Reynolds's portrait of Siddons as "The Tragic Muse." In a photograph of the event, Davis appears in full, eighteenth-century garb, seated on a mock throne, glaring down at a woman who reaches up to her in a gesture of devotion.[1] That an organizer of the event chose Davis to portray the eighteenth-century diva Sarah Siddons is a testament to the lasting quality of a category of identity that Siddons invented: the modern female superstar. The idea of the actress as a Queen, an untouchable ideal, an exemplar of femininity, and a sublime being originated with Siddons. Her celebrity status was the result of carefully crafted visual strategies on stage, on canvas, and in print that worked to convince audiences that she was, as William Hazlitt remarked, "tragedy personified. She was the stateliest ornament of the public mind."[2]

In the past ten years, there has been a significant amount of scholarship devoted to the study of Sarah Siddons, her fame and her after-life, or what I will call, the "Siddons effect": in other words, what audiences and observers saw, heard, and wrote about Siddons's theatrical performances, her portraits, her public appearances, her theatrical readings, and less frequently, her family and private life. Robyn Asleson, Shearer West and Heather McPherson have written eloquently about the cultural impact of Siddons's portraits, as well as her ability to manipulate her public image through a variety of visual materials.[3] Judith Pascoe, Catherine Burroughs, and Laura Rosenthal have explored Siddons's role as a literary and cultural icon.[4] Joseph Roach has explored the ways in which Siddons's extraordinary success led to an "acquisition of cultural authority" that depended in large part on the apparent whiteness of her skin. Roach writes of Siddons's fame: "Such idolatry also represents a symbolic version of the intergenerational contract famously set forward by Burke, 'between those who are living, those who are dead, and those who are to be born.'"[5]

David Román builds on Roach's argument that Siddons's status as a cultural icon provides a tangible way of understanding the connections between the past and the present. Román traces Siddons's cultural significance, and performative and visual afterlife, from Reynolds's portrait to Bette Davis's now-famous impersonation of her as the tragic muse, to the Hollywood classic *All About Eve*, to two contemporary exhibitions that featured Siddons at the Getty museum and the Huntington Library in Los Angeles, to end with a discussion of two "distinguished queer performance artists, Richard Move and John Kelly, whose recreations of Martha Graham and Joni Mitchell, respectively are legendary among a particular subculture and, as we shall see, timely to us all."[6] Román uses these various manifestations of "the Siddons effect" to establish a "genealogy of female celebrity and theatrical virtuosity."[7]

I would like to build on Román's argument that Siddons represents a kind of originary, or starting place, for ways to imagine a "geneaology of female celebrity and theatrical virtuosity," echoing both his anchoring of this tradition in Siddons's particular "brand"—to borrow a term from Joseph Roach—of celebrity, and pointing out how this tradition can be traced forward to the celebrated contemporary careers of male female impersonators. What Román ultimately sees as the power of Siddons's celebrity is based on the afterlife of her embodied performances: how these moments are recreated and re-imagined by the subsequent performances that they engendered. In other words, through Siddons, Román provides evidence that "performance archives its own past."⁸

This is a particularly powerful theoretical framework for thinking about what Siddons represents in the history of fashioning celebrity. What Romáan highlights about Siddons is that her celebrity became about the transmission of Siddons-as-subject to Siddons-as-object. Bette Davis's impersonation of Siddons-as-object/portrait represents an archive of Siddons's past performances that do not depend on textual evidence but instead on an embodied history—a kind of ghost effect. Thus, Siddons "ghosts the celebrity" of Bette Davis, whose role in *All About Eve* is all about how an actress can retain her persona as a "legendary star, or diva, to which the name and portrait of Sarah Siddons refer in the film."⁹

What I want to do in this chapter is to begin to think about the even more elusive figure of Sarah Siddons the subject. What is striking about scholarship on Siddons is the lack of attention to what Siddons wrote herself, about herself: specifically, 1) her notes to her authorized biographer Thomas Campbell, which exist as a complete manuscript that, later published by the Harvard librarian who discovered the manuscript as "The Reminiscences of Sarah Kemble Siddons," can be considered to be an original memoir; and 2) her "Remarks on the Character of Lady Macbeth," included in Campbell's biography, in which she provides an in-depth analysis of her signature role. Curiously, writings authored by Siddons have not been considered particularly relevant to the study of her celebrity. Román writes that, in reading about Siddons, "we are reminded that we have no direct access to Sarah Siddons, the stage performer. We know Siddons today only as an image, or rather, a series of images and textual descriptions. The primary traces of Siddons's celebrated career are the visual likenesses of her captured by painters of her day, and the textual accounts of her work and life, by those, such as Hazlitt, who put them down in writing."¹⁰ Cheryl Wanko writes in her study of thespian biographies that "very little evidence survives to show that she (Siddons) herself directed this (her) public image, except through the roles she chose and the ways in which she allowed portraitists to portray her."¹¹

But what about Siddons's own accounts of herself and her theatrical roles? I am by no means arguing that these writings offer "direct access" to Siddons. I do want to suggest, however, that it is vitally important to consider how these documents are significant to the study of Siddons's life, her career, and particularly, her strategies for fashioning celebrity. It is also important to consider why these writings have been generally ignored and left out of the central legacy of the "Siddons effect." Part of the answer to this omission has to do with Siddons's association with Queens.

SIDDONS AS QUEEN

Kristina Straub argues in *Sexual Suspects* that the public's fascination with the private lives of eighteenth-century players extended to surveillance over their bodies. Straub writes: "The public's gaze is seen in theatrical discourse as a powerful and often problematic act of control—even oppression—exercised over a body of individuals professionally vulnerable to surveillance and public scrutiny."[12] Siddons herself endured this kind of relentless public attention; however, unlike other female performers whose private lives and public antics created scandal, Siddons's unique position engendered another model of public fascination, a model similar to the worship of the British Monarchy. As Shearer West has proposed, Siddons's public and private roles represented "interlocking components;" her career was "anomalous" in a time when actresses were considered "dispensable or interchangeable."[13] The trope of Siddons as Queen, West explains, was a "persistent one, particularly in the latter part of her career."[14]

During Siddons's reign as the Queen of the British theater, the actual King and Queen, George III and Charlotte, were visible and popular public figures. Historian Linda Colley credits George III with revitalizing and revising the ways in which British subjects saw the monarchy. Largely through portraiture and public appearances, George III created an image of the royals as paradoxically ordinary and extraordinary, both remote and accessible.[15] Colley explains: "George III was on a different level from his subjects, the inhabitant of splendid palaces and the fulcrum of unprecedented ceremony; but he was also a husband, a father, a mortal man subject to illness, age and every kind of mundane vulnerability, and therefore, essentially the same as his subjects."[16] Like the King, Queen Charlotte used visual images to present herself as both royal and ordinary. Well-known artists, Thomas Gainsborough, Sir Joshua Reynolds, Benjamin West, and William Beechey, depicted the Queen as a fashionable, attractive woman whose duties involved both her regal obligations and her position as a wife and mother.[17] The same artists were also involved in painting portraits of Sarah Siddons. Portraits of Siddons that aided in promoting her celebrity emphasized many qualities portrayed in visual representations of Queen Charlotte.[18] Similar to depictions of the Queen, Siddons's portraits promoted the vision of her as both a public celebrity and a private individual.

In this chapter, while comparing portraits of Siddons and Queen Charlotte, I will consider how Siddons deliberately invokes images of royalty and maternity to envision and redefine the character of Lady Macbeth in her "Remarks on the Character of Lady Macbeth" and her own star persona in her *Reminiscences* (which I will refer to as her memoir). Examining Siddons's rarely read writings in relation to her affiliation with a variety of "Queens"—real Queens (Queen Charlotte), staged Queens (Lady Macbeth), and projected Queens (her own status as a Celebrity Diva)—reveals some of the mechanisms behind Siddons's strategies for fashioning her celebrity. By positing Lady Macbeth's character—and by extension, her own celebrity—as authentic and natural performances, Siddons effectively casts herself as a legitimate female star rather than an ambitious, power-seeking woman. At the same time, Siddons's writings reveal the paradoxical relationship between divas (or supreme female stars) and queens; or put more specifically, her writing reveal the ambivalent and often dangerous relationship between the actress's assumption of power and her actual social status.

SIDDONS AS DIVA

Considering Siddons's celebrity through her role as a diva, particularly in relation to her penchant for performing Queens and being visually represented as a Queen, suggests a more complex reading of her success than merely her ability to appear authentic by attempting to merge the perception of her private and public personas. Emphasizing Siddons's role as a diva highlights the variety of her performances and the constructed nature of her role as the Queen of the theater. What divas and Queens ultimately have in common is the fact that they are not ordinary or particularly real. Instead, they are powerful, excessive, and artificial. Wayne Koestenbaum writes in *The Queen's Throat:*

> Queens and divas understand each other. The diva believes—and this may not be grandiose delusion but truth—that she and the queen are secret sharers, conversing in winks and nods. The diva loves queens because pretending to be a queen is an occasion to divorce the body from the soul, to assume lofty and hieratic alienation; pretending to be a queen also helps the diva imitate figures from the past who might have ignored or abused her. The diva pretends to be royal, and at any moment her illusion might be shattered.[19]

While Kostenbaum is writing primarily about nineteenth- and twentieth-century opera singers, he explains that the category of diva can easily extend beyond the boundaries of opera. For Koestenbaum, the diva is a figure that engenders, represents, and creates "codes of extravagant female behavior."[20]

For Siddons, "personating Queens"—real and imagined—made it feasible for her to establish "codes of extravagant female behavior," to embody an unprecedented form of female celebrity, and to transform one of the most ruthless stage heroines into an exemplar of femininity. Using images of royalty and maternity as models for legitimate forms of theatrical display in her characterization of Lady Macbeth, in the building of her career, and in her representation of herself in her memoir, made it possible for Siddons not to appear to be too ambitious, too theatrical, or too independent. A closer look at Siddons's "Remarks on the Character of Lady Macbeth" and her memoirs, however, reveals that her success was achieved by careful staging, clever costuming, and diligent rehearsal. Dependent on public approval and subject to constant scrutiny, Siddons used her performances to gain power, re-script social hierarchies, and redefine gender roles. These documents indicate that Siddons was keenly aware of the delicate balance needed for a woman to sustain fame in the eighteenth century, a balance that was dependent on maintaining antithetical ideals of femininity that even the Queen herself could not fully transcend. Ultimately, Siddons's fame, which may have appeared effortless and natural, emerges as a highly constructed process, that left her at times exhausted, at times triumphant, but always aware of the power of her audiences to approve of her or destroy her.

The absence of a full discussion of Siddons's writings in the legacy of "The Siddons effect" suggests that there is something at stake in representing Siddons as a queen rather than emphasizing Siddons's role as a diva. In fact, the legacy of Siddons as the Queen of tragedy collapses the after-effects of her fame with her strategies for fashioning her celebrity. Thinking of Siddons as a diva emphasizes her self-conscious process of continuously performing visual, narrative, and theatrical acts of queenliness—a process that conjures the ghostly desires of Siddons-as-subject rather than only focusing on the after-life of Siddons-as-object. Returning once again to David Román, performance certainly embodies its own archive, but also contained within the archives of performance are significant traces of embodiment that materialize as strategies for fashioning celebrity in portraits and memoirs. Although we can never recover the definitive Siddons-as-subject, evidence does indeed survive that points to her direct involvement in imagining, shaping, and continuously re-inventing her public image.

THE "REMARKS" AND THE *REMINISCENCES* AS TEXTS

Out of all of Siddons's royal theatrical roles, she was perhaps best-known for her legendary portrayal of the doomed Queen Lady Macbeth.[21] Siddons's performance of Shakespeare's devious heroine was lauded by critics, was adored by audiences, and was the subject of numerous portraits, engravings, and her own notes on how to perform the part.[22] According to Siddons's "Remarks on the Character of Lady Macbeth," written sometime after 1815 and published in Thomas Campbell's *Life of Mrs. Siddons* (London, 1834), Lady Macbeth's duplicitous and ambitious persona is ultimately softened and counteracted by her madness and breakdown.[23] The sleepwalking scene, Siddons claimed, should be seen not as the confession of a guilty murderess, but as the triumph of Lady Macbeth's femininity and compassionate nature. In addition to her "Remarks on the Character of Lady Macbeth," Campbell's *Life of Mrs. Siddons* also includes excerpts from Siddons's "memoranda," or remarks on her own life. Siddons's "memoranda," however, also exists as a complete manuscript with an introduction, defined episodes, and an ending, which makes it possible to categorize the text as a memoir. The full text of the "memoranda," a document handwritten by Siddons, was misplaced sometime in the nineteenth century until it resurfaced in the 1940s in the Harvard library. William Van Lennep, the curator of Harvard's rare book room at the time, decided to reprint the full manuscript with the title *The Reminiscences of Sarah Kemble Siddons, 1773–1785*. Read together Siddons's "Remarks" and her *Reminiscences* provide evidence of her ambitious strategies for achieving fame and recognition.

The "Remarks" and the *Reminiscences,* as documents, pose some compelling questions because the texts are embedded within a biography written and edited by someone else. The "Remarks" are set off by quotation marks in Campbell's biography, comprising almost a whole chapter; the *Reminiscences* are interspersed throughout the biography. Both texts can be seen then as equally private and public documents. At the same time that they are authenticated by quotation marks, the excerpts of Siddons's writings are still part of the fabricated thread of Campbell's narrative. Having both texts embedded in Campbell's narrative allows Siddons to put forth an analysis and an opinion while still remaining within the authorized confines of another person's book. Her "Remarks" and her *Reminiscences* appear to be spontaneous and non-scripted, rather than a deliberate image-making strategy.

William Van Lennep describes the discovery of Siddons's memoir in the introduction to the text:

> *The Reminiscences of Sarah Kemble Siddons* is printed from a long lost recently discovered manuscript now in the Harvard College Library. Labeled at the top of the first page 'Fair Copy,' but containing, nevertheless, several

corrections and additions, the manuscript is entirely in the hand of Mrs. Siddons and occupies both sides of forty-four quarto pages. At the end are four unfinished lines of verse, headed: "To T. Campbell Esq."[24]

Siddons apparently wrote the manuscript for Campbell so that he could incorporate her memories into his biography. Read as a whole document, however, the text can be considered a short memoir that follows the format of an actor's autobiography. The narrative covers the highlights of Siddons's theatrical career, beginning with her first appearance on stage and ending abruptly with her last performance. Siddons composed the text while she was dying and hoped that her "imperfect narrative" would "perhaps have some interest for those few friends who may yet survive, to remember me and my appropriate qualities."[25]

Perhaps the most complicated issue involved with Siddons's memoir is the fact that, for many years, it was not considered a text at all. Biographers and critics still cite the *Reminiscences* primarily as "notes to Siddons biographer" without referring to the document as a separate manuscript.[26] The question of how Siddons meant this text to be read is a complex one for scholars and biographers. Considering Siddons's notes to Campbell as a memoir is particularly significant, since the tone and force of Siddons's narration is undercut and disrupted by the way in which Campbell revises and edits Siddons's words in his biography. What he chooses to include is as interesting as what he leaves out. The content of the memoir reveals that Siddons was tremendously involved in fashioning her celebrity status. She desperately wanted to be remembered as a star.

Much of our information about the innovation and impact of Siddons's performance of Lady Macbeth comes from a wealth of contemporary commentary about her actions and presence on stage. Her portrayal of Lady Macbeth went beyond the expectations of her early audiences. She established traditions associated with the role that would survive on stage in actresses' performances for generations to follow.[27] As Bernice W. Kliman notes, "Her performances are worthy of close study, because she may be the best actor who has ever played the role of Lady Macbeth and because actors have emulated her in many individual choices—if not the entire characterization."[28] Significantly, Siddons's "Remarks on the Character of Lady Macbeth" has garnered less scholarly attention than the extensive comments about her performances of the role, and the portraits of her as Lady Macbeth painted by a variety of well-known artists. Kliman writes, "She herself wrote about her intentions and about the character of Lady Macbeth, though many critics think she surpassed her own analysis."[29] And Russ McDonald suggests that

Siddons's "Remarks" "are to some degree a hindrance in that they are retrospective, summarizing a characterization shaped and tweaked for some thirty years. In other words, what they describe may not have been what spectators at Drury Lane saw in February of 1785."[30] Although the "Remarks" clearly cannot recapture exactly what Siddons did on stage, the document is an important record of how Siddons imagined and designed the role over many years in the same way that she invented and promoted a carefully crafted image of herself as a performer.

Catherine Burroughs, one of the few critics who consider the "Remarks" to be an important text in its own right, reads the document as evidence of Siddons's model for a method of acting that "had implications for living a more enlightened life off stage."[31] Using a passage from Siddons quoted by Thomas Campbell in the biography, Burroughs emphasizes Siddons's anxieties about the difficulties in portraying such an unlikable heroine. Burroughs explains Siddons's process:

> Schooling herself to tolerate negative characters in order to make herself more capable of empathizing with the strange, the threatening, and the despicable, she confessed that she had for several years, "perceived the difficulty of assuming a personage [Lady Macbeth] with whom no one feeling of common general nature was congenial or assistant. One's own heart could prompt one to express, with some degree of truth, the sentiments of a mother, a daughter, a wife, a lover, a sister &c, but to adopt this character must be an effort of the judgment alone.[32]

Burroughs argues that Siddons "persisted in trying to suspend her judgment about Lady Macbeth in order to inhabit the character in a way that would make more humanely explicable her variety of behaviors."[33] This displays her "sympathetic curiosity," a quality that allies her with other Romantic women writers.

Although Burroughs's reading allows for the complexities of Siddons's take on the role of Lady Macbeth, she does not consider the possibility that Siddons's humanizing of the character had more than "sympathetic" motivations. Siddons's project of portraying Lady Macbeth as a recognizable mother, daughter, and wife—a character whose nature at one time was "congenial"—was directly tied to promoting her own public image for audiences who had difficulty making the distinction between her identities on stage and off stage. As Judith Pascoe suggests, "Siddons as a wife and mother was just as public a persona as Siddons as Lady Macbeth, but the former role contained the latter one, rendering it less threatening to a society unused to demonstrable female desire."[34] Siddons's "Remarks on The Character of Lady Macbeth" can be read as a thinly veiled exploration of Siddons as the character of Lady Macbeth; in other words, it is a kind of autobiographical narrative disguised as notes on specific strategies for performance. Siddons's fascination with Lady Macbeth's diva-celebrity qualities—her entitlement, power, seductive charms, and ultimate destruction—are re-framed according to codes of acceptable femininity, a strategy that she echoes in the representation of herself as a celebrity diva in her own memoir.

QUEENLY MAKEOVERS

Throughout her analysis of Lady Macbeth in "Remarks," Siddons returns to Lady Macbeth's initial role as a would-be Queen, which of course involves acting as a gracious hostess to the soon-to-be-murdered King Duncan while doing everything she can to support her ambitious husband. Highlighting Lady Macbeth's beauty, strength, and devotion to Macbeth, Siddons is able to revise the more diabolical aspects of Lady Macbeth's character. From the outset, Siddons urges her readers to rethink their previous concept of a monstrously aspiring heroine:

> In this astonishing creature one sees a woman in whose bosom the passion of ambition has almost obliterated all the characteristics of human nature; in whose composition are associated all the subjugating powers of intellect and all the charms and graces of personal beauty. You will probably not agree with me as to the character of that beauty; yet, perhaps, this difference of opinion will be entirely attributable to the difficulty of your imagination disengaging itself from that idea of the person of her representative which you have been so long accustomed to contemplate.[35]

In this enticing introduction, Siddons admits that she has a new, original, and perhaps unwelcome, interpretation of Lady Macbeth.[36] Siddons contends that, despite Lady Macbeth's "dreadful language" and "remorseless ambition," she is essentially "feminine, nay perhaps even fragile." She has suffered in the past, and she uses those memories to fuel her motivation of her weaker husband. Separating Lady Macbeth's "ambition" from her true "nature," Siddons suggests that she is under some kind of unnatural spell that compels her to behave like a "perfectly savage creature."[37]

Siddons uses images of Lady Macbeth's "personal beauty" to soften the deviousness of her motives and sentiments in the first act of the play. She writes, "Lady Macbeth, thus adorned with every fascination of mind and person, enters for the first time, reading a part of one of those portentous letters from her husband. . . . Now vaulting ambition and intrepid daring rekindle in a moment all the splendors of her dark blue eyes."[38] Directing attention to Lady Macbeth's "dark blue eyes" gives readers a moment to visualize the "fascination" of Lady Macbeth's person. In a similar fashion, promoting "personal beauty" was an integral part of designing images of Siddons and Queen Charlotte.

GAINSBOROUGH'S BEAUTIES: PORTRAITS OF SIDDONS AND QUEEN CHARLOTTE

In portraits of Siddons as "herself," her elegant figure and classical features created the illusion of a larger-than-life grandeur. It was this grandeur that convinced critics that she was of a higher class. Thomas Davies writes: "The person of Mrs. Siddons is greatly in her favor just rising above the middle stature, she looks, walks, and moves like a woman of superior rank."[39] *The Morning Post* for Saturday, 30 December 1775, comments: "Her figure is a very fine one; her features are beautifully expressive; her action is graceful and easy, and her whole deportment that of a gentlewoman."[40]

Thomas Gainsborough's portrait of Siddons (1783–85) is a testament to her grandeur as a lady (figure 1). In this painting, Siddons is "out of costume" and playing herself, yet she is still in costume as a grand woman of society. She wears a white-and-blue-striped silk "wrapping gown" with lace sleeves.[41] She holds a fur muff in her hand, and a hat with feathers and bows sits gracefully angled on her head. Her hair is partially powdered with natural color showing through. She stares confidently and seriously into the distance; the soft folds of her dress contrast her angular features and the line of the black necklace across her pale skin. Although this portrait was clearly recognizable as Siddons, Gainsborough softened Siddons's features, particularly her characteristic nose. In a legendary story about the creation of this painting, Gainsborough became frustrated with Siddons's image, exclaiming, "Damn the nose—there's no end to it!"[42]

Gainsborough also manipulated aspects of Queen Charlotte's presence in his famous portrait of her, completed in 1781 (figure 2). In this painting, Charlotte stands against a backdrop similar to the West portrait. She is dressed in an elaborate "robe à la française"—a costume worn regularly at the royal court. She holds a delicate fan between her fingers as she gazes contently at the viewer. Aileen Ribeiro comments that, although the elaborate

FIGURE 1. Thomas Gainsborough. *Sarah Siddons*, 1785. © The National Gallery, London

mix of fabrics and lace in this costume could "easily look ridiculous," Gainsborough's skill in blending the "cobwebby" material of the dress with the Queen's powdered hair and flowered headdress against the landscape in the background makes this portrait a remarkable success.[43] Eighteenth-century observers of the image were impressed with the attractive representation of an otherwise ordinary looking Queen. Sir Henry Bate-Dudley remarked in the *Morning Herald:* "The Queen's is the only happy likeness we ever saw portrayed of her Majesty: the head is not only very highly finished but expresses all that amiableness of character which so justly distinguishes her."[44] James Northcote explains that the "drapery was done in one night by Gainsborough and his nephew; they sat up all night, and painted by candlelight. This in my opinion, constitutes the essence of genius, the making of beautiful things from unlikely subjects."[45]

Just as Gainsborough created the idea of status, wealth, and noble bearing with his portrait of Siddons, Queen Charlotte appears magically beautiful in his representation of her. Through visual imagery, both women were endowed with qualities that they did not innately possess. These qualities promoted their public images. Eighteenth-century observers' reactions to these portraits suggest that this is what the public wanted to see: a beautiful queen and a noble actress. Interestingly, these very different women participated in similar self-fashioning strategies. The goal of each was clearly to create an accessible image that sold her most attractive features. Queen Charlotte and Sarah Siddons had much in common; despite their disparate backgrounds, they were celebrities and public figures, subject to the same standards of judgment with respect to femininity and style.

Curiously, in her "Remarks," Siddons describes Lady Macbeth as having "dark blue" eyes. Siddons, herself, had dark brown eyes. Similar to the idealized visual makeovers performed in portraits of Siddons and of Queen Charlotte, Siddons's vision of Lady Macbeth is that of a woman more conventionally beautiful than Siddons herself. In her "Remarks," Siddons faced a task similar to that of eighteenth-century portraitists. In painting a likeable version of Lady Macbeth, she had to succeed at making "beautiful things from unlikely subjects."

ROYAL MOTHERS

One of the most difficult tasks Siddons faced in portraying Lady Macbeth's "personal beauty" occurs at the beginning of the play, when Lady Macbeth refers to the vexed possibility that she was once a mother. In the eighteenth

FIGURE 2. Thomas Gainsborough. *Queen Charlotte*, 1781. The Royal Collection © Her Majesty Queen Elizabeth II

century, emphasizing the virtues of domesticity and motherhood was a way of desexualizing the female figure, a process that was particularly important to the creation of a woman's public image. Popular portraits of Queen Charlotte and Siddons linked their personas to their role as mothers, presenting them as powerful figures because of their benevolent role as domestic guardians. Benjamin West's portrait of Queen Charlotte depicts her standing poised against a grand column with her children in the background (figure 3). The painting conveys the idea that the Queen's glory comes from her position as a wife and mother to the King's children, who will eventually rule the country.[46] West's image of Queen Charlotte suggests that eighteenth-century women could not be on stage or directly in the foreground without indirectly representing something else. In the painting, Charlotte's body, while beautifully clothed and positioned, is not a body of titillation or desire. She modestly gathers the folds of her costume in front of her lower torso, and her bosom is disguised by a large decorative bow. The small, tamed lap dog at her feet signifies the idea of domesticity and fidelity inherent in the Queen's personality. The production of children is, thus, not seen as the result of multiple sexual acts but as a duty and function of an eighteenth-century wife.

In William Hamilton's portrait of Siddons as Isabella from Thomas Southerne's *Isabella* (one of her most celebrated parts), Siddons's gestures and position signify her role as a devoted mother (figure 4).[47] The painting depicts the moment in the play when Isabella's reversal of fortune compels her to beg for food and money in order to support her family. Dressed all in black, Siddons looms above her son, her arms gracefully outstretched. She stares off in the distance with a look of pathos as she clutches the boy's hand.[48] Siddons's gestures recreate her presence on stage as a serious, accomplished performer, while lending credence to her "real life" image as a good mother and a devoted wife. This interplay of gesture, costume, and staging worked to promote the idea of Siddons as representative of the best qualities of her sex, while de-emphasizing the sexual nuances of her presence and her performances.[49]

In her *Reminiscences,* Siddons includes a description of her triumphant return to Drury Lane to play Isabella after her earlier, humiliating dismissal by David Garrick. Similar to her tactics in describing her particular portrayal of Lady Macbeth, Siddons uses the role of Isabella, the sacrificing mother, to frame her rise to stardom in terms of her maternal roles on stage and off stage. Siddons recreates the moment of her initial entrance: "The awful consciousness that one is the sole object of attention to that immense space, lined as it were with human intellect from top to bottom, and on all sides

FIGURE 3. Benjamin West. *Queen Charlotte*, c. 1779. Royal Collection © Her Majesty Queen Elizabeth II

FIGURE 4. William Hamilton. *Mrs. Siddons and Her Son in the Tragedy of Isabella*, 1785. Horace Howard Furness Memorial Library, University of Pennsylvania

round, may perhaps be imagined but can not be described, and never never to be forgotten."[50] The "awful consciousness" that Siddons describes is tied to the relationship between vision and power. The fact that there are so many people looking at her makes her a desired public spectacle, a being who solely occupies the attention of hundreds of spectators, marking the beginning of her life as a legitimate celebrity. This is a moment of joy for Siddons, but she is careful to balance it with a more private portrait of her family behind the scenes after the play. She writes: "On the general effect of this night's performance I need not speak. It has already been publicly recorded. . . . I reached my own fireside. I was half dead and my joy, my thankfulness, were of too solemn and overpowering nature to admit of words or even tears. My father, my husband and myself sat down to a frugal neat supper in a silence uninterrupted except by joyful exclamations from Mr. Siddons."[51] She goes on to further describe her father who, "lifting up his beautiful and venerable face, which was partially shaded by his silvered hairs," cried tears of happiness into his dinner plate.

Siddons is a master of getting her point across without making it seem as if she is applauding her own performance directly. By placing a private domestic moment after a description of a very public triumph, Siddons reinforces the qualities that allow her to be an icon: her devotion to her family, her humble, behind-the-scenes existence (she sits down to a "frugal neat supper"), and her apparent gratitude for the love of her fans. In her description, she sits "in a silence" that is only interrupted by her husband's exclamations and her father's tears. Siddons's role off stage, then, appears to be that of the ordinary wife and mother. She is the passive observer, while the men in the scene emote and react. Ironically, however, it is Siddons, and neither her husband nor her father, who has caused the moment of joy; it is her professional triumph that has put food on their table. It is important that Siddons stresses the idea of being "thankful" in order to appear modest even if at other points in the memoir it seems clear that she believes that she deserves every bit of her fame and fortune.

One of these scenes of self-congratulation is the moment when Siddons is given a new dressing room. She narrates: "I should be afraid to say how many times Isabella was successively repeated with still increasing favour. I was now highly gratified by a removal from my very indifferent and inconvenient Dressing room to one on the stage floor, instead of climbing a long stair case; and this room (oh unexpected happiness) had been Garrick's dressing room."[52] In this scene of backstage triumph, Siddons is not as careful about hiding her glee at supplanting Garrick, a man who almost ruined her career a few years earlier by breaking her contract at Drury Lane. Siddons's physical presence in Garrick's private space represents her triumph over his authority as a result of her newly crowned position as the rightful heir to Garrick's fame and fortune.[53]

Siddons knew that being given Garrick's old dressing room was a significant feat on many levels, and she goes on to describe how she feels about inhabiting his old quarters: "It is impossible to imagine my gratification when I saw my own figure in the self same Glass which had so often reflected the face and form of that unequaled Genius, not perhaps without some vague, fanciful hope of a little degree of inspiration from it."[54] Looking at herself in Garrick's mirror, Siddons implies that she is awed by the thought of Garrick's ghost and hopes that she, too, may be as successful as that great actor. However, Siddons's gratification additionally stems from seeing herself in the lofty position of inheriting Garrick's legacy of celebrity. Mirrors suggest an awareness of multiple identities. Siddons sees herself for a moment in the mirror the way that she hopes audiences will see her: as a formidable, rising superstar. Mirrors, like portraits and actors, also highlight distortions and illusions. Reflections never truly capture the thing itself, even though they may seem real. Siddons's desire to "ghost" Garrick's "genius" is fraught with the knowledge that the public controls her celebrity. She writes: "I well remember my fears and ready tears on each subsequent effort, lest I should fall from my high exultation."[55]

Using the scene of her dressing room as a potent central image, Siddons describes the complexities of being a celebrity. The liminal boundaries of the theatrical dressing room as both a private and public space dramatize Siddons's position as both subject and object of her own fame, as well as the tension inherent in her antithetical roles as diva celebrity and ordinary woman, wife, and mother. In her book *Designing Women: The Dressing Room in Eighteenth-Century Literature and Culture,* Tita Chico argues that "[t]he dressing room captured the collective imagination of eighteenth-century England because it represented the possibility that women could act independently and selfishly, a fear that was ultimately reshaped into a celebration of the belief that women would not act independently or selfishly if they were good mothers."[56] Siddons's depiction of dressing room scenes interspersed with touching domestic images underscores this ideological trajectory, but the fact that her dressing room is also a professional space adds another layer to this formulation. Siddons's job as an actress demanded that she act "independently and selfishly"; ironically, she was rewarded for her "performances" because she so consistently represented herself not only as a "good mother," but also as a noble queen.

While the role of Isabella was a perfect vehicle for Siddons's project of representing herself as a self-sacrificing mother and an emerging star, portraying Lady Macbeth as tenderly maternal would prove to be more of a challenge. In her "Remarks," Siddons attempts to reveal Lady Macbeth's hidden maternal instincts by translating her cruelest speech—in which she describes dashing out the brains of her mysterious child—into a more palatable psychological reading of the incident. According to Siddons, this is a moment of pure persuasion for Lady Macbeth: "Her language to Macbeth is the most potently eloquent that guilt could use. It is only in soliloquy that she invokes the powers of hell to unsex her. To her husband she avows, and the naturalness of her language makes us believe her, that she had felt the instinct of filial as well as maternal love."[57] Siddons imagines Lady Macbeth to be thinking: "I, too have felt with a tenderness which your sex cannot know; but I am resolute in my ambition to trample on all that obstructs my way to a crown. Look to me and be ashamed of your weakness."[58] Revised in this way, the line does not suggest that Lady Macbeth has harmed her child or even realistically would harm her child, but this is the most powerful image that she can conjure that would make Macbeth understand her deadly resolve. Siddons explains: "The very use of such a tender allusion in the midst of her dreadful language, persuades one unequivocally that she has really felt the maternal yearnings of a mother towards her babe, and that she considered this action the most enormous that ever required the strength of human nerves for its perpetration."[59]

Siddons's emphasis on Lady Macbeth's mothering instincts is significantly tied to her own performances and pregnancies. In April 1794, Siddons played Lady Macbeth at the lavish reopening of the new Drury Lane Theatre, while she was five months pregnant with her sixth child. This was not the first time she had performed while pregnant. In 1775, she gave birth to her second child, Sally, halfway through a performance at Gloucester; in 1782, eight months pregnant with her fifth child, Siddons played both Hermione in the *Distressed Mother,* and Nell in *The Devil to Pay at Bath*.[60] She was not shy about acknowledging that providing for her children was the main reason for her theatrical career. Siddons could be an adored celebrity because she was, by all appearances, also a devoted mother and wife. She remained in a passionless marriage with her husband, the unsuccessful actor William Siddons, and wisely avoided scandals associated with affairs and liaisons with powerful men—a practice that proved to be the downfall of many of her theatrical contemporaries. Although Siddons seemed to have the power to transcend the limitations of her own body during her performances, it is significant that audiences saw her appear as Lady Macbeth while she was pregnant.[61] The double nature of her persona as the character and the pregnant actress must have collided in these moments and helped to underscore Siddons's characterizations of Lady Macbeth as a potentially sympathetic figure.[62]

PERSONATING QUEENS

Siddons's "Remarks" and her *Reminiscences* both contain sections that focus on the "personating" or imitation of Queens. In her discussion of Lady Macbeth, Siddons describes the uncomfortable theatrical process of assuming a royal title under duress; and in her *Reminiscences,* she recreates her audience with the actual Queen, explaining that her talent for personating Queens was an invaluable skill to possess at court. Here the two narratives become even more directly tied to Siddons's strategies for fashioning her celebrity.

Once the murder of Duncan is accomplished, and Lady Macbeth becomes the "legitimate" Queen, her persona undergoes a significant transformation. Siddons writes, "The golden round of royalty now crowns her brow, and royal robes enfold her form; but the peace that passeth all understanding is lost to her forever."[63] Siddons explains how she portrayed Lady Macbeth's "loss of peace" on stage: "Under the impression of her wretchedness, I, from this moment, have always assumed the dejection of countenance and manners which I thought accordant to such a state of mind."[64] Suddenly, Lady Macbeth displays "striking indications of sensibility, nay tenderness and sympathy"[65] toward her husband. She becomes meek and repentant: "The sad and new experience of affliction has subdued the insolence of her pride and the violence of her will,"[66] and she loses her sharp ability to be duplicitous.

In the famous banquet scene, where Macbeth encounters Banquo's bloody ghost, Siddons describes the difficulty of conveying Lady Macbeth's vulnerable position:

> Dying with fear, yet assuming the utmost composure, she returns to her stately canopy; and, with trembling nerves, having tottered up the steps to her throne, that bad eminence, she entertains her wondering guests with frightful smiles, with over-acted attention, and with fitful graciousness; painfully, yet incessantly, laboring to divert their attention from her husband.[67]

Here Siddons emphasizes Lady Macbeth's discomfort with her newfound royal status; she "totters up the steps to her throne," which Siddons labels a "bad eminence," and is unable to naturally control her actions. She is overly solicitous and fitful. Siddons goes on to explain how difficult it is to perform this scene well: "What imitation, in such circumstances as these, would ever satisfy the demands of expectation? The terror, the remorse, the hypocrisy of this astonishing being . . . present, perhaps, one of the greatest difficulties of the scenic art, and cause her representative no less to tremble for the suffrage of her private study, than for its public effect."[68]

In her analysis, Siddons shifts the focus of this scene from Lady Macbeth's machinations to her own anxieties about performing the part. Siddons effectively invites the reader to equate their sympathy for Lady Macbeth's inner monologue with an appreciation of Siddons's (the actress's) own private struggle to understand and perfect her portrayal of the role. Siddons suggests that Lady Macbeth should be pitied because she is suffering so much from the dreadful knowledge of the crime in which she has participated. She then proposes that she should be admired for her skill in performing this complex train of emotions. Thus, both of these "illegitimate" Queens—the usurping Lady Macbeth and the ambitious actress Sarah Siddons—are asking to be exempt from harsh judgments about their presumptuous behavior: Lady Macbeth for her wrong doings, and Siddons for daring to inhabit a powerful and threatening female persona.

Interestingly, Siddons devotes a section of her memoir to her relationship with the real Queen. In narrating her interactions with Queen Charlotte, Siddons pays close attention to the negotiations of her carefully constructed performances. When she goes to the palace to read privately for the Queen, she describes the way that she felt in the awkward dress required: "One could not appear in the presence of the Queen except in a Dress (not elsewhere worn) called a saque, or Negligee, with a hoop, trebble ruffles and Lappets in which costume I felt not at all at ease."[69] During the performance, Siddons refuses to pause to take "some refreshment." She explains that she declined the honor, "altho' I had stood reading till I was ready to drop, rather than run the risk of falling down by walking backwards out of the room (a ceremony not to be dispensed with), the floor, too, being rubbed bright. I therefore remained where I was, till Their Majestys retired."[70]

As in her description of her anxious performance of Lady Macbeth in the banquet scene, Siddons is extremely aware of the theatrical conditions during her performances both on stage and off stage.[71] Unlike critics's representations of her effortless emotions and her natural gradations, or portraits that depict her in one powerful moment, Siddons illustrates that part of what she is always considering is the way her body appears to her audiences. If she walks backwards on the Queen's slippery floor, she might fall—better to go on reading than spoil the illusion by humiliating herself. While considering these humiliations, she is also wearing a dress that she thinks is unflattering and uncomfortable. Here her performance as an actress and as a royal subject overlap; both roles require certain physical gestures and movements. Siddons adds that, after her reading, she hears from one of the ladies who was present that "Her Majesty had expressd herself surprised to find me so collected in so new a position, and that I had conducted myself as if I had been used to a court. At any rate, I had frequently personated Queens."[72]

This witty remark demonstrates Siddons's understanding of the extent to which identities are based on calculated performances and visual clues that she had practiced, rehearsed, and perfected. Although Siddons is required to "perform" specific acts because she is in the presence of royalty, she remains the dominant figure in this scene. In Siddons's view, she is the one who understands how to manipulate the Queen's responses. She is therefore still in control. The Queen's authority here is symbolic and passive, similar to her presence in portraits. Siddons is the object of her gaze, but she is also an active subject in the scene. Siddons's ability to parody and applaud her own talent for "personating" Queens illustrates her awareness of the dynamics of fashioning her celebrity. She implies that the only moment she couldn't represent the Queen was when she was with the Queen herself; at the same time, she reveals her own anxieties about the reception of her performances. Audiences have to believe that she is a Queen so that she can assume a Queenly position; and even though she has perfected her royal affect, it is still only an effective illusion. Here Siddons's strategies for fashioning celebrity are clearly articulated through her own ideas about her performances and the effect these acts had on her audiences.

CELEBRITY SLEEPWALKING

In Siddons's analysis, Lady Macbeth self-destructs because, unlike Macbeth, she has had no outlet for her true feelings. Siddons explains, "His heart has therefore been eased, from time to time, by unloading its weight of woe; while she, on the contrary, has perseveringly endured in silence the utter most anguish of a wounded spirit."[73] This repression results in her collapse: "her frailer frame, and keener feelings, have now sunk under the struggle—his robust and less sensitive constitution has not only resisted it, but bears him on to deeper wickedness."[74] According to Siddons, Lady Macbeth's ultimate demise is the result of the sacrifices that she made for her husband. Her own pain leads her to redirect all of her attentions toward Macbeth. Siddons writes, "Yes; smothering her sufferings in the deepest recesses of her own wretched bosom, we cannot but perceive that she devotes herself entirely to the effort of supporting him."[75] This is not only a transformation from her formerly narcissistic monstrousness, but also a radical departure from the persona of her youth. Siddons suggests to her readers that as a child Lady Macbeth had no boundaries set for her and no limits on her power:

> Let it be here recollected, as some palliation of her former very different deportment, she had, probably, from childhood commanded all around her with a high hand; had uninterruptedly, perhaps, in that splendid station, enjoyed all that wealth, all that nature had to bestow; that she had, possibly, no directors, no controllers; and that in womanhood her fascinated lord has never once opposed her inclinations.[76]

In this passage, Siddons sounds very much like a contemporary actress employing a Stanislavski-inspired approach to understanding the inner workings of her character.[77] She creates a past and a set of memories for Lady Macbeth, which provide her with a psychological narrative and rationale for Lady Macbeth's actions. The description of Lady Macbeth's happiest days—her life in the "splendid station" where she had enjoyed "all that wealth, all that nature had to bestow" and ruled all around her with "no directors and no controllers" (not even her "fascinated husband")—are a far cry from what she descends to at the end of the play. As in the beginning of her analysis, Siddons returns to the details of Lady Macbeth's appearance: "Behold her now, with wasted form, with wan and haggard countenance, her starry eyes glazed with the ever-burning fever of remorse, and on their lids the shadow of death."[78]

Both of these tactics—giving Lady Macbeth a past and inviting readers to visualize Lady Macbeth's "wasted form"—are similar to strategies used in the portraits of Siddons and Queen Charlotte. In images of the actress and the Queen, viewers are asked to equate their visual personas with recognizable models of female identity. Charlotte becomes a dutiful mother and a lovely woman; Siddons becomes an aristocratic fashion plate and a woman who performs for the good of her children. With a strategic vision of the role, Siddons similarly transforms the ruthless Lady Macbeth into a noble heroine for her audiences. At the end of the play, Lady Macbeth is no longer an unnatural, cruel demon but a passionate, grief-stricken woman who gave up a life of comfort and glory in order to promote her thankless husband.

For Siddons's performance of Lady Macbeth to be effective, she must convince audiences that underneath Lady Macbeth's mask of ambition and cruelty lies a fragile feminine body that will ultimately be destroyed, an idea implicitly tied to Siddons's own exhausting career as an actress. Given that the "Remarks" were written at the end of Siddons's career, after many years of performing Lady Macbeth, the document might also be seen as conveying Siddons's subtle musings on the physical and emotional price she paid for her extraordinary fame.[79] The revised version of a domestic and oppressed Lady Macbeth in Siddons's "Remarks" is directly related to her attempts to dissociate her theatrical image from scandal, and to mitigate the stigma of her public role as a manipulative and powerful celebrity.

In a similar gesture toward the end of her memoir, Siddons relates one of the few incidents where her behavior was publicly criticized. When performing in Dublin, Siddons was asked to organize a benefit for the actor Mr. Diggs. According to Siddons, she managed to mount a performance of *Venice Preserved* after much scrambling and almost no rehearsal. Apparently, the manager of the theater felt that Siddons had cheated the actors out of their profits. By the time she returned to London, there was a "gathering storm," and the "public mind was thus poisoned against me." She describes the affects of the situation:

> Alas! How wretched is the being who depends on the stability of public favor! I left London the object of universal approbation, and on my return, but a very few weeks afterwards, was received on my first nights appearance with universal opprobrium—accus'd of hardness of heart, of the most sordid avarice and total insensibility to every thing and every body except my own interest.[80]

Siddons recreates the moment when she returns to the stage and is hissed and jeered at by the angry audience. Although a kind stranger in the front row tells her, "For heavens sake, Madam do not degrade your self by an apology, for there is nothing necessary to be said," she is dragged off stage by her brother, and she faints in his arms. Fortunately, she is convinced by her husband, her brother, and Mr. Sheridan to try to go on stage again. This time the audience is silent. She writes: "I was absolutely awe-struck and never yet have been able to account for this surprising contrast."[81] Siddons's fainting spell in this scene is a way of literally taking her body (and by extension, her conscience) out of the scene. Similar to the moment in *Macbeth* where Lady Macbeth "faints" to draw attention away from her guilty husband, Siddons's swoon at this moment is an attempt to garner sympathy from her audiences. Losing consciousness is also a way of conceding authority, which Siddons miraculously regains when she steps back out on to the stage apparently cleansed of her sins.[82]

Siddons's ability to triumph over accusations of self-interest, and to remain an object of public adoration, was an extraordinary accomplishment. Despite satirical prints of Siddons as a miser hoarding bags overflowing with gold coins, the idea of Siddons as a shrewd and calculating businesswoman was overshadowed by the idea of Siddons as an ideal representation of British femininity. Still, it is compelling that, with all her fame and fortune, Siddons would still want to rewrite the experiences that hurt her the most: her early difficulties with Garrick and the incident in Dublin. Koestenbaum's formulation that the diva pretends to be a Queen in order to "imitate figures from the past that might have ignored or abused her"—an imitation that is a "form of mourning-through identification," since "you imitate what you wish you could explain"[83]—seems directly related to Siddons's self-fashioning strategies. Siddons's gazing at herself in Garrick's mirror, and her performance of the role of Lady Macbeth off stage to avoid culpability for her actions in Dublin, point to the ways in which Siddons's self-fashioning strategies were aimed at relieving her own anxieties about the vulnerability of her celebrity status. But even more important is Siddons's role as a diva, effectively asserting her specific vision of herself both on stage and off stage. Through her narrative, visual, and theatrical performances, Siddons is for the most part able to use her imaginary role as the Queen of the theater to mask her negotiations as a theatrical diva. The attention that Siddons pays to the negative publicity directed at her celebrity suggests that she was aware that, as a fake queen, she might be held responsible for her actions, particularly for the very threatening assumption of a Queen's agency and power.

VISUAL ILLUSIONS:
SIDDONS AS "THE MURDER-LOVING MELPOMENE"
AND "THE TRAGIC MUSE"

While several portraits of Siddons as Lady Macbeth worked to convey her noble portrayal of the character to audiences—for example, George Henry Harlow's *Siddons as Lady Macbeth* (1814) and Thomas Beach's *John Phillip Kemble as Macbeth and Sarah Siddons as Lady Macbeth* (1786)—a less successful painting was William Beechey's *Sarah Siddons with the Emblems of Tragedy* (1793) (figure 5).[84] The portrait displays Siddons turning mischievously toward the viewer, holding a dagger in one hand and the mask of tragedy in the other. Fashion historian Aileen Ribeiro remarks, although Siddons wears "the traditional black dress of tragedy," the "pelisse gown with a white frilled collar" and "the white turban, exotic in inspiration,"[85] are

FIGURE 5. William Beechey. *Mrs. Siddons with the Emblems of Tragedy*, 1793, © National Portrait Gallery, London

unmistakably au courant for the 1790s. Siddons is thus dressed "as herself" in a contemporary costume, even while holding a theatrical mask and a prop from *Macbeth*.

The critic Anthony Piscine found the image vulgar and inappropriate. Rather than depicting "the murder-loving Melpomene," Beechey had instead created "a gypsey in sattin disporting at a masquerade."[86] Siddons's dual role in the portrait, as an actress and as herself, is what must have seemed startling and disturbing about this image for eighteenth-century viewers. In other portraits of Siddons as Lady Macbeth, she is clearly in costume, immersed in the character and a specific scene. Similarly, portraits of Siddons "out of character," such as Thomas Gainsborough's painting of Siddons as a grand society lady, do not display visual references to her career as an actress.[87] The natural, effortless, unconscious quality of theatricality that Siddons so carefully strategized and perfected is destroyed in Beechey's painting by her obvious unmasking—a gesture that marks her awareness of her own performances.

The failure of Beechey's portrait (never sold, it was found in his studio after he died) underscores that the key to a positive formulation of celebrity for an actress was to always keep the act of performance hidden.[88] Returning to image we began with, it is not surprising that the most enduring portrait of Sarah Siddons, Reynolds's "The Tragic Muse," portrays the actress as an allegorical Queen—a mythic representation of tragedy floating in the clouds. There she is separated from her "real" self, from the daily negotiations involved in being an actress, from the realities of her body, and from the manipulative tactics of fashioning her celebrity.

STAGING THE TRAGIC MUSE

In her memoir, Siddons writes a detailed account of the scene of the creation of the "Tragic Muse" in Reynolds's studio, an episode that occurs, significantly, right after she inherits Garrick's dressing room (figure 6). The anecdote is similar to a short play with Siddons as the heroine and Reynolds as the devoted admirer. In her negotiations with Reynolds, Siddons clearly sees herself as royal. She imagines that Reynolds treats her as Queen, which signifies that she has a Queen's power and authority. Siddons narrates:

> When I attended him for the first sitting, after many more gratifying encomiums than I dare repeat, he took me by the hand, saying, "Ascend your undisputed throne, and graciously bestow upon me some grand idea of

> The Tragik Muse." I walked up the steps and seated myself instantly in the attitude in which She now appears. This idea satisfyd him so well, that he, without one moments hesitation determined not to alter it.[89]

From the first moment, it is Siddons who is in control of this transaction. Reynolds asks her to perform the part in the painting. She makes an artistic decision and assumes a pose, and he loves it. Here, Siddons is not only the tragic muse; she is also Reynolds's muse. Siddons's control over the concept of the image renders the painting a true representation of her performance. Because she makes up the pose, the painting is not necessarily about tragedy, but about *her* ability to signify tragedy. Siddons further emphasizes her role as the muse by capitalizing the pronoun "She." Her grammatical flourish indicates both her majestic significance and her ability to play a role. The "She" depicted in the portrait is not a "real" representation of Siddons, herself, but rather a carefully constructed illusion.

Siddons goes on to relate that she not only contributed to the concept of the portrait, but she also graciously gave Reynolds artistic advice at crucial moments:

> When I attended on him for the last sitting, he appeared to be afraid of touching it, and, after pausingly contemplating his unequald glorious work, he said, "No, I will merely add a little more colour to the face." I then begged him to pardon my presumption in hoping that he would not heighten that tone of complexion so exquisitely accordant with the chilling and deeply co-centered musing of Pale Melancholy. He most graciously complyd with my petition.[90]

In this passage, Siddons suggests that, for Reynolds, her figure in the painting is analogous to her own body. The unframed, unfinished portrait becomes a kind of fetish object, a kind of undressed figure. Siddons remarks that he "appeared to be afraid of touching it." After gazing at his "unequald glorious work," Reynolds decides to add more colour to the face. At this point in the scene, the traditional relationship of artist-as-voyeur-and-creator and the woman-as-the-object-to-be-created has not been disturbed; however, Siddons enters the scene with her own set of desires. As another artist and inventor, she comments on her own image—her disembodied self on the canvas—and offers advice on how to make the ideal image better. Siddons "begs" Reynolds to leave her face pale in order to create the desired effect of chilling melancholy, which suggests that she wanted to be seen as "natural," without make up or additional artificial coloring. Reynolds graciously

FIGURE 6. Sir Joshua Reynolds. *Sarah Siddons as the Tragic Muse*, 1784, © Huntington Library, Art Collections and Botanical Gardens, San Marino, California

"complyd." The complying and begging in this scene suggest a negotiation of desires, a charged exchange that literally takes place over the brush strokes that create her image.

Siddons is the winner here—both in manipulating her image in the painting, and in conquering Reynolds's will. She continues:

> Some time afterwards, when he invited me to go and see the Picture finished and in the Frame, he did me the honour to thank me for persuading him to pause on heightening the colour, being now perfectly convinced that it would have impaired the effect, adding that he had been so inexpressibly gratifyd by observing so many persons weep in contemplating this favorite effort of his Pencil, and adding with his own benevolent smile, "You yourself, you know, can do no more than bring forth tears which, tho' you do not see, and sighs and sobs which, tho' you do not hear, you make us all so severely feel." [91]

Even when the picture is in the frame, and the transaction is complete, Siddons adds that Reynolds thanks her again for her wise advice and remarks that he is truly "gratifyd" by the overwhelming emotional response to the "favorite effort of his Pencil." Here, the flow of desires, the begging and complying over the unframed image, have been brought to a satisfying conclusion. And although the spectators are admiring the work of Reynolds's "pencil," Reynolds explains that he could not have done such extraordinary work without the power of Siddons's performances. He tells her that, although she does not "see or hear" what her audiences are doing, she is inevitably making them "feel" things severely and powerfully.

Siddons finishes the scene:

> I was delighted when he assured me that he was certain that the colours would remain unfaded as long as the Canvass would hold them together, which unhappily had not been the case with all his works. He then most gallantly and most flatteringly added, 'And to confirm my opinion, here is my name, for I have resolved to go down to posterity upon the hem of your Garment.' Accordingly, it appears upon the border of the drapery. Here ended this charming visit and, shortly afterwards, his precious Life.[92]

In a crowning flourish, Siddons ends this triumph by having Reynolds sign his name to the hem of her garment, metaphorically writing on her body. Thus, one of Reynolds's most famous images is, in Siddons's view, about his desire for her: his wish to possess her image and, in turn, her seduction of him. Once she has gotten what she wanted, she quickly writes him out of the picture: "Here ended this charming visit, and shortly afterwards, his precious life."

This reenactment of the portrait process illustrates Siddons's fantasy of her celebrated self, the pinnacle of her celebrity. It is significant that most historians discredit this version of events in favor of one of the following accounts of how the composition of the portrait was decided. Thomas Phillips writes: "Sir Joshua had begun the head and figure in a different view; but while he was occupied in the preparation of some colour she changed her position to look at a picture hanging on the wall of the room. When he looked at her, and saw the action she had assumed, he requested her not to move; and thus arose the beautiful and expressive figure that we now see in the picture."[93] Samuel Rogers provides a different story: "I was at Sir Joshua's studio when Mrs. Siddons came in, having walked rapidly to be in time for her appointment. She threw herself, out of breath, into an armchair; having taken off her bonnet and dropped her head upon her left hand—the other hand drooping over the arm of the chair. Suddenly lifting her head she said, 'How shall I sit?' 'Just as you are,' said Joshua, and so she is painted."[94]

In both of these narratives, Siddons pose is an "accident," and Reynolds seizes the moment, telling Siddons how she should appear. In Phillips's version, Siddons is looking at another picture while Reynolds is contemplating her image as it would look in a portrait, suggesting the duplicity of representation. In Rogers's account, art mirrors life; Siddons's theatrical everyday movements, in this case throwing herself on a chair, remind Reynolds of her persona on stage, providing a perfect idea for the painting.

Recently, X-rays have been taken of two versions of "The Tragic Muse": one completed in 1784; the other a copy from 1789. The X-rays indicate that Siddons's position on the throne remained constant. Other elements of the portrait—an angel in front of Siddons that was painted over in the final version, and a self-portrait of Reynolds as one of the shadowy figures in the background—were manipulated and revised.[95] What is interesting about this scientific evidence is how it reveals the mistakes inherent in each spectator's version of what actually happened in the creation of this painting, particularly the ways in which each narrator is specifically invested in his or her fantasy of the natural quality of artistic genius. For Siddons, narrating her own version of the events was a moment of true affirmation. She was actually being represented as she wished to be seen. She would now always be remembered as the undisputed reigning Queen of the British theater.

THE DIVINE MRS. S

Although Siddons's legacy as the tragic muse would provide a model for generations of actresses to follow, it is actually Lady Macbeth's rise and fall that represents a perfect paradigm for the paradoxes inherent in contemporary society's view of famous women. For successful women to be seen as sympathetic, they must be simultaneously passive and powerful, domestic and professional, compassionate and driven, divine and ordinary. In the end, Lady Macbeth's sleepwalking becomes oddly analogous to the task of every famous woman: to project a natural, passive, and unconscious mode of feminine power that softens the dangerous paradoxes of female ambition, desire, and success. Lady Macbeth's breakdown—the erasure of her own self-conscious performances—is also analogous to the legacy of the "Siddons effect" as a record of primarily what others saw, imagined, and constructed about Siddons without an emphasis on what Siddons wrote herself. Considering Siddons "Remarks" and her *Reminiscences* as documentary evidence of her strategies for fashioning celebrity provides a way of re-examining her place in the archives of female theatrical "genius and virtuosity." These writings also provide a link to a more intangible history of the effects of gendered performances in the creation of female identities, both real and imagined.

Siddons's fame created a new space for the actress by demonstrating that a woman could be worshipped and constantly on display. Her success in promoting her celebrity status, using visual, theatrical, and textual methods, gave other female performers a standard to imitate and aspire to. A late-eighteenth-century actress could now be a performer and be respectable if she could manage to follow Siddons's lead. For the other actresses in this study, this was not a simple task, particularly for those whose private lives included scandal and intrigue. Their attempts to fashion celebrity by manipulating eighteenth-century conventions would prove much more difficult. They would always live in the shadow of the reigning Queen of the theater, the divine Mrs. S.

Two

Mary Robinson's Gothic Celebrity

WHILE SARAH Siddons was able to cast herself as a respectable theatrical heroine, the actress, novelist, and poetess Mary Robinson (1758–1800) would always be best known for her brief and disastrous affair with the Prince of Wales. Robinson's attempts to portray herself as a desirable and sympathetic figure were ultimately overshadowed by the scandalous rumors about her notorious liaisons, her unhappy marriage, her spending habits, and her questionable morals. Her varied self-fashioning strategies suggest that contemporary ideas about the complexities of female celebrity, self-promotion, and public relations can be traced back to the eighteenth century, a world where image was everything.

The Prince's attention to Mary Robinson, which began with his falling in love with her during her performance of Perdita in Shakespeare's *The Winter's Tale* in 1779, marked her as the ultimate celebrity object of the moment: a position that she attempted to recreate and articulate through writing poetry, novels, articles, and essays, and posing for portraits for nearly twenty years after the affair had ended. Unlike her contemporary, Sarah Siddons, Robinson's celebrity never appeared to be natural or authentic. Instead, Robinson's fame was represented through her highly stylized self-constructions, her attention to fashion, and her prolific narrative performances. After the Prince's first declaration of desire—metonymically represented by the miniature he gives her as a gift with the inscription *Je ne change qu'en mourant*—this authentic moment of celebrity allure becomes Robinson's project of careful and deliberate reconstruction.

Robinson attempted to fashion her celebrity image as simultaneously seductive and vulnerable, designing her persona to be both unthreatening and desirable. In doing so, Robinson participated in acting out ideas about sexuality and female agency that were threatening and dangerous. It was particularly threatening that Robinson authorized and orchestrated her own objectification, and that those performances attracted the attention of several powerful men, most notably the prince himself. Because of her very public affair with the Prince, it was not possible for Robinson to be seen as entirely maternal or domestic. Robinson faced an unavoidable dilemma inherent in foregrounding her own body as a desirable object/commodity, while at the same time appearing to be authentic, natural, and feminine.

Robinson's use of Gothic strategies served as an effective tactic for negotiating her varied self-representations and for fashioning her celebrity. Gothic narratives create suspense, desire, and mystery for readers and spectators. Gothic ideology problematizes the relationship between reality and fantasy, illusion and truth, surface and depth, goodness and evil. The same ideas operate in the creation of an alluring celebrity persona. The celebrity is real and extraordinary, accessible and just out of reach. Celebrities create with their presence (textual, theatrical, and visual) a sense of desire and suspense. What will they say and do? How will the celebrity acknowledge me? There is always a paradoxical sense of presence and absence with a celebrity, since the presence of their image or narratives about them signals the absence of their "real bodies." Yet, possessing an image of a celebrity or writings by a celebrity is a fetishistic way of owning a part of that celebrity's persona. Celebrities tend to operate as ghosts, haunting the minds of their audiences long after they have ceased to be there in physical reality. Robinson's Gothic celebrity cannot be sustained because the "real" intrudes—her aging, damaged body ceases to matter, and she disappears. When Robinson has no more desirable models of femininity to enact and portray, she ceases to appear literally and figuratively. What I am calling Robinson's "Gothic celebrity" points to the ways in which celebrity identities materialized and vanished in late-eighteenth-century culture, revealing the limited and constructed nature of the process of image making.

In this chapter, I will focus on tracing the motif of Robinson's Gothic celebrity in two sets of materials that clearly represent Robinson's strategies for self-fashioning: a series of portraits of her painted right after her affair with the Prince of Wales ended badly; and her memoir, written in the last months of her life and published posthumously by her daughter Mary. In considering these particular portraits and the memoir together, I want to pay specific attention to the ways in which Robinson's use of fashion and costume in conjunction with Gothic tropes allow her to foreground the seductive, desirable qualities of her persona, and to subsequently disappear when those qualities signify the possibility of immorality or deceptiveness. Robinson creates her own celebrity allure by juxtaposing "real" and "imagined" identities in her portraits, and by highlighting and obscuring her "real" body through references to dress and costume in her memoir. In doing so, she participates in "embodying," acting out, and signifying fantasies and anxieties about female sexuality in late-eighteenth-century culture.

In looking at Robinson's Gothic celebrity as a process that highlights the contradictory and irreconcilable aspects of her private and public self-representations, I want to emphasize Robinson's strategy of self-representation as a process of moving between personas in order to fit and, at certain moments, to rebel against the desirable models of femininity projected by late-eighteenth-century culture. Excellent work has been done to establish the idea that Robinson fashioned herself as a variety of different subjects, particularly in her memoir, and that those identities represent shifting ideas about femininity and female subjectivity.[1] In her seminal article "Mary Robinson and the Scripts of Female Sexuality," Anne Mellor argues that Robinson's strategies for self-representation in her memoir follow four different "competing" narratives of the sexual nature of this "fair celebrity."[2] Mellor's competing narratives include Robinson as "a whore; an 'unprotected' and abused wife; a star-crossed lover; or a talented performer and successful artist."[3] I am interested in the ways in which Robinson uses Gothic strategies to move between and within these narratives. Rather than viewing them as competing or as contradictory, I see them as "intertextual" in that they establish Robinson's celebrity by working in relation to one another. The first three narratives are representations that stress Robinson's sexuality, vulnerability, and availability. The third narrative of Robinson as a Romantic artist is entirely informed by the first two.[4] Even when presenting herself as an author in her memoir, Robinson suggests the absence/presence of her seductive body, an idea that makes the purchase of her writings even more desirable.

Recently, Laura Runge has argued persuasively that Robinson's resistance to the labels "whore" and "prostitute" in her memoir reflects the history of anti-adultery discourse and the "legal and social developments concerning adultery and divorce during her lifetime."[5] In deploying "the repeated image of her public self in order to revise the trope of whore," and complicating "the story of her own adultery by dramatizing the libertinism of the elite lords of her acquaintance," Robinson "exposes the predatory nature of masculine power and its economic stranglehold over women."[6] In doing so, Robinson succeeds in distinguishing "between adultery and prostitution," aligning "her wage-earning labor with authorship and acting, but not with trade in sex."[7]

While I agree with Runge that Robinson distinguishes her identity from common prostitution and attempts, at times, to revise her position as a whore, I want to further suggest that both the sexual availability and desirability gained by presenting herself as a sexual object, and the sympathy gained by representing herself as a victim of predatory men, contribute to her strategies for self-representation. Her position as a "whore" or "fallen woman" is at times strategically productive in presenting herself as an accessible and desirable sexual object, and as a terrorized heroine. In her presentation of herself as a self-sufficient actress and author, Robinson is always reminding her readers of the consequences of these powerful assertions of agency, conjuring images of her debilitated and exhausted body while writing, and her state of anxiety while auditioning for a new theatrical role in her nightgown. By making her body both available and elusive through Gothic motifs, Robinson attempts to elicit, simultaneously, desire and compassion from her readers.

ROBINSON'S GOTHIC

It is perhaps not surprising that both the Gothic and celebrity emerge in the late eighteenth century as powerful discourses about the individual that complicate the relationship among categories used to classify and define identities.[8] Authoring oneself by marketing one's image suggested the possibility of revising one's identity, testing traditional boundaries of social status, modes of dress, and codes of behavior. The Gothic similarly stresses the opportunity to interrogate and, at times, to dismantle conventional modes of being. Anne Close has argued that Robinson uses the Gothic as a central motif for privileging her sexual experience and worldliness over the constraints of proper femininity. She writes, "Her Gothic argues that knowledge and experience, not chastity and filial obedience, are the most powerful attributes for a woman to cultivate—whether as a gothic heroine or as a powerful woman living and breathing in the turbulent world of 1790s England."[9] She proposes that Robinson presents herself as the Gothic heroine of her own story, "a move which simultaneously exploits familiar gothic conventions and reworks them to value and reward a woman like herself (who would not be considered as a suitable character in a gothic novel)."[10] While I agree that Robinson's representation of herself as a Gothic heroine exploits and reworks Gothic conventions, I want to stress that this strategy is not solely aimed at redemption of her self-image but also at seduction and self-promotion, a process which often involved emphasizing the very aspects of her persona that were the most suspect. I argue that the relationship of Robinson's use of the Gothic to the visual and theatrical aspects of her texts allows her to project a self-image that is paradoxically sexual and vulnerable, powerful and unthreatening.

Robinson's preoccupation with the Gothic is tied to the ways in which eighteenth-century audiences may have understood her public image. Writing primarily about Gothic drama, Jeffrey Cox argues that "[t]he gothic subverts morality and 'the natural order of things' by confusing sympathy and judgment, by finding 'noble' qualities in lower class figures and by offering sympathy to rebels."[11] The acts of posing for portraits after the collapse of her affair with the Prince, and writing her memoir at the very end of her life in a desperate attempt to make money, suggest that Robinson understood herself as a kind of rebel or outsider. Both the memoir and the portraits are evidence of Robinson's desire to revise her public image as an attempt to display her "noble" qualities to audiences, but they are also artifacts of her attempts to seduce and capture the attention of her fans.

In these self-representations, Robinson plays on the possibilities of her elusive ghostly body in order to appear likable and sympathetic while catering, at the same time, to her desire to market herself as a fashionable commodity. Robinson's fascination with the Gothic (she wrote several multi-volume Gothic novels and a play) reflects this interest in things irrational, but also a desire to revise the categories and conventions associated with the domestic. Robinson's Gothic is a Gothic pushed to its extremes. Her lengthy Gothic novels, *Vancenza* (1792) and *Walsingham* (1797), and her play, *The Sicilian Lover* (1796), all focus on reconfigurations of roles associated with the family and gender positions. In *Vancenza,* the main character discovers that she is having an affair with her brother. In *Walsingham,* two rival male characters fall in love when it is revealed that one of them is actually a woman who has been brought up disguised as a man so that she can keep her inheritance. *The Sicilian Lover* concerns a father's incestuous relationship with his daughter.

In her memoir, Robinson is literally writing about the ghost of her younger self. Her own fragile state is connected to the emotional act of recalling her past. Terry Castle has argued:

> A crucial feature of the new sensibility of the late eighteenth century was, quite literally, a growing sense of the ghostliness of other people. In the moment of Romantic self-absorption, the other was indeed reduced to a

phantom—a purely mental effect, or image as it were, on the screen of consciousness itself. The corporeality of the other—his or her actual life in the world—became strangely insubstantial and indistinct: what mattered was the mental picture, the ghost, the haunting image.[12]

Robinson echoes this new primacy of the "haunting image" in creating her multiple personas. Each of Robinson's "selves" can only be understood in relation to another of her identities, to the ghost of a former persona. The Gothic elements of the memoir work in conjunction with the visual elements to conjure various images of Robinson on the stage of the text, while others remain an unseen presence. Robinson's use of clothing—what she was wearing, what others were wearing, and how others viewed her outfits—is tied to the ways in which her various identities strategically appear and disappear throughout the memoir.

In her excellent study, *Fashioning Gothic Bodies,* Catherine Spooner uses the connections between Gothic literature and fashion to articulate new ways of understanding the problematic process of representing the female body and, by extension, female subjectivity. She argues that Gothic texts continuously foreground "surfaces" in order to interrogate an understanding of subjectivity that privileges a "surface-depth" model.[13] In other words, Gothic texts, with their emphasis on masks and disguises, complicate the relationship of the body to costume by suggesting the "erasure" or "effacement" of the body underneath the veil.[14] The subject can only be "read," then, through a series of visual signifiers that do not cover an "authentic" or real self underneath the costume. Spooner explains that in the world of the Gothic "external appearances are represented as more constitutive of personal identity than the apparently interior aspects of the self."[15] Thus, in Gothic texts, clothing often becomes the mechanism through which subjects are read, understood, and analyzed. Robinson's use of fashionable clothing to conjure images of herself in various situations throughout the memoir allows her to project versions of idealized femininity in order to direct attention away from her scandalous behavior and from her "real" aging body. Her focus on fashioning celebrity through visual roles helped to establish her fame and to hasten her downfall.

Robinson's emphasis on Gothic motifs in her memoir is also at work in her portraits. Like memoirs, which recall a life that has already been lived, portraits present an image that always invokes the idea of the absent body of the sitter. In Robinson's portraits, haunting doubling effects also occur in relation to the narratives of identity that each portrait represents. Gainsborough's portrait of Robinson as Perdita, for example, invokes her persona as the actress who plays the part of Perdita onstage, and the woman who plays the part of Perdita, or "the lost one," in real life. Robinson's theatrical roles, particularly as Perdita, are also tied to ghostliness. When an actress performs a part, her own body becomes in many ways intangible and indistinct.

As I have argued in the introduction, the Gothic phenomenon of judging identities through appearances and surfaces is also a central aspect of the mechanisms of celebrity culture. In his book *Celebrity,* sociologist Chris Rojek argues: "One might posit that celebrities are, in part, the projection and articulation of unconscious and subconscious desire. The public face of the celebrity contains traces of wishes and fantasies that are ubiquitous in popular culture."[16] Robinson's public face, as represented in her portraits and in visual representations of herself in her memoir, is charged with traces of her larger role as a celebrity figure. While these images gesture toward some kind of knowledge of the "real" Robinson, they are always elusively tied to the presence of the desires and anxieties projected by her audiences. Robinson's use of the Gothic in conjunction with visual imagery suggests her acute awareness of this connection between how she wished to appear and how her audiences wanted to see her.

STRIKE A POSE:
THE MANY FACES OF MARY ROBINSON

A significant number of unflattering representations of Robinson began to appear in the press as a result of her doomed affair with the Prince, which began in 1779 and officially "ended" in 1781. Perhaps to counteract these negative images, Robinson sat for four portraits by leading eighteenth-century painters George Romney, Thomas Gainsborough, and Sir Joshua Reynolds, between 1781 and 1784.[17] The portrayals of Robinson in these paintings vary from representations that signify her status as a fashionable lady to representations that refer to her position as an actress and a tragic figure. By presenting herself as an anonymous girl, a society belle, a romantic victim, and a literary heroine, Robinson effectively recasts herself in visually attractive and respectable eighteenth-century roles. Because Robinson commissioned, sat for, and most likely paid for all of the portraits (except the Gainsborough, which was commissioned and paid for by the Prince), it is safe to assume that she had some part in the artistic decisions being made.[18] As Robyn Asleson has suggested: "The publicity afforded by portraiture was simply too important to be overlooked, and a skilled performer such as Robinson would undoubtedly have participated in determining (or at the very least approving) the salient aspects of her pictorial representation."[19] Robinson's job as actress made it necessary for her to be familiar with the process of remaking herself using specific costumes, facial expressions, and poses. These portraits provide information about the way that Robinson wanted to be "seen" and the ways in which audiences saw her. In effect, they are artifacts of Robinson's strategies for fashioning her own celebrity.

This particular series of portraits of Robinson represents a variety of narratives of femininity that reflect late-eighteenth-century cultural fantasies and anxieties about gender, and more specifically, ambiguous desires surrounding the role of the English woman in the public sphere. The roles Robinson plays in her portraits gesture both toward her availability and toward her status as a famous person: a combination that creates a sense of desire for spectators eager to imitate and to possess Robinson's image. The portraits signal Robinson's glamour and authentic allure; simultaneously, they suggest her own theatrical participation in the management and manipulation of her career as a professional actress. Robinson attempts to complicate this contradiction between authenticity and theatricality by appearing in portraits as "herself," and in images that reference her identity as an actress and as an author. This sense of embodiment and elusiveness enacts, what I have been referring to as, Robinson's Gothic celebrity. By gesturing toward her "real" and "imagined" identities at the same moment, Robinson creates mystery, desire, and the potential for sympathy among her spectators.

The Gainsborough portrait (1781) is the only picture that alludes directly to Robinson's identity both as the Prince's mistress (she holds his picture in her hand) and as an actress (she is dressed in the costume of a Shakespearean shepherdess). The other portraits, Romney's *Mrs. Mary Robinson* (1781) and Reynolds's portrait of 1782, depict Robinson playing the part of a lady. In the Romney image, she is wearing a charming domestic costume; in the Reynolds portrait, she dons the guise of an aristocratic woman. Reynolds's later portrait from 1784 captures the Gothic mood and melancholy spirit that Robinson wished to convey in her writing. Although the four paintings present very different representations of Robinson, they are all advertisements for legitimacy.[20] These artists employ conventional elements of eighteenth-century portraiture to restage Robinson's identity and to promote her as a worthy and enticing celebrity.

In portraits by Romney and Reynolds, Robinson plays the role of an ordinary young woman. In these paintings, she is dressed as if she were "out of costume" in an attempt to present herself as having little to do with the theater. The emphasis on fashion in these images is significant: Robinson's *au courant* costume and accessories indicate that she is participating in a mode of acceptable eighteenth-century visual display. As a fashion model and a visual advertisement for clothing and style, Robinson is not on stage in a theatrical mode. In these portraits, she functions as a kind of mannequin. Similar to paintings of Siddons as a Grande society dame, which had the effect of translating her noble qualities onstage to her behavior and status offstage, Robinson's role as a "model" in these images redirects attention from her scandalous actions to the details of her outfits. Portraits of Robinson in and out of costume serve the double purpose of making her image seem accessible and ordinary for audiences, while featuring her body as an erotic object of display.

As I have argued in the previous chapter, the semiotics of fashion in portraits provides a way to read specific identities. Rojek explains that, as fashion became an integral part of modern culture in the eighteenth century, "sartorial appearance became a more significant feature of life strategy, since it conveyed immediately a façade of coherent lifestyle values and aspirations."[21] Robinson's costumes, then, provide specific clues about the visual narrative of identity projected by the portrait. We can catch a glimpse of what Robinson might have looked like dressed as an "ordinary" girl in a portrait by George Romney entitled Mrs. Mary Robinson, commissioned by Robinson and completed in 1781 (figure 7). Nothing about the portrait suggests Robinson's affiliation with the theater or with the Prince. Ten years earlier, Romney had painted another actress, Mrs. Yates, in the character of the tragic muse—a portrait that would later be compared to Reynolds's portrait of Sarah Siddons of the same name. Although Robinson sat for her portrait years later, at a different point in Romney's career, it is significant that the portrait is of Robinson playing the part of an anonymous girl, not as an actress or as a theatrical figure.

In the Romney painting, Robinson is wearing a modern dress with a shawl of lovely black fabric, a white fur muff, and a muslin cap. Her eyebrows are raised slightly as if she is tempting the viewer to challenge her. Her lips are drawn together, and her head tilts forward, further emphasizing the penetrating line of her gaze. Her accessories portray a woman of sufficient means—domestic yet fashionable. The muff, a stylish eighteenth-century item, is the central feature of Robinson's outfit, suggesting that she is participating as a consumer in the eighteenth-century marketplace.[22] While she is usually an object of consumption, selling herself on stage, her presence as a well-dressed "girl" emphasizes that she can easily assume the role of a character who participates in "real life" activities.[23] Robinson must wear recognizable eighteenth-century fashion items to market herself as a valuable commodity. In effect, she cleverly packages herself by equating the assumed value of the products she displays with her self-image.

FIGURE 7. George Romney. *Mrs. Mary Robinson*, 1781. By kind permission of the Trustees of the Wallace Collection, London

Robinson's role in this painting as both a consumer and an object of consumption reveals the ironies involved in fashioning celebrity. In order to be perceived as an "authentic" girl, Robinson must cleverly dress the part and draw attention to her stylish choices, a process that signifies artifice and theatricality. Furthermore, the muff, which can be read as a fashionable accessory for a "real" lady, has a more pronounced double meaning when worn by an actress—a professional occupation historically tied to promiscuity and prostitution. Robinson's "muff" (also a word for female genitalia) will always suggest her availability and sexuality. Robinson's role in this portrait as a kind of advertisement for a certain innocent girlish style "humanizes" or "legitimizes" her persona, momentarily obscuring her ties to scandal and adultery. However, the presence of the muff immediately suggests the possibility of an alternate identity that does not coincide with the persona ideally projected in the portrait.

Reynolds's portrait of Robinson, exhibited at the Royal Academy in April 1782, presents another view of the actress dressed as a fashionable lady (figure 8). At the time these portraits were painted, it was en vogue for aristocratic women to be portrayed in costume, particularly in costumes modeled after dresses used in seventeenth-century portraits by van Dyck and Rubens.[24] Often the artists themselves would have costumes in their studios that the sitter could wear. Sometimes, artists would combine elements of fashion from the past with embellishments from current fashion. Reynolds's portrait of Robinson is considered a costume piece. Robinson's pose and dress are reminiscent of Rubens's paintings (particularly *Le Chapeau de Paille* and a full-length portrait of Helena Fourment). Since Reynolds, in fact, had just visited Flanders in the summer of 1781, it is not unlikely that these images were on his mind.[25] Although elements of Robinson's costume invoke the past, the elaborate hat in the Reynolds portrait also seems consistent with Robinson's description in her memoir of the hat with feathers she wore to impress her husband's family.

Reynolds presents Robinson as a self-assured society beauty a different image from the one that she projects in the Romney portrait finished just a year earlier. In this painting, her expression is extremely composed, almost haughty (Reynolds apparently liked this portrait so much that he kept it hanging in his studio as a kind of advertisement for his own abilities as a portrait painter).[26] Although Robinson is playing "herself" in this image, she is also playing the role of a stylish celebrity. The image seems intended to provoke the spectator's desire to imitate Robinson's beauty and/or to possess her body. Robinson appears glamorous and alluring, and the portrait works to conjure an idealized fantasy of feminine beauty, grace, and confidence. At the same time, however, the image of Robinson as an object of stylish fantasy is also connected to the threatening possibility of her sexual agency, to her potential ability to transcend the social codes of traditional femininity, and to the boundaries of her class status as an actress/theatrical professional.

Whether Robinson's appearance was praised or parodied, it was always featured as the central aspect of her identity. While Siddons's persona was linked to her voice, theatrical gestures, and movements onstage, Robin-

FIGURE 8. John Hazlitt. *Mrs. "Perdita" Robinson after Reynolds*, 1782. By kind permission of the Trustees of the Wallace Collection, London

son was usually described in terms of what she was wearing. In *The Daily Advertiser* on 31 March 1783, one critic expressed a flattering view of Robinson's style: "There is a neatness and decency in the dress of the Perdita that challenges universal admiration; which if more frequently copied by our fair countrywomen would considerably add to their personal accomplishments."[27] Robinson is linked here to the "fair countrywoman" both by her clothing and by the way that she performs in her daily costumes. The fact that, in this spectator's opinion, Robinson could serve as a role model for "our fair countrywoman" is further evidence that actresses were seen, at times, to be "better" or more desirable than ordinary English women. For other contemporary observers, however, Robinson's costumes reflected her desperate attempts to appear desirable and to win her audience's approval. Leticia Hawkins comments: "Today she was a payasanne, with her straw hat at the back of her head, looking as if too new to what she passed to know what she looked at. Yesterday she, perhaps, had been the dressed belle of Hyde Park, trimmed, powdered, patched, painted to the utmost power of rouge and white lead; tomorrow, she would be the cravatted Amazon of the riding house: but be what she might the fashionable promenaders swept the ground as she passed."[28] Hawkins's emphasis on the theatrical, constructed nature of Robinson's appearance undermines the possibility of her authenticity and her ability to compete with "real" women. The image of Robinson that Hawkins conjures, with her face and hair "trimmed, powdered, patched, painted to the utmost power of rouge and white lead," is a nightmarish vision of excessive theatricality. In this picture, it is impossible to see Robinson's actual face underneath the layers of cosmetic products and potions, a metaphor for the idea that Robinson's authentic identity is similarly obscured and dangerously unreadable.

The ambiguous power of Robinson's public persona was reinforced by negative images and newspaper reports that reduced her identity to a phrase suggesting her affiliation with the Prince and her final role as an actress. Ironically referred to as "the Perdita," Robinson becomes a transparent or readable object, a commodity to be looked at, evaluated, and possessed. In May of 1782, *The Morning Herald* reports, "The Perdita was lately made captive by Lieutenant Colonel Banastre Tarl . . . n."[29] On 19 April of the same year, *The Public Advertiser* tells its readers, "The Perdita has been particularly successful in the commerce of this year. How immense must have been her *Imports* and *Exports* is Cognizable from this one circumstance: She has sat for her picture four times, viz. twice to *Romney,* once to *Gainsborough,* and once to *Sir Joshua Reynolds!*"[30] This parody of Robinson selling herself by posing for portraits suggests that there were limits to the extent to which a female celebrity could market and promote her image. Robinson's attempt to provide audiences with different versions of herself reinforced the idea that she was available for public consumption and complicated the narratives of femininity that she variously projected. As a public object of desire, she could not also be a respectable young lady; her status as "the Perdita" confirmed her value as an object to be passed around and owned.

CARTOONS/OVEREXPOSURE

While Robinson was sitting for portraits by Romney, Reynolds, and Gainsborough, various unflattering prints and engravings of her appeared in the press, along with humiliating letters and verses concerning Robinson and the Prince. In these images, Robinson's body is exaggerated through her costumes. An engraving by T. Colley published on 17 December 1782, entitled *Perdito and Perdita—or—the Man & Woman of the People*, is a good example of the public image that Robinson was trying to combat in her own self-representations (figure 9). Here, Robinson/Perdita is pictured gallivanting around in a carriage (she was famous for traveling in expensive carriages), while dressed elaborately in full riding regalia and a plumed hat. Next to her is a nauseous Charles Fox, a famous politician and admirer of Mrs. Robinson. It is Robinson, though, who holds the reins, literally and figuratively: a position the artist suggests she acquired by assuming the role of a society belle. Although her costume is different from the one that she wears in Reynolds's portrait, the idea of Robinson dressing as a lady of fashion is parodied and framed in this ridiculous context.

An equally unflattering anonymous print (figure 10) published in 1783 borrows from Farquhar's *The Beaux Stratagem*. Charles Fox and Prime Minister North, both suspected lovers of Mary Robinson, are Scrub and Archer. Robinson is cast as Gipsey. A copy of Reynolds's portrait of Colonel Banastre Tarleton hangs on the wall. Archer says: "And this colonel I'm afraid has converted the affection of your Perdita." Scrub replies: "Converted ay perverted my dear friend for I am afraid he has made her a whore." Robinson's pose and costume, which is similar to the one that she wore in the Romney portrait, except that the skirt of her dress is oversized, suggest perhaps that either one of the men, or both, could fit comfortably underneath. The connection that this artist proposes between Robinson's identity as an actress and her societal aspirations and liaisons illustrates that Robinson is not fooling anyone with her anonymous, lady-like disguises. According to her audiences, Robinson's "role playing" is degrading rather than legitimizing. The artist suggests that onstage and offstage actresses are masking their "authentic" identities as prostitutes.

In October 1783, an anonymous print was published depicting Robinson and the Prince as two halves of one figure (figure 11). The Prince wears gentlemanly attire, while Robinson wears a dress that reveals her right breast. The small heads of George III (who exclaims, "Oh my son, my son!"), Lord North, Fox, Banastre Tarleton, and Mr. Robinson (who bears the label "king of the cuckolds") are pictured in the background. The artist implies that,

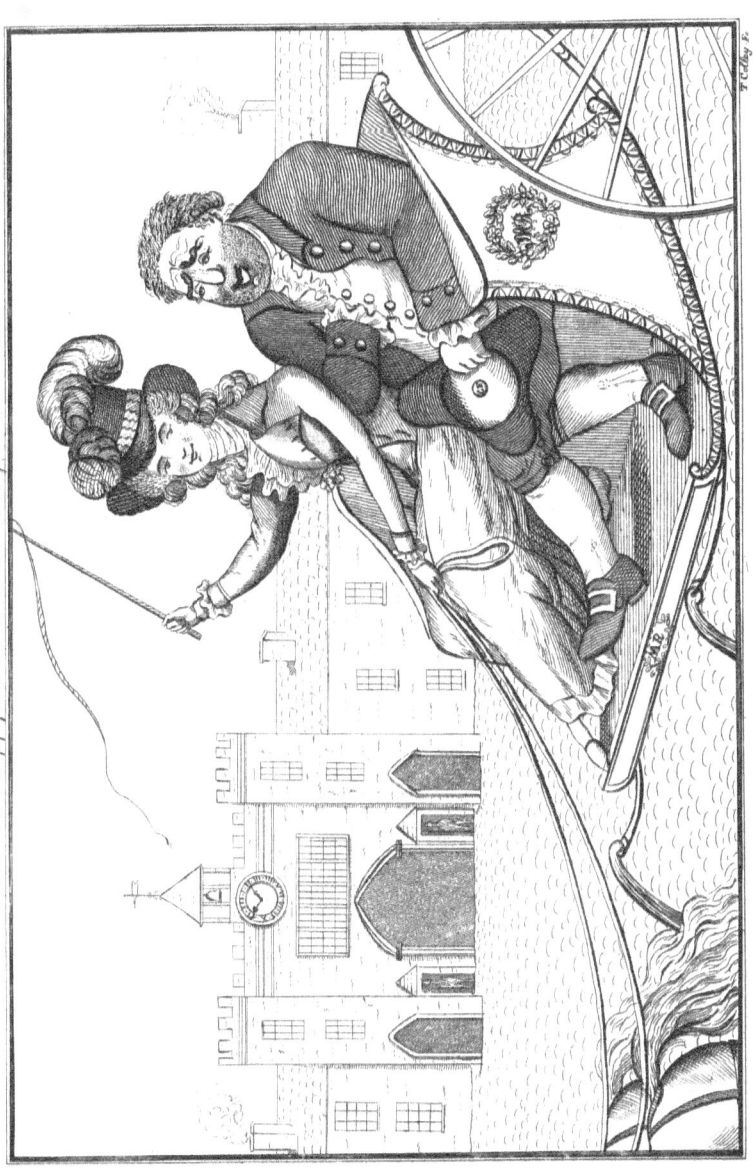

FIGURE 9. T. Colley, *Perdito and Perdita — or — the Man & Woman of the People*, engraving published 17 December 1782. © Trustees of the British Museum

FIGURE 10. Anonymous. *Scrub and Archer*, print published 25 April 1783. © Trustees of the British Museum

just as Robinson has worn her lovers out, she has also saturated the public with her image. Instead of appearing in a fashionable costume, she has been literally stripped of her disguises and pared down to the essential image of the breast—a symbol of sexuality, maternity, and female vulnerability. Although Robinson is undressed, the Prince remains clothed and unaffected. This juxtaposition serves as a chilling reminder that it is the gender of the body beneath the costume that dictates the possibilities of one's identity.[31] For women in the eighteenth century, fashioning celebrity involved different

FIGURE 11. Anonymous. *Florizel and Perdita,* print published 18 October 1783. © Trustees of the British Museum

rules than those for men, particularly men of rank. This satirical print, in particular, underscores the cultural anxieties around actresses fashioning their celebrity. When celebrity helps a woman to achieve a leap in class status that may, in fact, threaten the stability of the British monarchy, the consequences resonate deeply, and celebrity quickly transforms into notoriety.

ROBINSON AS PERDITA

Images of Robinson "in costume," or dressed in a specific role, link her theatrical personas with her tumultuous life offstage. These portraits suggest what Rojek terms "the intertextuality of celebrity,"[32] or in other words, the "interplay between the narrative of celebrity and the historical, cultural and socioeconomic contexts to which celebrity is attached."[33] The Gainsborough painting of Robinson (figure 12), for instance, finished in 1781, is a very different picture from the Romney and Reynolds portraits because its impact depends on the spectator's knowledge of specific events happening in the world outside of the painting.[34] This portrait creates a fantasy narrative that revises the sordid details of the "real" relationship between Robinson and the Prince.

The portrait presents Robinson as an innocent victim of an unfortunate romantic attachment, not as an active participant in the affair. Even though the liaison between Robinson and the Prince had ended, this painting is a kind of testament to his affections. The romantic pastoral setting that frames Robinson is typical of Gainsborough. She stares off pensively into the distance while holding a miniature of the Prince in her left hand and a handkerchief (perhaps for drying her tears) in the other. A dog—a symbol of faithfulness and sensitivity—sits lovingly by her side, a sad substitute for the Prince himself. Visual clues in the portrait provide a trajectory for the spectator, who is asked to equate the fragile delicacy of Robinson's elongated figure with her vulnerability and despair.[35]

The portrait's imaginary landscape and narrative suggest a literary moment. The viewer is directed to see Robinson as "Perdita" from Shakespeare's *The Winter's Tale,* which was the role that she played the night she met the Prince of Wales. Her father, the paranoid King Leontes, ruthlessly abandons Perdita at the beginning of the play. She grows up believing that she is a shepherdess only to discover that, when she is ultimately rescued by a Prince and reunited with her family, she is actually a princess. This Cinderella story has obvious parallels to Robinson's own situation. Dressed as Perdita (which in Latin translates as "the lost one") Robinson has been wrongfully deserted and still has hopes of being rescued by a new "Prince." She is also a legitimate princess, even though she wears the costume of a common shepherdess. The context of this portrait ultimately attempts to reframe real events by substituting fictional parallels. Here, Robinson is the indisputable victim of circumstances beyond her control.

In a review of the three portraits on 19 April 1782, *The Public Advertiser* pronounced the Gainsborough painting as one of his "few failures" because the portrait was not a true "likeness" of the sitter.[36] Romney's *Mrs. Mary Robinson* was described as "second in point of merit" to Reynolds's portrait of Robinson finished in 1782.[37] Reynolds's image of Robinson garnered the most praise: "The countenance was grave and sensible, the likeness very

FIGURE 12. Thomas Gainsborough. *Mrs. Mary Robinson (Perdita)*, 1781. By kind permission of the Trustees of the Wallace Collection, London

strong and the coloring correct. The artist has certainly not done so much on the score of beauty, as the Fair original has claim to. . . . But of the three portraits Sir Joshua's [is] beyond comparison the best."[38] Not surprisingly, it was the portrait of Robinson as a society belle that received the most critical acclaim. The reviewer even goes so far as to point out that the beauty portrayed in the portrait does not do justice to Robinson's authentic beauty, suggesting the spectator's desire to see the image of the actress as a nearly perfect representation of the actress's real body. Interestingly, it was the threat of the "authenticity" of Robinson's stylish celebrity persona (in other words, her beauty and charms could possibly give her power) that led to prints and articles satirizing her attempts to legitimize her image. Once Robinson's image became inextricably associated with questions of notoriety, she shifted her tactics once again, creating a new version of herself as an authoress.

ROBINSON AS A ROMANTIC HEROINE

In the same year that the double torso print of the Prince and Robinson appeared, Robinson suffered a miscarriage that left her frail and barely able to walk. She sailed for France the following year and did not return to England until 1788. Before she left England, she sat for one more portrait by Reynolds entitled *Mrs. Mary Robinson* (1784, which presents her as a wistful romantic heroine (figure 13). This portrait seems designed to suggest a new mode of celebrity tied to Robinson's blossoming literary career. Robinson selected this image to be the frontispiece of her *Poems* (1791) and her *Lyrical Tales* (1800), which suggests that she wished to associate this image with her authorial persona.[39]

Reynolds conveys the emotional strain of Robinson's illness and self-imposed exile by depicting her in profile, as she turns dramatically away from the viewer. She is wearing a white muslin gown with a pink sash. The black necklace around her neck emphasizes the whiteness of her skin and, perhaps, the poignant separation between her active mind and her inactive body.[40] Her figure is set against the backdrop of a dark sky and a tempestuous ocean. Robinson loved this type of romantic scenery. In her memoir, she explains that her state of mind often reflected the rustic sea landscape of her childhood: "I was naturally of pensive mind and melancholy character. My reflections on my changes of fortune, frequently gave me an air of dejection, which perhaps excited an interest beyond what might have been awakened by the vivacity or bloom of juvenility."[41]

FIGURE 13. Sir Joshua Reynolds. *Mrs. Mary Robinson*, 1784. By kind permission of the Trustees of the Wallace Collection, London

Reynolds's second portrait of Robinson has an "intertextual" relationship with the other portraits discussed in this essay. Robinson's body turning away from the viewer suggests a turning away from previous representations that emphasized her fashionable body toward an image that suggests the value of her interior self—her intellect and emotional sensibilities. Unlike the previous images, where Robinson stares directly at the viewer narcissistically inviting the spectator's gaze, in this painting she looks away, which has the effect of emphasizing her role as an object to be looked at rather than a subject to be reckoned with. The romantic features of the painting, the natural outdoor setting in particular, suggest that Robinson's persona is natural and unstaged. The portrait also ties Robinson's image to the tumultuous realities of her situation, creating a narrative of romantic sympathy and feeling where Robinson is cast once again as a fashionable victim of circumstances beyond her control. However, this image can also be seen as a calculated performance of romantic literary femininity—a role that would ideally soften the complex relationship between Robinson's authenticity, her theatricality, and by extension, her public and private selves.

Robinson's refusal to engage the viewer directly can be read as a deliberate bid for celebrity attention. In effect, she asks the viewer: how can you get me to look at you again? The image can be seen as a moment of self-consciousness similar to the moment Siddons creates when she looks at herself in Garrick's mirror in her new dressing room. Robinson's awareness of her celebrity persona invokes the idea of several identities here: the idealized Gothic/romantic heroine; the introspective "authentic" Robinson caught in a moment of self-absorption; and the actual Robinson—the ghostly, paralyzed body behind the image on the canvas. This image captures the effects of Robinson's Gothic celebrity by alluding to all three selves simultaneously and projecting them as inextricably linked.

Robinson's portraits exist today as ghostly examples of her attempts to fashion her celebrity. The various personas projected in these images represent fantasies of late-eighteenth-century femininity. Spectators' reactions to these images reveal competing desires surrounding the threatening presence of women in the public sphere. Robinson's portraits demonstrate the potentially seductive power of female celebrity to disrupt, revise, and complicate traditional conceptions of female identities. In her portraits, Robinson could be an innocent girl, a stylish aristocrat, a lost princess, and a literary heroine. At the same time, however, Robinson's inability to fully adopt these personas in her real life led to her inevitable fall from public favor. Ironically, audiences preferred the illusion of her theatrical personas to the complexity of her "real" self, a paradox that she attempts to recreate with her use of Gothic motifs in her memoir.

GOING GHOSTLY: ROBINSON'S GOTHIC MEMOIR

Using her talents as an author, Mary Robinson adapted elements of late-eighteenth-century literary trends to present herself as a legitimate heroine in her *Memoirs of the Late Mrs. Robinson,* published posthumously by her daughter in 1801. Written while she was ill and still suffering from the rheumatism that plagued her for most of her life, the story focuses on the vicissitudes of her youth and early adulthood. Robinson recalls her childhood and education, her courtship and marriage to Mr. Robinson, and her debut and successes on the stage, and ends abruptly with her affair with the Prince of Wales. The portion of the narrative that she actually wrote covers only the first twenty-two years of her life. The memoir is finished and edited by a "friend" (Robinson's daughter) who informs the reader in the preface that her mother's dying wish was the publication of this last work.[42]

What sets Robinson apart from other thespian memoirists is the fact that she was both an actress and a professional author. She was, therefore, deeply aware of the literary concerns of writing a life-narrative, as well as the issues involved in crafting a female character who would be sympathetic to eighteenth-century readers.[43] Robinson's strategies of self-representation in her memoir are based on an understanding of character drawn as much from her experience writing novels, poetry, and plays, as they are from her experience performing characters onstage.[44] As her story progresses, her various identities are designated by relevant costume changes. When she finds herself in a difficult or suspicious moment, she reappears in a different outfit, leaving the phantom of her guilty self in the wings. Robinson writes her memoir as a celebrity ghost. Capitalizing on the Gothic potential of her own history, she attempts to juxtapose sympathy with seduction in order to create a narrative that captures her reader's attention, desire, and compassion.

The beginning of Robinson's memoir resembles the early chapters of a sentimental novel. The reader soon realizes, though, that all is not what it appears to be. When Robinson was ten years old, her father, William Darby, deserted his wife and children to supervise a whaling expedition off the coast of Labrador. From there, he sailed to America where he took up with a mistress who would be his companion for the rest of his life. Ironically, Robinson repeats her father's behavior later in life by leaving her philandering husband to pursue an ill-fated affair with the Prince. Robinson goes to great lengths in the memoir to convince readers that her father was not entirely responsible for his actions. Her own indiscretion becomes, then, strangely justified, not only because of the evidence that she provides of Mr. Robinson's activities, but also because she, like her father, succumbs to her passion. She cannot resist the Prince's power and seductive charm.

This is the perfect setup for a Gothic novel where the heroine is seduced by forces beyond her control, away from the traditional safety of the domestic space. She is lured into the dark interiors of a castle ruled by a mysterious villain. The difference is that, in the Gothic novel, the heroine is a passive victim of circumstance, not an active performer. Although Robinson elicits the reader's sympathy by detailing her own suffering at the betrayal of her father, and later her husband, her story is as much about her status as a victim as it is about the triumphs of her performances.

Robinson begins the memoir by describing her birthplace as a dwelling on an important site of British history:

> At the period where the ancient city of Bristol was besieged by Fairfax's army . . . a great part of this venerable *Minster* was destroyed by the cannonading before Prince Rupert surrendered to the enemy; and the beautiful Gothic structure, which at this moment fills the contemplative mind with melancholy awe, was reduced to but little more than one half of the original fabric. (vol. 1, 1–2)

The crumbling Gothic monastery is a Romantic image, which lends legitimacy to Robinson's education, as well as her literary and aesthetic sensibilities. The image of ruins is also connected to the idea that the self that Robinson creates in her memoir is a self of both the past and the present. Robinson writes about her Gothic birthplace, while at the same time she, too, has become a ghostly figure. With this dramatic description, Robinson locates herself and the reader somewhere in the mythic, military lore of Britain's past. She is born on British soil, on land fought for and conquered by British soldiers. Her claim of British origin, however, is mitigated by the fact that the site of her birth—"a beautiful gothic structure"—is now in ruins, reduced to "one half of the original fabric." Robinson's rooted claim to British identity is from the outset crumbling, fading, temporary, and "besieged."[45]

Robinson goes on to describe the architecture of her birthplace in more detail. Echoing the beginning sequence of Ann Radcliffe's *The Mysteries of Udolpho*, in which Radcliffe describes the chateau of Monsieur St. Aubert, Robinson leads her readers up a winding staircase to an inner chamber with narrow windows and an iron-spiked door. She writes: "In this awe-inspiring habitation during a tempestuous night on the twenty-seventh of November, 1758, I first opened my eyes to this world of duplicity and sorrow" (vol. 1, 4). The recurrence of "duplicity and sorrow" in Robinson's life frame what she would like us to see as a potentially "normal" childhood—a youth that might have led to the life of lady. Although she will attempt in this first volume of her memoir to represent herself as a worthy heroine by describing her family, her coming of age, her education, her courtship, and her marriage, such conventional images of the eighteenth-century literary heroine are undercut by a more sinister strain.

The Gothic scenery of her birthplace is one of the initial clues that the configurations of family and of domestic space are also marked by darker qualities. Throughout the memoir, Robinson describes domestic events that occur in Gothic spaces: her own birth, her pregnancy, and her daughter's first words. Gothic spaces are dark, narrow, secretive, and circuitous. The castle is typically a locus of entrapment for the heroine, and the site of her "discovery"—a revelation that usually leads to the uncovering of the secret that unhinges the plot.

Robinson describes her father as a man of "strong mind and high spirit" (vol. 1, 5). Her mother, who was not considered "handsome," was the grandchild of Catherine Seys, "a woman of great piety and virtue" (vol. 1, 5), who was distantly descended from the philosopher John Locke. The only daughter in a family of three sons, Robinson describes herself as more mysterious than her brothers:

> All the offspring of my parents were, in their infancy, uncommonly handsome, excepting myself. The boys were fair and lusty, with auburn hair, light blue eyes and countenances particularly animated and lovely. I was swarthy; my eyes were singularly large in proportion to my face, which was small and round, exhibiting features marked with the most pensive and melancholy cast. (vol. 1, 11)

Apparently, Robinson's swarthy visage, and her pensive melancholy air, endeared her more to her parents, particularly her father, who she "strongly resembled." Robinson links the mysterious darkness of her outward appearance to the details of her early childhood, a youth "tinctured with romantic and singular characteristics" (vol. 1, 12). For Robinson, her early years provide proof that "the mind is never to be diverted from its original bent; and that every event of my life has been more or less marked by the progressive evils of a too acute sensibility" (vol. 1, 12).

Robinson's use of the words "romantic," "singular," and "sensibility" indicates that she is thinking about her past through the lens of late-eighteenth-century literary conventions. She sets up the elements of a legitimate domestic situation—a relatively wealthy father, a mother descended from gentry, and animated, blue-eyed siblings—at the same time, she foreshadows the possibility that everything is not what it appears to be. Her differences, marked by a mixture of Gothic and romantic characteristics, set her apart. Her nursery, located in the depths of a Gothic monastery, exposed her to organ music and to the sublime affects of choral "chaunting" (vol. 1, 15). Once she learned to read, her favorite pastime was memorizing epitaphs and monumental inscriptions. Her favorite poems were Pope's "Lines to the memory of an unfortunate mistress" and Mason's "Elegy on the Death of the Beautiful Countess of Coventry" (vol. 1, 15).

Robinson's use of literary references establishes her early education and literary sensibility; however, this practice is an interesting transference from the past to the present. These poems refer indirectly to her own persona: She is both the "unfortunate mistress" and the "beautiful countess," and both poems can be read as musings on her Gothic celebrity. Throughout her story, she relies on her ability to present herself as an "unfortunate mistress," a persecuted Gothic heroine, and a "beautiful countess," a stylish and desirable figure. At the same time that Robinson emphasizes the importance of her early intellectual development, she provides a striking image of her "small and round" face, "large" eyes, and "melancholy" features. The vision of her childlike face, marked already with the sensibilities of a mature adult, is a tantalizing image designed to make readers curious about the woman that she will become.

Despite the gloomy overtones of her early childhood, all was well in the Robinson household until her ninth year, when "a scheme was suggested to my father as wild and romantic as it was perilous to hazard" (vol. 1, 18). The scheme was to establish a whale fishery off the coast of Labrador and to "civilize" the "esquimaux Indians" in order to "employ them in the extensive undertaking" (vol. 1, 18). Robinson's mother reacted badly to the proposal, fearing for the future of her children and the safety of her husband. Empathizing with her mother's position, Robinson rationalizes her father's desire for adventure. She writes: "In the early part of his youth, he had been accustomed to a sea life, and, being born an American his restless spirit was ever busied in plans for the increase of wealth and honour to his native country" (vol. 1, 19).

Ultimately, William Darby gives in to his "restless spirit." He abandons his family for America and eventually takes a mistress. He returns to England a few years later with his new "wife," but objects to the way that Mary and her mother have managed to support their family by opening a school for young girls. Looking back on her father's betrayal, an event that marked the first in what would be a series of abandonments (the prince, and then, her companion Colonel Banastre Tarleton), Robinson sees her own passion linked to her father's desire for excitement and adventure. She explains: "This deviation from domestic faith was the only dark shade that marked my father's character. Yet, though his mind was strongly organized, though his understanding capacious and his sense of honor delicate even to fastidiousness, he was still the dupe of his passions, the victim of an unfortunate attachment" (vol. 1, 32). Robinson's description of her father's character is a foreshadowing of her own feelings about her doomed affair with the Prince, which she documents in the memoir, as well as the desertion of Colonel Tarleton after her paralysis. Because of her father's desertion, Robinson becomes a fatherless daughter—an illegitimate woman. However, she recasts herself as a passionate heroine and resurrects her character as a classic victim.

Robinson's father appears only a few more times in her memoir. She mentions that he threatened to "annihilate" (vol. 1, 48) her mother if she allowed her to go back on the stage and that he was of no help to them financially. Despite his tyrannical qualities, Robinson justifies her father's actions by explaining that, during the short periods of time that she spent with him, "His conversation was generally of a domestic nature, and he always lamented that fatal attachment which was now too strongly cemented by time and obligations ever to be dissolved" (vol. 1, 45).

Robinson's sympathy for her father is inextricably tied to her attempts to gain sympathy for her own position as a married woman taken in by a "fatal attachment." Using her father as a double for herself and her own passions displaces her own guilty body onto her father's persona, blurring gender roles and complicating questions of entitlement and authority. Robinson suggests, through this doubling, that her father's authority to choose passion over reason has somehow been passed onto his daughter. She also presents her father as a character with a combination of positive and negative characteristics, preparing her readers for her own complex representation of herself. The debate Robinson stages between passion and reason is a particular feature of Gothic narratives, which tend to privilege extreme emotion over rational sentiment. Cox argues that this upsetting of the usual "order of things" is what gives Gothic narratives a political and even revolutionary valence.[46] Robinson uses Gothic reconfigurations of domestic acts and arrangements to indirectly suggest that women should have the power to make choices based on passion and emotions. Because Robinson uses her father's actions as a substitute for her own, her "guilty" inheritance is legitimized momentarily by her use of Gothic tropes and strategies.

MONSTROUS MOTHERS

Robinson's father's desertion creates a domestic nightmare that truly initiates her as a Gothic heroine. She has now become a full-fledged victim, and the

Gothic tone of the narrative is further emphasized by the appearance of Meribah, the headmistress of a boarding school that Robinson attended. From the outset, Meribah provides a sharp contrast to Robinson's own mother. According to Robinson's account, her mother lost her father because of her "unconquerable timidity" (vol. 1, 21). Such antipathy toward her mother's weakness may explain Robinson's attraction to the eccentric intellectual Meribah, who was her teacher and an alcoholic. Robinson describes her as "one of the most extraordinary women that ever graced or disgraced society. She was mistress of the Latin, French and Italian languages; and she was said to be a perfect arithmetician and astronomer. . . . [A]ll that I learned I learned from this woman" (vol. 1, 33). In her lucid moments, Meribah encouraged Mary to develop her interest in literature and to write poetry. Mary became her constant companion: "She [Meribah] made no scruple of conversing with me (sometimes half the night for I slept in her bed chamber) on domestic and confidential affairs. I felt for her a very sincere affection" (vol. 1, 34). However, in her darker hours, Meribah's addiction often "deprived her of every power, either mental or corporeal" (vol. 1, 33).

Meribah's strength and intellect are not powerful enough to curb her addiction. A few years after Robinson leaves the boarding school, a strange woman comes to her door in rags:

> I observed a woman evidently laboring under excessive affliction; I instantly descended and approached her. She bursting into tears asked if I did not know her. Her dress was torn and filthy;—she was almost naked;—and an old bonnet which nearly hid her face, so completely disfigured her face that I had not the smallest idea of the person who was then almost sinking before me. (vol. 1, 40)

Robinson soon discovers that the woman is Meribah Lorrington. She is penniless and filthy, a ghost of her former self. The Meribah episode, part nightmare and part morality tale, is a strange commentary on the power of appetite and addiction. Echoing Robinson's sentiments about her father and, by extension, her own restless spirit, Meribah's grotesque transformation underscores the potential tragedy of giving in to one's weaknesses. Meribah is a complicated figure because she is both a maternal mentoring presence in Robinson's life, as well as a symbol of madness and destitution. Meribah's madness is also connected to her brilliance and to her "masculine" education. Robinson is attracted to Meribah's knowledge at the same time that she fears its power. She finds her own writing exhausting, and writes of her younger days: "Alas! How little did I then know either the fatigue or the hazard of mental occupations! How little did I foresee that the day would come, when my health would be impaired, my thoughts perpetually employed in so destructive a pursuit" (vol. 1, 185).

Perhaps the most significant aspect of this episode is the haunting image of the "filthy," "naked," and "disfigured" Meribah, whose terrible afflictions are described through the details of her costume. Robinson's rendering of Meribah borrows from conventional imagery of mad women in late-eighteenth-century literature. However, unlike the typical deranged heroine who wears a white dress (often torn) with wild loose hair and wandering eyes, Meribah is an aged Ophelia, stripped of the youth and beauty that would make her persona romantic and sympathetic. Meribah is clearly the cause of her own demise. The fact that Robinson doesn't "recognize" her is a distancing strategy, a way that Robinson can assume a moral position at the same time that she feels pity for Meribah's situation.

Meribah's presence in the text, right before Robinson begins to narrate the section on her theatrical career and her affair with the Prince, seems equally connected to Robinson's sense of her own body. As she writes the memoir, she is aged and disfigured, unrecognizable as her former youthful, desirable self. She, like Meribah, has been a victim of her own passions and desires. Meribah's state of ruin is specifically described through her lack of clothing—a metonym for an inability to dress oneself, to disguise oneself, and to invent a persona to mask one's "real" self. Meribah inhabits a body that has ceased to matter—a self that is only visible to those who dare to look. This is Robinson's worst nightmare: to be in a position where self-fashioning is impossible.

DRESSING FOR SUCCESS: A HEROINE COMES OF AGE

In the beginning of her memoir, Robinson adapts conventions of eighteenth-century fiction—specifically from the Gothic and the domestic novel—to present herself as a legitimate literary heroine. This strategy works well for the section of the memoir that details her childhood. At the point in her story where Robinson makes the decision to become an actress, however, she is faced with a dilemma: How can she be a sympathetic character while pursuing a professional career based on inauthenticity and spectacle? Robinson solves this contradiction by "dressing" in various costumes. Her focus on clothing—what she was wearing, why she was wearing it, and the affect her costume had on the others present—allows her to appear in acceptable guises at points in her narrative where her body becomes the focus of her story.

Robinson relies on the notion that her identities will be read through external signifiers that suggest sympathetic female roles. She also uses descriptions of her dress to facilitate the progress of the plot, which becomes more of a Gothic mystery as Robinson's performances become more suspicious.

In effect, Robinson's use of the Gothic tropes of doublings, ghosts, and disappearances give her a narrative strategy to counteract her theatrical self-fashioning. Robinson vividly recounts the details of her costume on the night that she met Mr. Robinson. She writes: "It was then the fashion to wear silks. I remember I wore a nightgown of pale blue lustring, with a chip hat, trimmed with ribbands of the same color. Never was I dressed so perfectly to my satisfaction; I anticipated a day of admiration—Heaven bear witness it was a day of fatal victory" (vol. 1, 58).[47] Robinson's reflection on her own sense of style is a reference to her position as fashionable celebrity. She relies here on the assumption that her readers will be able to conjure images of her in the fashions of the day—either from her portraits or from her presence on stage, or around town. The irony of never being "dressed so perfectly" on a "day of fatal victory" is also a classic set up for a Gothic plot in which Robinson plays the role of the innocent heroine, and Mr. Robinson is cast as the dark and mysterious stranger.

At first, Mr. Robinson presented himself to Mary and her mother as a man of good prospects. He claimed that he had a rich uncle, a "probable advancement in his profession," and a sincere affection for Mary. He proved himself through indefatigable visits and presents for Mary's mother, as well as providing a great "source of comfort" when both Mary and her brother fell ill with smallpox. Of the potentially disfiguring illness, Robinson writes, "I felt little terror at the approaches of a dangerous and deforming malady; for, I know not why but personal beauty has never been to me an object of material solicitude" (vol. 1, 61). Robinson's assertion that she has no concern about her personal beauty is a way of characterizing herself as a likeable character, one who is more preoccupied with internal qualities of strength, intellect, and moral goodness than exterior, superficial attributes.[48] Although she recovered from smallpox with little or no scarring, at the time she was writing her memoir Robinson was exhausted and fading. In this moment, Robinson is perhaps referring to her present condition, which is a way of recasting her vanity and focusing instead on her position as the naive victim of Mr. Robinson.

Robinson agrees to marry her ardent suitor, rejecting Garrick's pleas for her to pursue a theatrical career. She describes her adjustment to the idea of being married in terms of accepting a new role—a role that required a significant costume change. She writes: "As soon as the day of my wedding was fixed, it was deemed necessary that a total revolution should take place in my external appearance. I had till that period worn the habit of a child; and the dress of a woman so suddenly assumed sat rather awkwardly upon me" (vol. 1, 69).

Understanding Robinson's description of her strange marriage ceremony depends on wardrobe details. For the event, she is dressed in the "habit of a Quaker." But afterwards, she wears "a dress of white muslin" and a hat adorned with "white ribbons" (vol. 1, 69). The second costume is significant because when a friend of Mr. Robinson's remarks that she was "*dressed like a bride*" (vol. 1, 71; Robinson's italics), Robinson realizes that her husband wants to keep their marriage a secret. Ironically, in this scene, Robinson is playing the part of a bride, when she actually "is" a bride. She is reminded that her dress only signifies marriage if her husband acknowledges their union. While clothing is usually an indication of a specific identity, Robinson's role as a bride is just another disguise, and this deception provides proof of Mr. Robinson's potential to be a Gothic villain.[49]

The confusion of costume signifiers in this scene has significant implications for Robinson's "real" body. If she is understood to be a bride, then she is not in a compromising position with Mr. Robinson. If she is just playing the role of the bride, then her body (her virtue) is threatened. The ambiguity of the "status" of Robinson's body is significantly tied to fashioning her celebrity. If she presents herself as an unknowing victim of Mr. Robinson's diabolical plot, then she is somehow more justified in her adulterous affair with the Prince. However, presenting her body as available for circulation and fantasy in this scene emphasizes her position as a desirable commodity, reinforcing the image of herself as a seductive celebrity. Thus, Robinson is able to represent herself as vulnerable and available, seductive and demure.

LOOKING LIKE SOMETHING HUMAN: ROBINSON'S NEW ROLES

As Robinson matures into her new role as a wife, she frequently uses descriptions of her dress to signify her role in a given scene, as well as to signify the difference between herself and others. For instance, when she first meets Mr. Robinson's gloomy family, she is wearing "a dark claret colored riding habit with a white beaver hat and feathers," whereas her sister-in-law emerges in "a gaudy colored chintz gown, a thrice bordered cap with a profusion of ribbons, and a countenance somewhat more ruddy than was consistent with even pure health" (vol. 1, 87–88). She describes her other sister-in-law as equally objectionable: "Miss Robinson rode on horseback in a camlet safeguard, with a high crowned bonnet. I wore a fashionable habit and looked like something human" (vol. 1, 91). Even though she was "taunted perpetually on the folly of appearing like a woman of fortune," Robinson still insisted on dressing herself as a lady, distinguishing herself from her vulgar relatives.

Robinson's depiction of her tasteless in-laws provides more clues about her husband's true nature. Aside from his dubious business dealings, Mr. Robinson also had a questionable sense of domestic devotion. Robinson learned soon after their marriage was made public that Mr. Robinson had a mistress. The scene where Robinson describes confronting this woman emphasizes her use of visual and theatrical details. When she arrives at the woman's house, a "dirty servant girl," who informs her that the mistress is not at home, greets her. Left alone in the drawing room, Robinson takes it upon herself to open the door leading to a private chamber. On the bed, she finds "a new white lustring sacque and petticoat" (vol. 1, 113). Just as the part stands for the whole in Robinson's analysis of her ill-bred in-laws and their poor fashion choices, the "white" dress and undergarment on the bed replace the actual body of the mistress. The visual signifier of the unworn costume stands for the other woman, as well as for Mr. Robinson's betrayal. While she is staring at the dress, there is a knock on the door. Robinson re-enters the drawing room, and the mistress appears, wearing "a dress of printed Irish muslin, with a black gauze cloak and a chip hat" (vol. 1, 114). At first, Robinson plays the role of an innocent bystander, asking the mistress if she is "acquainted with Mr. Robinson?" (vol. 1, 114). The mistress admits that she is and takes her gloves off, revealing a ring that belongs to Mr. Robinson. Although Robinson does not divulge her identity, the reader is led to imagine that something in her expression causes the mistress to notice Robinson's costume, which Robinson describes as "a morning dishabillé of India Muslin: with a bonnet of straw: and a white cloak bordered with lace" (vol. 1, 114).[50] When the mistress fully digests these visual clues, she offers Mrs. Robinson her ring and exclaims, "You are Mr. Robinson's wife, I am sure you are!" (vol. 1, 115).

In this scene, Robinson uses codes of eighteenth-century fashion and theatrical gesture to differentiate herself from the mistress. The reader is asked to compare the character's costumes: the mistress wears Irish muslin (less expensive), and Robinson wears India muslin (imported, exotic, more expensive). The mistress wears a black cloak in contrast to Robinson's more innocent and virginal white cloak. Robinson's careful staging of the scene, her movement from the outer to the inner chamber, her discovery of the dress, and the exchange of the ring, reinforce the notion that subjectivity is based on disguise and revelation. The mistress recognizes Robinson through the differences in their costume, just as the audience understands the illicit aspect of the situation through the visual signifier of the dress on the bed. Robinson has cast herself once again as a well-dressed victim of circumstances beyond her control. Costumed in white, Robinson becomes the innocent worthy heroine; conversely, the mistress plays the role of the scheming seductress. However, the presence of the disembodied costume on the bed suggests that there is more going on in this scene. The ghostly dress refers, in fact, to both the mistress and to Robinson herself. Robinson's discovery of Mr. Robinson's affair sets the stage for her own infidelity, which occurs just after the birth of her first child. The ghostly dress, then, foregrounds the strategic erasure of Robinson's sexualized body, making it possible for her to appear momentarily pure and innocent; furthermore, the costume foreshadows the possibility of Robinson's own scandalous behavior.[51]

MOTHERHOOD AND THE PRINCE

Soon after her introduction to society and her encounter with Mr. Robinson's mistress, the focus of Robinson's narrative shifts again from copious details about the fashions, tastes, and attitudes of the public world, to her more private feelings about becoming a mother. Instead of portraying her own costume changes, Robinson describes sewing dresses for her unborn child. Finding herself pregnant at such a young age, with a husband who was still being pursued by his many creditors, forced Robinson to become something of a recluse, spending her time, she recalls, "making my little infant's wardrobe: my finest muslin dresses I converted to frocks and robes; with my lace I fondly trimmed them. It was a sweetly pleasing task and I often smiled when I reflected that, only three years before this period, I had dressed a waxen doll, nearly as large as a new born infant" (vol. 1, 131). Even though these domestic activities were a far cry from her usual life of parties and appearances, Robinson writes that she "little regretted the busy scenes of life; I sighed not for public attention" (vol. 1, 132). Here, images of dolls and babies draw attention away from Robinson's own body. Robinson's projection of herself onto her child transfers the narrative back to the realm of the domestic. Interestingly, however, Robinson carefully avoids presenting images of her pregnant body, keeping the imagined fantasy of her innocent desirable self in the minds of her readers.

In this section of the memoir, Robinson tries to underscore her maternal sensibility, her faithfulness to her cheating husband, her concern for her unborn child, and her desire to be with her own family. She describes the stages of her dread when she is forced to leave her mother and return to Mr. Robinson's home to give birth to her child:

> I felt a severe pang at the idea of quitting my adored mother at a moment where I should stand so much in need of a parent's affections: my agony was extreme: I fancied that I should never behold her more; that the harshness and humiliating taunts of my husband's kindred would send me prematurely to my grave; that my infant would be left among strangers; and that my mother would scarcely have fortitude sufficient to survive me. (vol. 1, 135)

These sentiments, along with the descriptions of her feelings of alienation and isolation, leave the reader with a sense of the limited options available to her. Robinson emphasizes the fact that, as Mr. Robinson's wife, it was her duty to obey him and, in a sense, to be his prisoner. Much like Mary Wollstonecraft's heroine Maria in her novella, *The Wrongs of Woman*, Robinson represents herself as an emotionally fragile heroine trapped by circumstances beyond her control. In both texts, the Gothic elements of narrative become fused with the realities of life for eighteenth-century women.[52] No sooner had her lovely child opened her eyes to this "world of duplicity and sorrow" (vol. 1, 4) than Mr. Robinson was arrested. The family spent nearly ten months in prison. The more trapped Robinson becomes by her unbearable domestic situation, the more her body—her costumed, theatrical figure—disappears. The reader has no sense of what Robinson looked like in prison. Instead of describing her dress, Robinson focuses on the development of her internal, intellectual, literary psyche. These descriptions are significantly marked by references to weakness, melancholy, and despair. Robinson writes: "I chose captivity for the subject of my pen, and soon composed a quarto poem of some length; it was superior to my former productions, but it was full of defects, replete with weak or labored lines" (vol. 1, 170).

Once out of prison, the Robinsons had no money. Mary tried to write and then considered the prospect of returning to the stage: "the idea rushed like electricity through my brain" (vol. 1, 186). Although she was pregnant again (she lost this child soon after she was born), Mr. Sheridan came to see her at home while she was still "dishabillé" in her nightgown. He asked her to recite a few passages from Shakespeare and was delighted with her talents. Mr. Garrick (now retired), Mr. Sheridan, and Mr. Brereton decided that she should make her debut as Juliet. Robinson describes her fears about performing in light of her domestic state,

> The only objection which I felt to the idea of appearing on stage was my then increasing state of domestic solitude. I was, at the period Mr. Sheridan was first presented to me somewhat advanced in that situation which afterwards, by the birth of Sophia, made me a second time a mother. Yet such was my imprudent fondness for Maria, that I was still a nurse; and my constitution was very considerably impaired by the effects of these combining circumstances. (vol. 1, 189–90)

Robinson's concerns about her body, and her admission that she is still breast feeding her older child, are poignant reminders of the physical and emotional demands on actresses. (Siddons acted Lady Macbeth when she was six months pregnant) Coming right before the moment of her "debut" (which takes up far more narrative space), Robinson's domestic concerns are a reminder to the reader that her main reason for performing is to support her family.

The image of Robinson auditioning for these men at her home while pregnant, wearing informal attire, is a startling visual reference. Is this image supposed to be read as a moment of sympathy, where the heroine is forced to give up her privacy in order to support her family; or as a moment of voyeuristic pleasure, where the "undressed" celebrity heroine allows the public to view her talents? The effect of this juxtaposition can be read as another Gothic disappearing act. Robinson's sexualized body is replaced with a maternal body, which leaves traces of Robinson's guilt and culpability mostly out of view. This double image of Robinson as seductive ingénue and new mother allows her readers to feel sympathy and desire at the same moment, the perfect combination for fashioning female celebrity.

After describing the initial success of her theatrical debut, Robinson breaks her narrative sequence to address the reader directly.

> I transcribe this passage on the twenty-ninth of March 1800. I feel my health decaying, my spirit broken. I look back without regret that so many of my days are numbered; and were it in my power to choose, I would not wish to measure them again:—but wither am I wandering? I will resume my melancholy story. . . . It was now that I began to know the perils attendant on a dramatic life. It was at this period that the most alluring temptations were held out to alienate me from the paths of domestic quiet—domestic happiness I cannot say, for it never was my destiny to know it. (vol. 2, 11)

In the process of detailing her allure as an actress, Robinson stops to redirect the reader's attention to her authorial presence. She invites us to imagine her ghostly figure—a body whose "health is decaying" and whose spirits are broken. While this self-conscious moment is designed to solicit sympathy for the narrative she is about to tell, it also creates a palpable amount of suspense. Readers are being prepared for Robinson's affair with the prince. She uses her Gothic celebrity here to create a sense of excitement and compassion. Her identity as a serious Romantic author is juxtaposed with the promised seductive allure of her former persona as the Prince's lovely mistress.

ROBINSON'S LAST PERFORMANCE

Although Robinson had been on the stage for nearly two years before meeting the Prince, she became an overnight media sensation once he chose her as his mistress of the moment. Robinson takes full advantage of this in her memoir, recreating in detail the moments leading up to her performance of Perdita in *The Winter's Tale,* before the Royal family in 1779. She was nervous before the play and recalled that Mr. Smith, who was to play her father, Leontes, joked, "By jove, Mrs. Robinson you will make a conquest of the prince for tonight you look handsomer than ever" (vol. 2, 37). In true Cinderella fashion, Robinson denies any prior thoughts of seducing the Prince and describes in detail the moment that their eyes met:

> The Prince's particular attention was observed by everyone. . . . On the last curtsy, the royal family condescendingly returned a bow to the performers; but just as the curtain was falling my eyes met those of the Prince of Wales; and, with a look that *I shall never forget,* he gently inclined his head a second time; I felt the compliment and blushed my gratitude. (vol. 2, 39; Robinson's emphasis)

The power of Robinson's performance is analogous to the power of celebrity status. Her appearance disrupts class boundaries, social constructs, the divide between the audience and the actors, and the separation between Robinson-as-Perdita and Robinson-as-herself. In this instant, she has achieved a perfect state of fame—recognition by the heir to the English throne, the "ideal" man, and the ideal audience. At the same time, this moment of celebrity recognition, when Robinson is able to escape the realities of her "real" life, is also a haunting reminder of what will be. Her readers have been led through the narrative in anticipation of this very moment and the inevitability of her demise afterward. Robinson will always be trapped by her domestic role, by the need to care for and support her daughter, and by the consequences of her doomed liaison with the Prince. Thus, the moment when her body matters most is also the moment that signals the price of her celebrity and her own futile attempts to recapture its original authentic moment.

Robinson and the Prince became associated for a short while. Cartoons in the press depicted Robinson as Perdita and the Prince as a smitten Florizel. Although the affair ended quickly, and Robinson negotiated a deal with the Royal Family for a monthly allowance in exchange for his incriminating letters to her, none of these financial details are included in the section of the memoir that was written by Robinson. Robinson insists that the Prince was responsible for their clandestine correspondence and that he sent her a miniature of himself with an inscription that read: *"Je ne change qu'en mourant;* Unalterable to my Perdita through life" (vol. 2, 47).[53] Curiously, Robinson's "authentic" portion of the memoir ends abruptly and is continued by a "friend" just at the point in the narrative where she is invited to "Meet the royal Highness in his apartments."[54]

The "friend" in question is Robinson's daughter, who managed to find a lengthy letter written by her mother that picked up the narrative right where it ended. The mysterious letter that continues the memoir is written to an anonymous male friend in America. Robinson did have a long relationship with Colonel Banastre Tarleton who was stationed for a period in America; however, the text fits so seamlessly into the narrative that it seems as if the references to this person were added in order to provide an audience for this "letter." Who, then, wrote this portion of the memoir? Most scholars agree that Robinson's daughter, Maria, herself an unsuccessful novelist, wrote the letter in her mother's voice in order to make the story appear to be more complete and authentic, or perhaps the original letter existed in fragments that Maria pieced together in order to finish the text. Even more compelling is the idea that at this point in her story, Robinson was no longer able to use Gothic strategies to fashion her celebrity, so she disappears as an authorial presence. Robinson cuts off her story just at the point where her performances begin to have consequences, and she cannot resort to literary categories to rescue her reputation. In true Robinson fashion, the secret of who wrote the letter and the rest of volume two is the memoir's Gothic paradox. Robinson ultimately becomes the ghost that haunts her own story.

While Robinson could negotiate strategic disappearances at points in the memoir where her body became enmeshed in scandal and intrigue, off stage her ability to project idealized images of herself became increasingly difficult. In the same way that she vanished from her memoir, she gradually disappeared from public view. Despite Robinson's associations in her later years with notable figures, including the Duchess of Devonshire, Sheridan, Fox, Coleridge, Godwin, and Wollstonecraft, she died virtually alone with only her daughter left to mourn her passing. A segment of the author Jane Porter's diary reveals what society thought about Robinson near the end of her life. She writes about the moment when she heard of Robinson's death:

> I pleaded a nervous headache, and made that an excuse for the tears which poured down my cheeks. . . . I one moment despised myself, for being ashamed to avow feelings, which I could not condemn, and the next I excused myself from the conviction that it was only a prudence due to my sister and myself not to publish a conduct, which however guilty, would draw on us the disrespect of many of our friends, and most likely the scandal of the world.[55]

Ultimately, Robinson's visual, narrative, and theatrical attempts to rescue her damaged reputation were thwarted by the menacing scrutiny of public opinion. Her status as an adulteress and an actress would follow her until her death in 1800.

Robinson's final poem entitled "All Alone" ends, significantly, with a reference to dressing and adornment:

> My Father never will return,
> He rests beneath the sea-green wave:
> I have no kindred left to mourn
> When I am hid in yonder grave;
> No one! To dress with flowers the stone:—
> Then—surely I am left alone![56]

The image of Robinson's bare grave stone is perhaps a fitting end for a life spent dressing, disguising, and fashioning identities. The limits of Robinson's success in fashioning her celebrity suggest the ways in which celebrity is tied to an actress's ability to project idealized narratives of femininity through written, visual, and theatrical strategies. Robinson was able to partially reinvent herself because of her talents as an actress and an author. In the end, though, despite her use of Gothic strategies, a process aimed at creating meaningful links among her varied self-representations, she could not reconcile her public reputation with the personas that she hoped would make her seem valuable in the eyes of eighteenth-century audiences.

The ideals of eighteenth-century femininity that Siddons and Robinson cultivated in their self-fashioning strategies would be alternately parodied and ignored by the actress Mary Wells, the subject of the next chapter. Wells deviated so far from the norm in her self-representations that her contemporaries labeled her mad, disturbing, and wildly eccentric. Wells's unique brand of theatricality looks forward to characterizations of nineteenth-century madwomen, who, in acting out on their desires, challenged and threatened Victorian ideals of feminine domesticity and passivity. For Wells, fashioning celebrity meant creating all her own rules.

Three

Mary Wells's Notorious Celebrity

IN 1791, John Russell exhibited a painting at The Royal Academy titled, *Portrait of a Lady and Three Children*.[1] The lady, who was later revealed by *The Morning Chronicle* to be the actress Mary Wells, sits gazing down at her three lovely daughters. The children are captured in a moment of carefree innocence. One child uses a feather to tickle her sister who is holding a basket of flowers. The daughter closest to Wells gestures playfully toward her mother. Wells smiles contentedly at her little ones with a mixture of protectiveness and pride. With her large eyes, cherubic mouth, and subtle dress, Wells is the ideal of feminine domestic beauty in this portrait.

What is absent from the painting, however, is just as interesting as what is depicted. The most striking omission is the image of the father, Edward Topham, who was Wells's lover but not her husband. After her identity was revealed, the portrait became known as "Mrs. Topham and her three children."[2] Art historian Marcia Pointon observes in her book, *Hanging the Head*, that a missing father in an eighteenth-century family portrait is often "a deliberate narrative device that sharpens the perception of the patriarchal."[3] Thus, the most powerful figure in the family constellation is even more significant when alluded to but not represented. In the Russell portrait, the fantasy of legitimacy, intimacy, and naturalness that this painting conveys would be ruined by Topham's presence. Without him, the painting is simply titled, *Portrait of a Lady and Three Children*.[4] There is no hint that Wells was an actress, that her relationship with Topham was not traditional, or that the family is not respectable. With Topham in it, the painting would represent an illegitimate family—a domestic fraud.

The Topham family grouping is placed against a nonspecific background instead of a decorated room, or a designated domestic space. The stage-set quality of the backdrop reinforces the illusion of harmony that is going on at many levels in the painting. By 1791, Topham and Wells were no longer together. He had accused her of being mad (she claims in order to make room for his next mistress), and she had left him for playwright Frederick Reynolds. In subsequent years, Topham would separate Wells from her children. They grew to be lovely gentlewomen, while their mother spent her days in and out of debtor's prison, performing her imitations of other famous actresses and writing her memoirs in order to "prove" her sanity. Her daughters married well and, ultimately, wanted nothing to do with their eccentric mother.

A few years later, James Northcote, assistant and biographer to Sir Joshua Reynolds, exhibited his painting Mrs. Wells as Hebe (figure 14) at the Royal Academy, in 1806.[5] The "Lady" was later identified to be Mary Wells. Hebe, the goddess of youth, cupbearer of immortality, and wife to Hercules, was a popular subject for eighteenth-century artists.[6] In Northcote's portrait, Wells wears a fashionable and alluring classical costume of white gauze, which covers her breasts but leaves her shoulders exposed. Her hair flows naturally in the wind.[7] Wells stares intently out at the viewer while opening the sacred cup. An eagle is at her side, looking up at her expectantly. Significantly, Hebe offers the promise of immortality to the viewer more directly than to the eagle.[8] Thus, Northcote's *Mrs. Wells as Hebe* can be read as an image that suggests a struggle between sexuality and control. Hebe dominates the bird, a symbol of a male god and of masculine power; she has something that it wants.[9]

As in the previous portrait, *Portrait of a Lady and Three Children*, what is significant about this painting also lies in what is not represented. In 1806, Wells was forty-three years old, her career was nearly over—badly damaged by her bouts of madness, her stints in debtors prison, and her very public marriage and divorce to the Moorish Jew, Mr. Sumbel. Why, then, would Northcote depict her as Hebe the goddess of youth? Was it an ironic commentary, or a gesture of positive publicity for a failing friend? Is the character of Hebe supposed to signify Wells's goddess-like qualities, thus associating the image with other depictions of ladies in mythological costumes? Or was this a reference to Wells's career as an actress, when she offered up her own body as a fantasy of youth and desire for her audiences?

We may never be able to answer these questions about the circumstances surrounding Northcote's painting of Wells. What is clear, though, is that the role that Wells plays as Hebe in Northcote's portrait is very different from the one she plays in Russell's portrait of her as Mrs. Topham. These characters—the sexualized goddess and the loving mother—represent the extremes

FIGURE 14. Thomas James Northcote. *Mrs. Wells as Hebe*, 1805. © Art Gallery of Ontario, Toronto

of Wells's experience from her very public role as an actress to her more private life as the working mother of three children. Both portraits are advertisements for legitimacy. Despite their diverse approaches, Northcote and Russell depict Wells playing recognizable eighteenth-century female personas. As we have seen, this strategy for fashioning celebrity worked beautifully for Siddons, who was able to establish seamless connections between her public and private personas; and at times, for Mary Robinson, who attempted to use visual images of herself to create a sense of her sexuality and vulnerability. For Wells, however, these idealized versions of her image were so far from the reality of her situation that they exist today as evidence of her vexed strategies for fashioning her celebrity, as well as the illusions associated with her desperate bids for fame and recognition.

Wells's most significant attempt to gain public acknowledgment was her lengthy three-volume autobiography, *Memoirs of the Life of Mrs. Sumbel, Late Wells,* published in 1811. The memoir includes details of her career in the British theater as an actress, singer, and comedienne (she was famous for her imitations of Sarah Siddons and Dorothy Jordan); her liaisons with famous men; episodes of her alleged madness and treatment by Dr. Willis (the same doctor who "cured" George III); and her exotic marriage in debtors prison to Mr. Sumbel, who divorced her because she would not abide by the laws of Judaism. Although the varied nature of Wells's life was not atypical of a late-eighteenth-century actress, her connection to questions of madness is what sets her apart from other performers. It is unclear from Wells's memoir, or from contemporary commentary about her life and career, what constitutes the difference between characterizations of Wells's insanity and descriptions of her theatrical behavior.

As we have seen with Siddons's and Robinson's autobiographies, reading eighteenth-century actresses' memoirs can be a complicated task because the narratives are not transparent documents of theater history. Although a memoir, as a text, can be read for specific information about an actress's life, her own representation of herself within the memoir is clearly manipulated and designed to appeal to reading audiences. In writing their memoirs, actresses made certain assumptions about what the reading public already knew about their life and career. The memoir, then, serves as an attempt to explain, clarify, revise, and redirect those public perceptions. Thus, the actress's memoir as a specific genre is a work that is always negotiating between the worlds inside and outside of the text.

Wells's autobiography is an excellent example of this process of negotiation. Described by one of her contemporaries as a "noted and infamous woman,"[10] Wells's antics off stage provide a backdrop for her self-characterization in her memoirs. She attempts to capitalize on her reputation as a notoriously eccentric celebrity; at the same time, she claims to be writing her memoirs to prove that the accusations of madness leveled against her by her former lover, playwright and journalist Edward Topham, were false. The problem with this approach is that her own story—her characterization of herself—ends up reinforcing perceptions of her instability and narcissism. Because she so clearly departs from narrative conventions associated with depictions of eighteenth-century heroines, Wells represents herself as a mad character whose unpredictability, obsessive desire for attention, and spectacular visual appearance serve not as justification for her renewed fame, but as sad evidence of her status as a societal outcast.

Reading Wells's memoirs along with visual images of her and characterizations of her theatrical personas on stage and her strange behavior off stage written by her contemporaries, I suggest that in the late eighteenth century the possibilities for female celebrity are linked to narratives of desirable and acceptable female identity in the same way that madness is defined in opposition to constructions of "normal" feminine behavior. Just as Siddons's celebrity became linked to models of femininity based on royalty and maternity, and Robinson's celebrity can be seen as characterized by Gothic strategies, Wells's celebrity became associated with madness and notoriety. Wells's peculiar theatricality on stage was initially read by her audiences and contemporaries as comedic, eccentric, and amusing, while her odd behavior off stage became increasingly labeled as "infamous," "outrageous," and "mad." While Wells's risky performances led to her initial success as a talented mimic and fearless comedienne, her attempts to translate those performances offstage in order to promote her celebrity eventually led to her demise.

Public reaction to Wells's performances on stage, off stage, and in print, points once again to a significant set of cultural anxieties circulating around the ambiguous status of actresses at the turn of the nineteenth century—anxieties that centered around actresses' potential ability to rise in class through their liaisons with prominent men, and their ability to support themselves individually through their profession. As actresses increasingly became the focus of celebrity culture, the agency they gained through their celebrity status carried with it a sense of privilege that was not gained by the traditional venues of birth or marriage. Robyn Asleson has argued that late-eighteenth-century actresses were "essentially the only group in Georgian Britain with both the power and the license to orchestrate public perceptions of themselves—chiefly through carefully contrived stage performances but also through myriad forms of personal propaganda and self-fashioning."[11] Considered through this frame, Wells's mad behavior, which involved a series of strange events where she acted, as Fanny Burney remarked, as if she were "accustomed to indulge herself in all her whims,"[12] could be considered both a symptom of and a reaction to negotiating her role as an identifiable public figure capable of attracting attention through fame. The fact that Wells's unusual performances were read as evidence of her madness is directly tied to the ways in which late-eighteenth-century audiences participated in the shaping of guidelines and boundaries for female celebrity. Audiences expected that female celebrities would embody and enact specific performances of femininity. Wells not only defied these expectations, she seemed to deliberately perform in reaction to them: evidence perhaps not of her madness but of her dark satiric sensibility and of her subversive strategies for fashioning her celebrity.

Wells's repeated assertions of her celebrity contradicted accepted notions of female propriety and agency. Unlike Sarah Siddons, whose diva celebrity was celebrated and reinforced by her audiences, Wells's assumptions about her status as a diva eventually became out of touch with the expectations and desires of her audiences. In Wells's case, acting as a notorious diva, both off stage and on stage (through her mimicry or "ghosting" of famous actresses such as Siddons and Dorothy Jordan as well as her outrageous representations of herself), signified her theatrical and delusional sensibility. As Wayne Koestenbaum has argued, the other side of the adored diva is the monstrous diva. He explains, "The diva is demonized: she is associated with difference itself, a satanic separation from the whole, the clean, the contained, and the attractive."[13] In addition, the diva's "codes of extravagant behavior" are so fascinating because she is able to challenge traditional notions about identity through the spectacle of her acting out. Koestenbaum continues, "Our social selves—the selves that believe in order and humility and staying in one's proper sphere—are shattered by the liberating spectacle of a diva standing up for herself against propriety."[14] Jacky Bratton makes a similar point about the power of mimicry on audiences:

> On a social level, mimicry is a threat to our own sense of ourselves and of our dignity—people rarely like to see themselves "taken off"—and more importantly, to the confidence with which we recognize not only other individuals but classes of individuals by their manner and appearance, and so make the stream of decisions and recognitions upon which our positioning of ourselves in society depends. The mimic may be a loose cannon in a social situation, and one of the deep roots of the opprobrium which fuels anti-theatrical prejudice is here, in moral disapproval and deceit about who we are.[15]

Looking at Wells's celebrity through the framework of her talents as a mimic, as well as her eccentric assumptions of divaness, is an alternative way of assessing the significance and impact of her misdirected strategies for fashioning celebrity. What made Wells so threatening in her own lifetime is, I believe, connected to her disappearance from the official record of theatrical history. Siddons and Robinson were attractive to late-eighteenth-century audiences for many of the same reasons they have become alluring subjects for contemporary scholars: Both actresses fit into recognizable models of female celebrity, even if their own writings challenge and attempt, at times, to dismantle or revise these assumptions. Wells's resistance to categorization and the bizarre—and at times, impenetrable—nature of her writings have made her an unruly and difficult subject. Unlike Siddons and Robinson, who promoted their celebrity by highlighting the fantasy that audiences could have access to their "real" selves, Wells's strategies for fashioning her celebrity had the opposite effect. The authenticity that Siddons appeared to embody and that Robinson sustained as a seductive illusion was absent with Wells whose ties to madness, mimicry, and theatricality rendered her deviant, other, and unrecognizable.

MARY WELLS was born Mary Davies on 16 December 1762. Her father, Thomas Davies, was a wood carver and guilder in Birmingham; her mother was a tavern keeper and a provincial actress with a "modest career" in Bath, York, and Gloucester.[16] She begins her memoirs with a brief sketch of her early childhood, establishing that she has no claim to genteel origins. She writes:

> An illustrious pedigree is generally uppermost in the minds of actors and actresses. From their personating royalty, and being so often clothed in splendid dresses, they frequently imagine themselves what in mimic scenery they only represent. . . . I beg leave to premise that, in conjunction with the most noble and ancient families on earth who boast of the unadulterated blood of ancestry, I am originally descended from Adam and Eve.[17]

In this opening passage, Wells articulates several important ideas: the wish of the actor/actress to associate himself or herself with "illustrious pedigrees"; the natural tendency for them to believe themselves of a higher rank because they so often impersonate royalty; and the sad fact that they are only "representing" what they mimic for a short period on stage. Her own understanding of such ironies leads her to explain that she, like everyone with "unadulterated blood," descends from Adam and Eve. From the outset, then, it is clear that Wells understands the tricky cycle of representation that she is engaged in as an actress. Convincing a spectator that you are someone else is part of an actress's seduction. Like Hebe offering a fantasy of youth, an actress offers a fantasy of availability. However, at the beginning of Wells's memoir (which is by its genre supposed to be a testament to who she really is), she explains that she understands the difference between representation and reality, and she continues to capitalize on the slippage between the two. Her description of Adam and Eve as her ancestors is a clever commentary on the conventions of the beginning of memoir, where the author must account for her illustrious pedigree or lack thereof.[18]

Wells's father's claim to fame was digging up the root of the mulberry tree at Stratford-upon-Avon in order to make a box for the actor and theater manager, David Garrick. Wells recalls: "He had a medal given to him at the time, for the design, which his partner had carved."[19] Her father's partner, Mr. Griffith, apparently took advantage of him by attempting to seduce Mrs. Davies, Wells's mother. Griffith subsequently managed to have Davies thrown into prison and later put into a madhouse where he died.[20] Soon after, Griffith abandoned Wells's mother, who became a keeper of a tavern that was popular with actors and introduced young Mary to the theatrical scene in Birmingham. Wells made her acting debut playing the Duke of York in *Richard III*. Next, she played Cupid in the *Trip to Scotland,* followed by Prince Arthur in *King John*. She then went to Bath and was engaged by Mr. Palmer. In her memoir, Wells writes: "though the salary was small (a humble five shillings per night) still the circumstance is sufficient to prove to the world that my theatrical career did not commence among strollers."[21] Interestingly, Wells reveals that her parents were of "modest" origins, but she distinguishes herself from other actors who began their careers with strolling companies, providing evidence that she has always been a legitimately paid actress. She also writes that Garrick "made overtures to my mother to take me as an apprentice."[22] Mrs. Davies answers: "If others choose to apprentice their children to the stage, she did not, considering it a sure road to the destruction of the innocence of her child."[23]

Wells's inclusion of this exchange, something that she "remembers" after almost thirty-five years, is an interesting comment on the idea that acting was still very much associated with prostitution. Although she includes outrageous anecdotes of her behavior later in life, and makes no apologies for her illegitimate children, she still wants to establish her past as a time of innocence and her mother as a protective figure. She explains: "Long since I have learned by sad experience, that, for the female part of a family, a mother's presence is absolutely necessary."²⁴ Given that Wells is shunned later in her life by her own daughters, it is significant that her own memories of her loving mother tie her in some way to a domestic past. This material about her childhood seems to be an attempt to establish herself as a sympathetic character and to present the memoirs as a typical story of a young girl coming of age.

Wells misses an opportunity to present herself as classic eighteenth-century heroine/victim in her description of her marriage. In 1778, Wells met her husband, actor Ezra Wells, while playing Juliet to his Romeo. The marriage did not last long. Shortly after the ceremony, Mr. Wells sent Mary's mother a note, which indicated his disinterest in his new wife: "Madam, as your daughter is too young and childish, I beg you will again for the present take her again under your protection."²⁵ Wells later finds out that her husband has left her for one of her "brides maids." While Mary Robinson makes the most of her philandering husband's desertion in her memoirs, Wells pays little attention to Mr. Wells's escape. Wells's status as an abandoned woman did not seem to have a negative affect on her blossoming career. Much of the next section of the memoir is a laundry list of Wells's most successful roles and reviews.

In 1778–80, Wells played singing parts in Bristol and Plymouth. She made her debut on the London stage on 1 June 1781 at the Haymarket Theatre as Margery in *Love in a Village* and Mrs. Cadwallader in *The Author*.²⁶ Reviewers established Wells's beauty and her talent for comic roles as her strong suits. *The Morning Chronicle* described "a beautiful young actress of the name of Wells, who has for some time been the Thalia of the West."²⁷ *The Public Advertiser* wrote: "Mrs. Wells appeared for the first time as Madge at this theater. The lady has established her fame as an actress in characters of this nature; and her last performance of Margery confirms that the final decision stands good."²⁸ Along with compliments about her performances, critics also introduced the idea that Wells's behavior needed to be a bit more refined. A writer from *The Westminster Magazine* reported that "when her manières have acquired a little more urbanity, she will be a very good performer."²⁹ Perhaps there was something about Wells's theatrical presence that provided early indications of the strange events to follow.

WELLS, MIMICRY, AND CHARLOTTE CHARKE

According to Annabel Jenkins (the actress and author Elizabeth Inchbald's biographer), Wells was known from her early career to be an enormously talented mimic. She apparently rivaled the great comic actor Tate Wilkinson, whose theater company she acted with in the early 1780s.[30] Tate Wilkinson was the protégé of the notorious mimic Samuel Foote. Theater historian Jane Moody cites Foote as the first actor to create a "new kind of theatrical celebrity based on the mimicry of famous performers and other public figures."[31] Foote's "Diversions," a performance piece of imitations of other actors, marked a new kind of relationship of the actor to an emerging culture of celebrity in the middle of the eighteenth century. Moody goes on to argue that, through these theatrical parodies, Foote "capitalized on an intense uncertainty in eighteenth-century culture about the ability of public figures to create their own celebrity through the agency of media and their control and manipulation of images, institutions, and performances."[32]

Wells's mimicry of other actresses on stage, particularly of Sarah Siddons, can certainly be seen as an extension of this type of theatrical practice. And like Foote, who received both positive and negative responses to his imitations, Wells's ability to send up other performers was both fascinating and threatening. Unlike Foote, who established himself as an actor/gentleman amassing a small fortune and "mixing in fashionable circles,"[33] Wells's increasingly marginal social status, coupled with her tendency to perform offstage in a variety of eccentric ways, marked her brand of mimicry as dangerous and unstable. Wells also used herself as a subject for mimicry, performing exaggerated versions of her own character on stage and off. These performances can be linked to her notorious predecessor—the actress and author Charlotte Charke.

Charke's memoir, *A Narrative of the Life of Charlotte Charke* (1755), has received the most critical attention of any eighteenth-century autobiography written by an actress. Reasons for this include Charke's relationship to her famous father, the actor and author Colley Cibber, (the narrative was written as a ploy for his attention and is at times as a direct reflection on his memoirs), and Charke's appeal to scholars of feminist theory, performance theory, and queer theory. Charke's varied performances on stage and off, which are described in detail in her memoir, provide very rich material for discussions of identity and performativity, as well as for the relationship between gender and the construction of the self.[34] While a comprehensive comparison of Charke and Wells is beyond the scope of this chapter, Charke's ties to mimicry are useful in thinking about how Wells's eccentric performances were familiar and unfamiliar to late-eighteenth-century audiences.

As a child, Charke was famous for imitating her father, Colley Cibber, by putting on one of his enormous wigs—an anecdote which she chronicles in detail in her memoir—and for adopting a variety of characters and professions, including masquerading off stage as man. Like Charke, Wells's theatrical abilities translated off stage in unsettling ways. Unlike Charke, however, who is very clear throughout her narrative that these imitative strategies are necessary for her economic survival, Wells is far less convincing in her portrayal of herself as a woman forced to seek out creative, and often desperate, alternatives to conventional acting practices. Charke relies on her audience's knowledge of her famous father and their contentious relationship in the writing and marketing of her memoirs. Her narrative strategies are often designed as a direct copy of her father's text.[35]

Sidonie Smith argues that Charke's theatrical cross-dressing (her self-conscious performance of masculinity and masculine authority) is analogous to her inability to construct a self in her autobiography: "A woman dressed as a man, Charke cannot place herself comfortably within the narratives of her culture. She is truly 'peerless.' With no self-illumination and self-reflectiveness, she cannot discover who and what she is."[36] According to Smith, Charke's mimicry points to her inability to inhabit her own subjectivity and her ultimate alienation from the socially sanctioned "narratives of her culture." While Charke has been consistently read through her father and through the ambiguities of cross-dressing (both literally and figuratively), Wells's departures from normative models of identity (femininity and heterosexuality) are less clearly defined. In fact, her exaggerated performances of herself—which have no distinct origin—are seen as mad and outrageous precisely because they have no legible or legitimate counterpart.

Kristina Straub suggests persuasively that Charke's mimicry calls into question the very nature of the categories that she attempts to inhabit (masculine), and that she would "naturally" be associated with (feminine). Straub writes:

> Her [Charke's] mimicry of her father's text marks her own distance from the masculine role she puts on, but it also marks that role as a role, gestures toward the artificiality—and tenuousness—of the masculinity that she, in turn, puts on. Charke's cross-dressing indicates her failure to be her father, but it also throws into relief the constructed ambiguities, and even self-parodying nature of that father's authority.[37]

These questions of artificiality and tenuousness are at work in Wells's deliberate mimicry of Sarah Siddons. Wells denaturalizes the authenticity of Siddons's celebrity and "authority" as the queen of the theater by imitating Siddons on stage and by copying Siddons's strategies for marketing her public image. While Wells's mimicry of Siddons can be seen as a form of flattery or of pure business savvy, I suggest that Wells's strategies for fashioning her celebrity through imitation also contained a subversive element. Wells's ability to copy Siddons disrupted the fantasy that Siddons was an authentic and distinct original, and that her fame was achieved through little effort or self-invention.

WELLS AND SIDDONS

Wells had her first chance to act in a tragic role in 1783, when she played the lead role in *Jane Shore*—a role popularized by Siddons. Wells writes in her memoirs that Siddons wanted to have nothing to do with her: "Mrs. Siddons refused to play Jane Shore with me; upon which Mr. King, the manager of Drury Lane theatre, advised me to play the part myself. . . . On the reason for Mrs. Siddons' refusal I shall make no comment."[38] Wells's refusal to comment is a not-so-veiled reference to the animosity between the two actresses. Siddons was the most sought-after actress in London and clearly did not wish to be associated with Wells.

In 1784, Wells played Isabella (another part that made Siddons famous) at Covent Garden. *The Morning Chronicle* compared Wells's performance to Siddons's famous interpretation of the role:

> On Thursday night Mrs. Wells made her appearance in Isabella; and although the audience went with such strong prejudices in favor of the fashionable Melpomene, yet never did Mrs. Siddons draw more genuine tears from an audience. . . . She (Mrs. Wells) has a beautiful face, with most expressive features, which no doubt are much in her favor; but that in which she excels, is her following nature, and concealing all the study of art in representing the character.[39]

The Public Advertiser also compared Wells to Siddons, declaring that "both these actresses posses a quality which no other actresses have on the English stage—they are *always,* whether speaking or not speaking, in their part."[40] The reviewer's comment that the actresses were both "always in their part" is significant given that being associated with their roles had very different consequences for each actress. For Siddons, her status as the "tragic muse" was a position that allowed her to become a superstar and to carve out a respectable position for an actress in the eighteenth century. Wells, however, was recognized primarily for her skill in playing comic roles. She was often cast as the available coquette, a role that only added to the speculations and rumors about her activities offstage.

Images of the two actresses by John Downman illustrate the differences in the way they were "seen" by audiences. Downman depicts Wells wearing a fashionable dress of the period with a lovely hat (figure 15). Wells has beautiful features in this portrait, which presents her as an object of desire. The details of her pretty costume (her powdered hair and fancy hat) also present her as a kind of eighteenth-century fashion plate. Wells's dress, a muslin-wrapping gown, was a chic garment for ladies of the day. Such portrayals contributed to Wells's growing popularity and visibility among curious theatrical spectators.

Downman also drew an image of Siddons (figure 16) in a style similar to his depiction of Wells. It was an unpopular portrait of her. One critic wrote: "Mrs. Siddons whose frown is tragick, and whose Countenance is masculine, is drawn like a pastoral coquette."[41] A comparison of these two images suggests that Wells and Siddons were viewed as different types of actresses. Wells's beauty and facility with comedy made her the equivalent of an eighteenth-century pin-up girl. Siddons's success in performing tragic heroines, specifically Shakespearean women, lent her persona an air of legitimacy that was misrepresented by Downman's frivolous portrait of her in an exaggerated, frilly costume. In the public eye, the careers of Siddons and Wells represented the opposite of the spectrum: while Siddons's performances signified all that was lofty and admirable about British femininity, Wells's comedic flair threatened to extend it to outrageousness, excessiveness, and unpredictability—qualities that were dangerous for a society that expected women to be dignified, demure, and in full possession of their emotions.[42] Siddons seems to have known that Wells was in a different category from her, and she did her best to disassociate herself from the actress. Despite Siddons's attempts to distance herself from Wells, Wells continued to haunt Siddons, inventing a variety of strategies for mimicking Siddons's methods for fashioning celebrity.

THE MUFF PORTRAITS

In another ploy to copy Siddons, Wells had her portrait painted by Sir Joshua Reynolds, in an obvious attempt to imitate Gainsborough's successful portrait of Siddons as a grand society lady holding a muff (see chapter 1, figure 1).[43] In the painting, Wells wears a striped wrapping gown and an elaborate hat similar to the costume Siddons wore in the Gainsborough portrait.[44] Her figure, like Siddons's, is shown in profile. The most striking feature of the painting is the enormous muff that Wells holds in her lap. The comparison of the two paintings was not lost on the newspapers of the day. *The Daily*

FIGURE 15. John Downman. *Mrs. Wells*, 1792. © Trustees of the British Museum

FIGURE 16. John Downman. *Mrs. Siddons*, 1787. © Trustees of the British Museum

Universal Register for 27 August 1787 declared that Wells had "sought with eagerness to copy out the example of the prodigious Mrs. Siddons."[45] *The Times* focused on the excessively proportioned muff: "Sir Joshua is a wag, and declares that muff work is very comfortable this cold weather. He likes to encourage commerce too, and takes his fee—half in cash, half in kind. Indeed Becky's (one of Wells's nicknames) kindness was never questionable."[46]

Muffs in portraits of actresses draw attention to the complex boundary between fame and notoriety for eighteenth-century women: in certain images, muffs function as signs of aristocracy and glamour; in others, of crass accumulation and overt sexuality. For Siddons, an actress without a "reputation," the muff signifies her dignified, stylish presence as an aristocratic woman. For Wells, the muff is a sign of her overt sexuality and bad taste. Wells's unpredictable behavior off stage, and her very public affairs with various men, made her an obvious target for an attack that links selling her body directly to selling her public image. Still, there are several questions that remain unanswered about this portrait. The most obvious, perhaps, is why is the muff so big? Clearly, Reynolds was an extremely accomplished artist who understood the effect of proportion and perspective. We do not have notes pertaining to the circumstances of the painting, but it seems possible that the size of the muff may not have been solely his idea. Did Wells ask for the muff to be very large in order to out-do the size of the muff in the Siddons's portrait? Was the muff covering a pregnancy or the aftereffects of a pregnancy that Wells was trying to hide? (She did give birth to a daughter around the time that this painting was completed).

Comparing the Wells portrait to a painting by Reynolds of the aristocratic Lady Skipwith (figure 17) completed in the same year, 1787, it is interesting to note that Lady Skipwith's incredibly tiny waist is as exaggerated and out of proportion as Wells's enormous muff (figure 15). Lady Skipwith's emaciated body, a sign of her stylishness, status, and innocence, is a stark contrast to Wells's unsubtle attempt at marketing her public image. In the Skipwith portrait, the threat of a woman on public display is mitigated by visual clues that suggest containment and control. The portrait, painted for her husband, Sir Thomas George Skipwith, signifies Lady Skipwith's ownership by her husband; her grace and elegance is also an indicator of his wealth and prosperity. For Wells, the actress who belongs to everybody and nobody, the threat of display is unconfined and multiple. The image suggests the possibility of actresses' availability for circulation in nontheatrical circles, the threat of their rise in class status, the potential reality of their financial independence, and in Wells's, case the obviousness of her inauthenticity. In mimicking Siddons's pose and dress, Wells parodies the act of attempting to be something

FIGURE 17. Sir Joshua Reynolds. *Selina, Lady Skipwith*, 1787. © The Frick Collection, New York

one inherently is not. The key to Siddons's celebrity was her ability to market herself as a paradoxically authentic actress and a natural performer. Wells's muff mimicry exposes more than her own desire to be looked at and to be compared to Sarah Siddons—it reveals a strategic process of fashioning celebrity that operates with a specific series of visual clues, theatrical strategies, and narrative projections based on a set of late-eighteenth-century feminine ideals. Actresses' ability to fashion their images according to these codes led to their relative success or disappearance from public view. Wells's skills at imitation onstage did not translate well to her activities off stage. When she attempted to assume the privileges of Siddons's established celebrity status, her persona became associated with madness, deviance, and unavoidable notoriety, a characterization that she attempted to market and manipulate in her representation of herself in her memoir.

TOPHAM AND WELLS: A MAD VICTIM

Wells met Edward Topham, the playwright, officer, and journalist, when she was presented with an epilogue that he wrote for her benefit on 15 April 1785. She explains in her memoir: "The different necessary interviews we had, from my frequently rehearsing the epilogue before him, created a mutual esteem between us. I was captivated with the beauty of his mind: he made me an offer of his hand; but as we could not be legally united in this kingdom, he proposed going to Italy."[47] Wells never married Topham (presumably because she was already married), but she does "remove to his house" on Bryan Stone Street, where she became the mother of three children. Like Mary Robinson, who portrays herself as a doomed heroine in her memoirs, Wells presents herself similarly as the victim of a thoughtless and selfish man. She apparently trusted that Topham would marry her and warns her female readers against the dangers of believing in false promises. She writes, "But that woman who can confidently listen to the empty promises of a *man* deserves every misery the world can inflict."[48]

While Robinson makes the most of her passive status as an unfortunate victim of circumstance, Wells integrates her pleas for sympathy with descriptions of her various activities. Instead of appearing fragile and vulnerable, Wells emerges in her memoirs as a modern workingwoman able to juggle the demands of a growing family and successful careers as an actress and a journalist. After three years together, Topham and Wells moved to the Beaufort buildings where they established a newspaper called *The World*.[49] Wells had as much if not more responsibility for writing and editing the paper than Topham. She explains: "I have in the course of conversation, often heard the expression, *seen a great deal of the world,* but, for my part, I saw *too much of it*—for the principal burden of carrying it on fell at last upon my shoulders."[50]

In her memoir, Wells includes several letters between herself and Topham, which illustrates the degree to which he relied on her skills and her opinions. After Wells gives birth to their third child, Topham writes: "My dear Pud, I wish you joy on all being over, and on a boy—this is right. Pray take care of yourself and when you have been quiet some time take care of *The World*."[51] In another letter, he asks her to send a reporter out to get the scoop on a new story: "There has been a good deal in the paper about boxing. Old Broughton lives by the waterside at Lambeth. If Samuel for his amusement, has a mind to walk there and get a few historical anecdotes of boxing from Broughton, of and about the men of his time, it would be a good article."[52] At the end of the letter, he writes: "I hear with great pleasure that the numbers of *The World* printed on Friday, were two thousand and six hundred. That's a credit to *you,* you old Pud."[53]

In addition to taking care of *The World* for Topham when he was out of town, Wells was also caring for three small children and honoring her contract at Covent Garden (for seven pounds per week). In the 1785–86 season, her roles included Rosalind in *As You Like it,* Portia in the *Merchant of Venice,* Eugenia in *The Birdcage,* and Satira in *Alexander the Great.* In 1786–87, she appeared as Belinda in *The Provok'd Wife,* Lady Percy in *Henry IV,* and Sophia in *Bonds Of Judgement,* a farce by Topham. In September 1787, Wells performed at the Royalty Theatre in a scene titled, "Ourselves; or The Realities of the Stage," which included "Extracts from some of the principal Female Performers." In 1787–88, she earned eight pounds a week at Covent Garden, playing roles such as Mrs. Page in *The Merry Wives of Windsor,* Angelina in *Love makes a Man,* and Hermione in *The Winter's Tale.*[54] Wells's demanding schedule suggests that she was still sought after professionally, despite rumors circulating about her mental instability.

According to Topham, by 1792 Wells's condition was so extreme and her behavior so hysterical that he felt she should be removed from public life. In a letter declaring Wells's insanity, he writes: "Of her madness there is not now a doubt; and she is better even where she is than in society, to alarm and distract everybody she sees."[55] Topham's anxiety about Wells's distracting performances suggests that there was much at stake for a woman who was acting out of control. Even though Wells was an actress trained to perform in public, Topham implies that she dangerously crossed the boundaries of acceptable interaction. Despite Topham's assertion that Wells was genuinely ill, others believed that her insanity was an act to attract attention. Those who knew Wells wondered if she was acting hysterically on purpose or if she was truly out of her mind.[56] In a letter to a friend, Sarah Siddons offered a telling observation about Wells when they were both in Weymouth in the summer of 1789: "Mrs. Wells is here and is either *really* mad, or affects to be so, opinions of her malady are various, I for my own part think it put on, entre nous."[57]

Wells may have "put on" her madness to ally herself with the growing trend of "nervousness" developing in fashionable circles. A popular eighteenth-century diagnosis of madness focused on the state of an individual's "nerves," a condition that was diagnosed by observing the subject's behavior. By the middle of the eighteenth century, people of fashion, particularly women, began to complain of being "nervous." This condition of anxiety and agitation became known as "The English Malady."[58]

Although nervous disorders were originally associated with the upper classes, the trend soon became more widespread. In 1807, Dr. Thomas Trotter writes about the enormous increase of cases of "neuroses" undoubtedly brought on by the very public spectacle of George the III's madness and recovery. If acting nervous was another way of acting wealthy, Siddons and others may have seen Wells's madness as a calculated performance not only to gain attention, but also to feign association with a fashionable malady.

Along with nervous disorders, another eighteenth-century mental condition associated with Wells's unusual behaviors was the diagnosis of mania. Drs. William Babington and James Curry define manic insanity in their "Outlines of a course of lectures on the practice of medicine, as delivered in the medical school of Guy's hospital (1802–1806)," as "false perceptions or erroneous conclusions, continuing during the waking state, leading to various acts not natural and customary with the patient, often dangerous to his own, or to others' personal safety."[59] Here, the definition of mental instability is explained in terms of a patient's acts or performances. When a patient acts in a way that is considered to be abnormal or dangerous, he can be classified as insane. Mania was a diagnosis applied to King George III's condition, which was marked by his unusual behaviors and actions.

WELLS AND THE KING: COWSLIP'S MAD

Wells would certainly have been aware of the king's precarious condition, as well as his particular love for the theater and for specific actresses. In the summer of 1789, the king traveled to Weymouth for a seaside respite with the specific desire to see his favorite actress, Sarah Siddons, perform in the theater. Not surprisingly, Wells also appeared in Weymouth attempting to secure theatrical employment. In one of the most famous anecdotes about her madness, it was reported that Wells hired a yacht to attract the attention of King George III. She allegedly followed him in the boat and placed herself on a "gun mounted on the deck, on which she sat astride singing 'God save the King.'" A contemporary observer, the critic John Bernard, described the events: "Whenever his Majesty cast his eye over the blue element," there was Wells's boat "careering in pursuit of him; the infatuated woman reposing on the deck, in all the languor and sumptuousness of Cleopatra." Upon hearing that Wells was following him, the King exclaimed, "Wells, Wells! Wells again!—Cowslip's mad!—on sea, on land haunts me everywhere!"[60] Whether or not the exact details of the story are accurate, this visual image of Wells stalking royalty while playing the role of a doomed queen indicates that her theatrical tendencies were linked to the possibility of her madness.[61] The king also refers to Wells as Cowslip, the name of one of her most popular roles in O'Keefe and Arnold's *Agreeable Surprise,* indicating that even for royalty Wells's persona off stage was inextricably linked to her roles on stage.

What makes this anecdote about the king even more interesting is the fact that the king was recovering from his own bout of insanity at the time. Beginning in 1788, the issue of George III's competence and stability had transfixed the nation. George III's madness was played out publicly through newspapers, gossip, and caricatures at exactly the same time that Wells was also going "mad." Theatrical displays and spectacles similarly characterized the King's madness. However, while the King's madness threatened the stability of a nation, Wells's madness was an eccentric inconvenience. The fact that the Cleopatra incident occurred in Weymouth at the same time that the King was there to see Sarah Siddons suggests that Wells's theatrical displays may have been staged to draw attention away from the more "serious" actress, Siddons, and to capitalize on what she believed to be her most desirable assets—her body and her seductive charms. However misguided this plan might have been, Wells's ability to stage her own bizarre theatrical promotional stunt may not be an indication of her madness but, rather, an example of her subversive attempts to market her public image.

POOR, WEAK, AND INJURED WOMAN

Interestingly, Wells does not mention the Weymouth anecdote in her memoirs. In fact, her main goal in much of the first volume is to counteract public ideas about her insanity by describing her doomed romantic relationship with Topham. Adapting tropes from popular eighteenth-century fiction and drama, Wells maintains that her "madness" was originally caused by Topham's cruelty. Confined to her bed after giving birth to her fourth child two months early, Wells overhears a conversation about Topham's affair with another woman, a lady whom she believed to be "her bosom friend." She explains:

> The fatal words reached my ear: to think that the man would behave so for whom I gave up everything—peace of mind reputation!—My state of health being so delicate and the horrid expression worked so much upon me at the moment, that I was immediately seized with a milk fever. My feelings received such a shock, that in the height of it I must have mentioned the abominable fact, which never enters my mind but I am agitated to a great degree.[62]

On first reading, this "abominable fact" appears to be Topham's infidelity. Wells goes on to explain that, in order to avoid the scandal associated with Topham's affair, she decides to "give out to the world that I was mad" and that anything she said "was not to be regarded" an idea "which was most industriously circulated abroad."[63] She then claims that she was advised to "take shelter under Dr. Willis," in order to avoid "being arrested, *that the world might know that I was under the care of a doctor who cured insanity.*"[64]

Here is where the narrative becomes confusing. Would Wells have been "arrested" for her illegitimate relationship with Topham or for Topham's affair? Probably not. A more plausible explanation is that the "abominable fact" she reveals during the height of her mad milk fever had something to do with her shaky financial situation at the time. Wells uses her stay with Dr. Frances Willis, the king's personal physician, then, as a public relations strategy. Capitalizing on the publicity of the king's madness, Wells promotes the image of her own instability so that she can elicit sympathy, and so that she can avoid being arrested for her debts and thrown into prison. Although Wells initially attempts to portray herself as a heroine wronged by a cruel and heartless man, she ends up revealing her own participation in representing herself as a mad character.

Wells's retreat to Dr. Willis's farm provided her with some escape from her creditors and from Topham. Predictably, Willis's fame as the doctor of the king forever associated her with questions of madness. As if she were acting in her own tragic play, Wells writes in her memoir:

> Oh tempora! O mores!—it was but rehearsing that part of the drama which he had laid out for me to act; and it was forming plot and counterplot in the most masterly manner, at the expense of the feelings of a poor, weak injured woman, and the innocent offspring that she brought into the world. I made a sacred promise, from that moment, we should be platonic lovers, and kept my word: thus is explained his afterwards allowing me to be dragged from prison to prison. . . . Sooner than explain my case to the world, I chose to be unhappy.[65]

Adapting elements of eighteenth-century drama, Wells casts Topham as the diabolical mastermind of her downfall and presents herself as a sympathetic victim.[66] She emphasizes her domestic role as a mother and dramatizes the effects of Topham's cruelty. Wells goes on to admit that she kept all of her sorrows to herself "sooner than explain my case to the world I chose to be unhappy." The idea that she has remained "silent" up until the publication of the memoir ironically frames the narrative as a final act—or a last attempt to clear her name—rather than a ploy to make money or to attract attention.

Wells further claims that Topham added to her misery and questionable reputation in his "sketch of his life" in the seventh volume of *Public Characters,* a narrative that she recognizes to be "the production of his own pen."[67] Wells writes that, in his essay, Topham:

> praises my beauty at the expense of my sense, and where he describes my madness in such *glowing* colors: but who is there who would not be *mad* at any man's conduct who could act as he had done? If my behavior afterwards in the King's Bench displeased him, why ever suffer me to go there unless the *mad plot* would be imperfect without my *martyrdom?*[68]

Wells's rereading of Topham's disguised narrative of self-promotion in her memoir is significant in several ways. Her comment that she recognizes the text to be a "production of his own pen" reveals Topham's narcissistic strategies for improving his public image. Wells suggests with this pointed comment that her memoirs, written clearly in the first person, take on more authoritative weight than Topham's third-person exposé of his own life. In her memoirs, Wells declares that Topham wants her to appear mad so that he can get her out of the way. She insists that her "martyrdom" is a result of his maneuverings, not her own instability. To provide further proof of Topham's plot against her, Wells includes the previously mentioned fragment of a letter that Topham supposedly sent to her mother. He writes: "'In regard to poor Mrs. Wells, she will of course be taken out on proper certification of her lunacy to the Lord Chancellor, which I am putting in a proper train. Of her madness there is now no doubt; and she is better even where she is than in society, to alarm and distract everybody she sees.'"[69] Wells sees this letter as evidence of Topham's callous behavior. In her version of the story, Topham's betrayal was strategically planned and executed.

Both Wells and Topham suggest the possibility that "milk fever" led to Wells's madness. But in *Public Characters,* Topham specifically links Wells's mental state to her anxieties about her acting career. He explains: "Mrs. Wells, in her eagerness to appear in a particular part, to oblige the manager of Covent Garden, too soon after a lying-in of her last child, produced a revolution of her milk which afterwards flew to her head, and occasionally disordered her brain."[70] In other words, Wells was trying to do too much, dangerously allowing her professional responsibilities to interfere with her domestic duties as a mother. Ironically, Topham was only too happy to have Wells leave her newborn to supervise his newspaper, but the prospect of her performing conflicted directly with her ability to take care of his children. Topham's damaging characterization of Wells as a neglectful mother and an ambitious actress contributed to an image of her as an unnatural woman who tested the boundaries of propriety and respectable behavior at the cost of her own mental stability.

In *Public Characters*, Topham describes Wells's madness as a complete change in her personality. He writes:

> The brightest coruscations of genius, the tenderest feelings of the tenderest heart, the noblest efforts of the most enlightened or most reflecting mind, the most exact discretion, the most rigid reserve, all may, or may not, take an opposite direction; and chance and mad momentary impulses alone decide the character. To view this change is the severest pang the heart can feel: to lament over it is to be mad ourselves.[71]

The changeability that Topham describes as characteristic of Wells's illness sounds very similar to the task of an actress—to be willing and able to transform oneself to another character at whim. Topham's use of the terms "discretion," "reflection," and "rigid reserve" further indicate that he believes Wells's madness is connected to her improper, and particularly, unfeminine behaviors. Her actions are impulsive, manic, and characterized by multiplicity. Topham's presentation of himself as a worthy gentleman distances his persona from the irrational, deranged Wells. Framing her illness as an unavoidable tragedy, Topham is able to rescue his own reputation while furthering Wells's already tarnished public image. The competing versions of Wells's madness in these narratives reflect the extent to which representations of her are based on texts that were aimed at self-promotion. Ironically, while Wells and Topham spent most of their relationship collectively promoting themselves and their theatrical careers through the newspaper they ran together, in the end they fought bitterly against one another in their memoirs. The texts provide modern readers with a revealing look at the ways in which their personal and professional associations unraveled. Wells's madness becomes a convenient trope in both narratives: for Wells her madness provides a way to present herself as a tragic victim; and for Topham, Wells's madness provides a way of justifying his separation from her and his attempts to distance himself from her damaged pubic image.

THE ADVENTURES OF SOPHIA STRANGEWAYS AND MARIE ANTOINETTE: STAGING PARODIES OF HERSELF

Other figures in Wells's life used her alleged madness and her theatrical persona as material for their own creative works. The dramatist Frederick Reynolds, Wells's new companion after her break with Topham, wrote several roles for Wells that seem to draw from both fact and fiction. One of these "portraits" is the character of Sophia Strangeways in Reynolds's farce *Notoriety* (1793).[72] A character in the play describes Ms. Strangeways as multi-talented: "She's an authoress, an actress, a musician, a painter and in short everything."[73] At one point in the drama, Sophia is accused of acting improperly in her advances toward men. She is threatened with being "sent to the country, and lock'd up for life."[74] When told that she must never show her face again in "society," Sophia retorts, "In fashionable life, loss of character makes one's reputation; but what is to become of me! If I am sent to the country, I shall die, I know I shall, and so suddenly, I shan't have time to write my own life, and run down half my acquaintance."[75] Later in the play, Sophia makes a telling comment about the popularity of women's writing: "I did write morally and what was the consequence? I had made a sum of money by a Novel called 'Seduction'—and lost it all by writing an 'Essay on Charity.'"[76]

The role of Sophia Strangeways seems to parody Wells's own experience in important ways. Reynolds makes fun of the fact that she has many professional identities and that she continues to market herself even when her reputation has become questionable. He also includes the possibility that she is mad. The idea that Sophia/Wells should be sent to the country and "lock'd up for life" is a version of what occurred between Wells and Topham. Reynolds also parodies the way that the public reacts to women writers and professional women in general. Sophia makes fun of the notion that women are encouraged to write moral essays but only make money with popular fiction. What is significant about these connections between life and art is that, in performing this role, Wells was, in fact, playing a parody of herself. In creating the character of Sophia, Reynolds points to the theatrical layers involved in fashioning celebrity. Even in a comic context, Sophia's many roles and attempts to "sell" herself are connected to the threat of madness, of being "lock'd up for life." Here Wells and Reynolds deliberately capitalize on the notoriousness of Wells's persona offstage to market her character onstage. Siddons's strategies for fashioning celebrity involved translating the nobility of the characters she played on stage to the private representation of her persona offstage. Wells's theatrical imitations of herself have the reverse effect: a parody of her ridiculousness off stage becomes less threatening and comic onstage. The fact that the play itself is about the ironies and pitfalls of fame in the eighteenth century stages a kind of postmodern, metatheatrical moment in which Wells is enacting the process of fashioning celebrity through deconstructing its elements in performance. The creative collaboration here between Wells and Reynolds suggests that, at least at this moment, Wells was entirely aware of the subversive potential of her celebrity persona and that she participated in the marketing of herself as a parodic subject.

In addition to his portrayal of Wells through the character of Sophia Strangeways, Reynolds also wrote about his experiences with Wells in his memoirs. According to Reynolds, he and Wells arrived in Calais "in the middle of March 1792."[77] They stayed for three months and returned to England after receiving a letter that cleared Wells of her financial obligations. Wells then decided to live in seclusion in Sussex, which created such a stir in the neighborhood that "she philanthropically resolved, before she shut out the world forever, once more to indulge its curiosity,—and give a masquerade!"[78] After this display of her "dramatic talents," she became the toast of the town. Returning to London, Reynolds reports that she "appears on the stage every evening," and each morning she was seen in "a new, and conspicuous chariot with four fine horses, outriders and the usual paraphernalia of a splendid equipage."[79] In London, Wells is still "alarmed" by her creditors, and she decides to take up residence in Gretford so that she can be near Dr. Willis. Wells writes: "Lodgings were taken for me at a farm-house in the neighborhood, where I went under the name of Wilson."[80] Reynolds describes his visit to Wells's country retreat in his memoirs. He and Wells dined with Dr. Willis. Afterwards, they followed the doctor's advice and retreated quietly to Wells's farmhouse. Reynolds notes that the house was, "at least, ten miles from any market town," leaving him famished during the day and fearful at night that they would be attacked by "smugglers." Wells, by contrast, was apparently delighted by the rustic quality of her surroundings. In one instance, Reynolds noticed that the neighboring farmer, his wife, and the peasantry regarded Wells with a suspicious degree of curiosity. He discovers that "with the aid of broken English, conjoined with her beauty, her fanciful dress, and elegant appearance, she should succeed in making these artless countrymen believe she was the Queen [Marie Antoinette]."[81]

Wells pretending to be the exiled queen of France in the middle of the British countryside can be seen as both theatrical and slightly off-balance. As

Reynolds makes clear, her odd theatrics work in her favor in this instance. Her audience, rural peasants, is ready and willing to believe that the woman speaking broken French in a fancy dress is the real thing. Such a leap of faith, though, is as much about the spectators as it is about Wells's ability to perform the part of a queen. Wells's parody of royalty—specifically of a foreign, persecuted queen—is an ironic commentary on female power and theatricality. As in her portrayal of the doomed Egyptian Queen, Cleopatra, Wells's mockery of majesty reflects her own desire to be worshipped at the same time that her eccentric performance demonstrates that the perception of royalty is artificial—anyone can play a queen. Wells's mimicry of queenliness is also tied to her attempts to fashion her celebrity through copying Siddons, who had cornered the market on performing queens. By assuming her own "royal" status, a role that is clearly an exaggerated fantasy, Wells deliberately defies reality and makes fun of the audiences that believe her to be the thing that she represents. Wells is in effect challenging her audience's willingness to accept female celebrity as real and legitimate. Her performance of Marie Anoinette in the countryside is an enactment of the foundation of what made Siddons such a successful star—the illusion that Siddons was a queen, a fantasy for the audience that effectively masked her deliberate strategies for fashioning her celebrity.

A VIOLENT AND OUTRAGEOUS WOMAN

Wells's odd behavior, as challenging and subversive as it may have been, had significant consequences for her life in the "real" world. The question of how to "read" Wells's actions—as deliberately theatrical or mentally unstable—arises once more with the episode in her memoirs when she describes visiting Dr. Willis's farm again—this time, with her three children. Unfortunately, when Wells arrives, she discovers that the doctor is not at home. Mrs. Willis, who recognized Wells as a former patient of her husband's, and who "conceived that a person once mad must always remain so,"[82] called for her son, Dr. John Willis. Wells narrates:

> On entering the room where I was, with his hat on and a keeper with him carrying a straight-waistcoat, I immediately perceived that he took it for granted that I was actually mad, and was determined to treat me accordingly. My temper, which was never one of the most placid, was at such treatment worked up into a pitch of frensy: upon which he ordered a pair of blisters to be put to my legs, which orders were immediately executed.

> I remained in this situation an entire week, when my children's governess came down, and being persuaded also that I was mad, took them away from me.[83]

Before her children leave, Wells manages to slip a note to her eight-year-old daughter with directions to deliver it "with her own hand on her arrival in London"[84] to Wells's friend, Mrs. Hemit, who can help her to escape. Once she receives the letter, Mrs. Hemit goes to find Dr. Willis to ask him if Wells was in fact mad. He replies: "not she indeed, I now perceive; but she is the most violent outrageous woman I ever saw."[85]

Dr. Willis gives Mrs. Hemit permission to take Wells away from the house, but he will not arrange for a carriage to transport them. Instead, they walk. Wells describes the situation:

> I was doomed to walk four miles, with my legs raw from the blisters on a scorching hot day. On our arrival at the inn, my friend asked for some rags to dress my blisters; from our appearance and such a request, the people conceived that we had escaped from a mad-house, and dispatched a messenger to Dr. Willis's, to let him know that two ladies, one in a melancholy, and the other in an outrageous state of madness, had ordered a chaise for London, and inquired if they should permit them to proceed. He returned for answer, that we might go to the devil.[86]

Wells's retelling of her escape from Dr. Willis's home highlights the theatricality of the anecdote. Wells's attention to the details of the characters' actions, dialogue, and costumes draw the audience's attention to her violated body as the focal point of the dramatic action. However, because the scene also involves her children and her role as a mother, the question of how the scene is supposed to be read becomes less clear. Wells's domestic situation, something she could have used to elicit compassion from her readers, is framed in an unconventional context. Why does she bring her children to Dr. Willis's when she knows that she has been there formerly as a patient? Instead of worrying about her children's well-being or safety while she is being held against her will, she uses one of her daughters to secretly help her to escape. Her inclusion of Dr. Willis's reaction to her plight is telling. He confirms that she is not mad but, rather, "violent" and "outrageous."

Wells only adds to her extreme portrait of herself with her description of walking four miles in the heat with raw blisters on her legs. The visual image of the two women, exhausted and bedraggled, arriving at an inn and asking for bandages for Wells's wounds, leaves little doubt as to why Wells might have been perceived as unstable. Despite all of the details that point to the possibility of Wells's madness, there are circumstances that do seem beyond her control as a woman without the safety and security of an acceptable position in society. The expectation that she should lead a domestic life without the protection and financial backing of a husband is something that she suggests might lead to a tendency to behave in unusual ways.

It also seems clear that Wells's madness is equally tied to questions of performance, identity, and celebrity. The spectators (and readers) in this anecdote are not willing to accept Wells, who once played the part of a madwoman, as capable of playing the role of a caring mother. This is the difference between performing onstage and performing in one's "real" life. The ability to switch roles onstage is an asset; off stage, such a gift is seen as dangerous, especially for women. What is particularly threatening about Wells is her willingness to merge her public and private personas. If she is publicly known to be a madwoman, she cannot also be a sane mother. The memoir continuously recreates this uncomfortable separation between what Wells wishes to convey and what her audiences understand from her performances. The more theatrical Wells becomes, the more inappropriate her behavior appears to be, and the easier it is for Topham to dismiss her. After the second Dr. Willis incident, Topham made sure that Wells was separated from her children. The rest of her narrative is full of stories about her wild attempts to see them.

MRS. WELLS AND THE MOOR

By 1796, Wells was back in prison at the King's Bench for debts connected to her brother-in-law. In August of the same year, she moved to Fleet Prison where she met her next husband, Joseph Sumbel, a Moorish Jew.[87] The dashing and unpredictable Sumbel was educated in Europe and appointed Moorish Envoy to the Court of St. James in 1794. He was sent to the Fleet Prison for contempt of court when he refused to answer questions "concerning a large quantity of diamonds in his possession."[88] Wells describes in her memoirs how she became acquainted with "the sultan." After spying on him, Wells learns that he had been "asking a number of questions concerning me."[89] She continues: "Let any woman on earth tell me that she is not fond of being inquired after, and I will immediately say to her that she is both a coquette and a hypocrite!"[90] Wells's apparent defensiveness indicates that she anticipates some criticism for her liaison with Sumbel. Still, she goes on to describe the events around her marriage and subsequent divorce in great detail.[91]

Wells sets the stage for her relationship with Sumbel by establishing the visual details of Sumbel's quarters and the shady supporting cast of characters that surround him. Sumbel invites Wells to dinner in his room, which was "fancifully hung with pink satin"[92] and populated by other Turkish dignitaries. One man, Abbo, "took a fancy" to Wells and made her a proposal of marriage, which she promptly declined. According to Wells, Abbo was so incensed that he later returned to the prison to "assassinate" her, but due to "timely notice," he could not get through the prison gates.[93] Soon after their first meeting, a mysterious man offers to get Wells out of prison. Sensing a rival, Mr. Sumbel immediately proposes to Wells, and she accepts. Wells acknowledges that she was walking into a trap. She explains that in marrying Sumbel: "I obtained my liberty in one way, though I had just given consent to lose it in another."[94]

In order to avoid the obstacle of her marriage to Mr. Wells, whom she hadn't heard from for over twenty years, Wells decides to become a "Jewess" and to be married according to the laws of the Jewish faith. On 16 October 1796, *The Post and Morning Gazetteer* reported their "Extraordinary Marriage":

> On Thursday Evening last, the marriage ceremony in the Jewish style, was performed in the Fleet, uniting Mrs. Wells, late of Covent Garden Theatre, to Mr. Sumbel, a Moorish Jew detained for debt in that prison. The ceremony was solemnized with all the Jewish magnificence. The bridegroom was richly dressed in white satin, and a splendid turban with a white feather; the bride, who is now converted to Jewess, was also attired in white satin, and her head dressed in elegant style with a large plume of white feathers.[95]

The spectacle of Wells's strange marriage provided the newspapers with great scandalous material. *The Morning Herald* of 17 October joked: "Mrs. Becky Wells late of every theatre in this kingdom, has extended her *known good nature* so far as to *marry a Moorish Jew*. . . . Some Christian Wags joked with her respecting the ceremony of *circumcision,* but Mrs. Sumbel—for that is her present name—silenced them by an assurance that she had tried her husband's *attachment.*"[96] The writer connects Wells's theatricality to her abundant sexuality and to questions of deviance. As we have seen, the actress-as-prostitute was a familiar construction, but the actress associated with a Jew (another social "other" in eighteenth-century society) provided even more fodder for satire and public humiliation.[97]

Wells includes a letter that she wrote in response to this article where she defends her choices:

> Sir—In your paper of Thursday last, it was said "Mrs. Wells was always an *odd genius,* and her becoming a Jewess greatly gratifies her passion for *eccentricity.*" In answer to this, I beg the favor to insert in your paper, that it is not any passion for *eccentricity* that has induced me to embrace the *Israelitish Religion*—it is studying and examining with great care and attention The Old Testament, that has influenced my conduct.[98]

In this letter, Wells sounds very much like Sophia Strangeways, the character that Reynolds created for her in his play *Notoriety*. She argues that she is not eccentric or odd, but that she has chosen to adopt Judaism because she finds the Old Testament so interesting. She has already admitted to her readers, in volume one of her memoir, that conversion was a way to get around the fact of her previous marriage. The clever idea of presenting herself as a scholar is a testament to Wells's desire to present herself favorably in public, despite the idea that it would have been considered mildly eccentric for Wells to write to the paper on her own behalf in any situation. In this forum, Wells depicts her acceptance of the Jewish faith as just another role that she must throw herself into.

Wells admits that with her marriage to Mr. Sumbel, she got more than she bargained for. She writes: "I now found for the first time in my life, the difference betwixt celebrity and Notoriety."[99] It is compelling that Wells deliberately points to the line that she has attempted to balance throughout her career between fame and notoriousness in reference to her relationship with Sumbel. Even though this is perhaps the most "eccentric" extended anecdote in the text, Wells seems to have fashioned the story so that it would fit into an understandable framework for eighteenth-century readers who would have seen the exotic Sumbel as an "other" to the more familiar and recognizable English actress Wells. Readers might have also identified with Wells as a victim of her husband's cruel authority, particularly because Wells models him after Shakespeare's irrational Othello.

Soon after their marriage, Wells learned that Mr. Sumbel was as abusive as he was wealthy. He was extremely jealous and kept Wells under close observation wherever they went. Although she lived in luxury, wearing fancy clothes and diamonds, Mr. Sumbel would remove her jewelry and commit them "to the care of an iron chest"[100] when she returned from a night out. Wells, in fact, was not even allowed to see the diamonds unless she was in the presence of Mr. Sumbel. "And as to money," Wells explains, "I was never suffered even to have a shilling in my pocket, for fear I should run away."[101] Here, Wells associates her new husband with negative stereotypes of Jews and their concern for money. Wells explains that Sumbel's excessive attention to her jewels frequently resulted in violence. One evening, when she was preparing to take off her earrings, "he seized hold of one of them, and tore it entirely through my ear."[102] These details prepare the reader for Wells's ultimate decision to leave her husband.

One of Wells's strategies for sympathy is to depict Sumbel's Moorishness as the opposite of her own Englishness. When describing a trip that the two take to see her children in the country, she uses visual clues to differentiate herself from her husband. From the outset, it is clear that they are not suitable traveling companions. Mr. Sumbel insists on riding with his entire entourage in full Turkish costume. Wells reports that, because of their strange appearance, they are often turned away from the village inns that they encounter. Mr. Sumbel, or the "moor," as she begins to call him in reference to Shakespeare's Othello, becomes more and more irate and critical. With no money and no resources, Wells is left to accept the situation. She writes: "On we went, half the twenty-four hours in British simplicity, the other half in African grandeur. One hour I fancied myself the once happy *Cowslip,* and the next I knew, to my inexpressible sorrow, that I was the wife of a Moorish *nobleman.*"[103] Interestingly, in this passage, Wells gives equal weight to her roles both onstage and offstage. Wells recalls her former days in the theater and bemoans her lost reputation as an alluring comic heroine. She was once the beloved "Cowslip." Now, she is instead the wife of a cruel "Moorish Nobleman." In this comparison her role as a successful actress—a role that highlights her British femininity—is framed as more legitimate than her current position as the domestic prisoner of a foreign man.[104]

The moor finally agrees to let Wells continue on her own to Lincolnshire to visit her children with the stipulation that, while she is away from him, she should "neither sleep nor undress" herself.[105] Wells agrees to these strange demands and travels to see her daughters. After a long, tiring journey, she is reunited with her children, who are thrilled to see her. Wells writes: "The first object I beheld was my dear eldest daughter. . . . The little sports woman, the huntress of the Wolds, was deeply absorbed in her favorite task: when her eye caught the chaise entering the lawn she screamed—'Our mother!—Our Mother!"[106] After relating her joy at the "six little arms at one moment encircling my neck," Wells describes her own arms, which are "swollen immoderately and very painful" because she had obeyed her husband's orders and not taken off her dress during her journey.[107] In this instance, Wells's dress becomes a metaphor for the confining and cruel relationship that she has with her husband. Her wardrobe in this scene is not symbolic of a loftier character like Marie Antoinette. Rather, Wells is costumed in her own version of a straightjacket. Her clothes, once symbols of her beauty and success as an actress, are now fragile and sad reminders of her situation and of the impossibility of representing herself as an alluring celebrity.

Wells's marriage to Mr. Sumbel and their eccentric behavior (Sumbel threatens to "sell" Wells and to shoot her) resulted in her final estrangement from her family. Wells describes being shunned by her daughters as she passed them on the road several years later: "My eldest daughter (Mrs. Ford) perceiving me, desired my daughter Maria to ride at a gallop, and told the groom to follow her, that he might not perceive me. They informed me that they were on their way to Scarborough, to order dresses for a ball. . . . At length my daughter Harriet wrote to me to let me know that I must not think of residing in the neighborhood as her father would not allow it."[108]

In October 1800, Wells sent her daughters hats decorated with cowslips, an emblem of her famous role in *The Agreeable Surprise*. Her daughters, Juliet and Maria, wrote to her without acknowledging directly that she was their mother: "For the very elegant and tasteful present we have this morning received, we are bound to return you many thanks. We wept over them: and while we wear them shall remember to whose kindness we are indebted for them."[109] Wells refers to Topham's letter, in which he quips ironically: "Could I add anything more grateful to your feelings than the above, I would do it. The taste displayed is all your own. I shall never see them worn, but the flowers will remind me of the happiest days of my life."[110] Topham's suggestion that "the taste" Wells displays is "all her own" is a poignant reminder of Wells's lost career and of the class divide that now separates her from her children. Topham separates himself from Wells using specifically elitist language that signals his participation in contemporary debates about taste in relation to class status. His reference to Wells's questionable style here is a thinly veiled insult about her gaudiness, lack of culture, and refinement. Although Wells is the mother of his children, Topham makes it clear that she is now not a suitable role model for them. Her theatricality and exuberance, once qualities that made his days "the happiest," are now indications of her instability and potential deviance.

WELLS IN PUBLIC: UNRECOGNIZABLE PERFORMANCES

Topham was not the only person who found Wells's behavior to be eccentric and unrefined. The celebrated novelist Frances Burney documented a strange encounter with Wells in a letter written to her sister Susanna Phillips in June

1792. While visiting John Boydell's Shakespeare Gallery in Pall Mall, Burney describes being followed around the rooms by the actress Mary Wells. Burney's inclusion of the Wells anecdote in her letter, which is framed narratively as if it were a scene in a novel, is perhaps the best evidence we have of how Wells behaved in public and the ways in which her "audiences" perceived her as menacing, crazy, and above all presumptuous. Upon entering the gallery, Burney, her father, and friend Mrs. Crewe noticed "an extremely handsome woman, who was parading about with a nosegay in her hand."[111] After sitting too close to Mrs. Crewe on a bench, striking various strange poses, and dropping her nosegay dramatically in front of Mr. Burney, Wells began to sing passages "without words or connections," further alarming the group. Burney writes: "By the looks we-interchanged, we soon mutually said, This is a Mad woman! . . . We were going to run for our lives when Mrs. Townshend whispered to Mrs. Crewe it was only Mrs. Wells the actress! And said she was certainly only performing vagaries to *try effect*, which she was quite famous for doing."[112] Burney goes on to describe Mrs. Crewe's reaction in detail:

> It would have been food for a Painter to have seen Mrs. Crewe during this explanation. All her terror instantly gave way to indignation—and scarcely any pencil could equal the high vivid glow of her Cheeks. To find herself made the object of Game to the burlesque humour of a bold player was an indignity she could not brook, and her mind was immediately at work how to assert herself against such unprovoked and unauthorised effrontery.[113]

Mrs. Crewe then tries to complain about Wells's behavior, mentioning the names of the people in her party to one of the proprietors of the gallery, which makes Burney very nervous because the anecdote may "get into all the newspapers."[114] Wells overhears this interchange and apparently exclaims: "It's very hard, very cruel indeed to take such notice of people in public. The Public's open to us all, and we have all a right to behave how we please. And it's very hard, and very cruel in people to be so soon affronted. And one person is as good as another in a public place."[115] Burney responds by attempting to dissuade Mrs. Crewe from "competition with this lady," describing Wells as "a wild, half-crazy woman, accustomed to indulge herself in all her whims as I had witnessed in Weymouth, where absurdly as she behaved, she was opposed by nobody, and seemed always to regard herself as a privileged person." Mrs. Crewe answers: "I don't understand such privileges. If she assumes them as hers, what in the meantime is to become of ours?"[116]

Mrs. Crewe's remark is telling. If Wells assumes the privilege to act in any way she pleases because of her celebrity and her potential power to influence the public sphere (i.e., her ability to get things into the newspapers), what will happen to those who are supposed to have privileges as a result of their "actual" status in British society? This is a clear expression of the anxiety that Wells's behavior instilled in spectators outside of the comfortable boundaries of the theater. While Wells's antics were certainly annoying, the most galling aspect of the incident, according to Mrs. Crewe, was the boldness of her behavior as an actress in relation to a group of people who were clearly above her in social status.

Wells's counter assertion that "the public's open to us all" can be read as a powerful and poignant statement about the possibilities for female celebrity. At the same moment that the establishment of female celebrity generates a new kind of status and agency for women in the public sphere, the audience's assessment of those performances is ultimately the most powerful indicator of a celebrity's success or failure. The initial description of Wells as a "mad woman," and the subsequent revelation that she is only an actress "performing vagaries for effect," are particularly telling. Wells's "unauthorized effronteries" represent the opposite of "natural" celebrity seduction, where audiences are drawn to an individual because of his/her authentic beauty or talent—an illusion perfected by Siddons.

The Burney group's response to Wells reveals inherent cultural assumptions about celebrity status for women in the late eighteenth century. Actresses were tolerated in the public sphere only if they remained "under control." Wells's habit of indulging herself in all of her "whims," a typical accusation leveled against many modern celebrities, is dangerous because it threatens established social codes and hierarchies. Celebrity status suggests that an individual's performance can win them a certain agency or privilege that they otherwise would never have obtained. Wells's performance of celebrity privilege can thus also be read as an ironic commentary on the process of fashioning celebrity. The public may be "open to us all," but there are still limitations on and expectations of feminine behavior that intangibly structure and script the ways in which women are allowed to act and the ways in which audiences are led to respond to their performances. Wells's performance in the Shakespeare Gallery is also an exaggerated representation of herself as an actress. There is something about Wells's performance for performance sake here—a performance without role models or boundaries—that crosses the line between eccentricity and parody, and into the realm of madness and deviance.

FINAL PERFORMANCES

Wells seems to have understood that her fame later in life was partially based on her questionable reputation. She includes a story in the last volume of her memoirs about receiving an invitation to "Countess Dowager B's" house for the evening. The next day she visits another woman who was also asked to the same gathering. Much to Wells's surprise, this woman declares that she is looking forward to the performance of Wells's "Imitations" to be given at the party. A glance at the bottom of this guest's invitation reveals that she was indeed the promised entertainment. Wells writes: "I felt myself hurt at it: though aware that to my public character I owed the honor of my invitation, I was not pleased at the idea of the party being given to exhibit me."[117] In typical Wells fashion, she pretends to have lost her voice when she is asked at the party to interrupt her card game and give her imitation of Siddons as Isabella. She recalls: "The lady who knew my real motive overheard our conversation and was almost convulsed with laughter at my *acting*."[118]

Wells's awareness of her own "public character," and her acknowledgment in her memoir of the various forms of "acting" that she needed to do on a daily basis in order to survive, is perhaps the most significant evidence of her strategic involvement in fashioning her celebrity. The public's desire to see Wells's "Imitations" suggests the extent to which celebrity and fame were now rooted in eighteenth-century culture. The fact that one could mimic famous people in order to gain recognition for oneself indicates that fame was a commodity. A famous persona could be copied and manipulated, bought and sold by an entirely different person. Wells's choice of Siddons and Jordan as models reflects the extent of these actresses' public recognition value, but it also illustrates Wells's own belief that she was equal in talent to those women and, therefore, should also have achieved a similar celebrity status. Wells's performance of illness in this anecdote can be seen as a small act of resistance in her refusal to perform according to her audience's expectations of her. Ultimately, the larger schema of her outrageous self-representations on stage, off stage, and in print can also be read as a series of resistant performances, which were inevitably understood by spectators as evidence of her madness and instability.

Although Wells repeatedly claimed to be writing her memoirs in order to rescue her already damaged reputation, the narrative seems to have accomplished just the opposite; after its publication, Wells all but disappeared from public life. Her final documented performance was a benefit that she gave for her mother on 4 December 1815. She lived her last years in a boarding house on Cavendish Street, caring for her mother, who died in January 1827 at the age of 95. Wells became ill and died only two years later on 23 January 1829. She shares a grave with her mother in the churchyard of St. Pancras.[119]

At the same moment that Wells disappeared from public life, she also nearly vanished from theatrical history. The same qualities that led many to dismiss Wells as notoriously eccentric in her own lifetime have also led scholars to ignore her impact on late-eighteenth-century theater. Despite the fact that she "knew everyone and everyone knew her" in the late-eighteenth-century theatrical world, scholarship on Wells has been limited, and the extent of her influence on historical figures who have received far more attention—such as Sarah Siddons, Elizabeth Inchbald, and Mary Robinson—has been largely unrecognized.[120] That Wells was considered unstable points to a growing ideological separation between British actresses such as Sarah Siddons and Fanny Kemble, who were considered to be theatrical heroines, and lesser-known female performers who were unable to sustain their celebrity by fashioning themselves as idealized feminine subjects. Ultimately, the accusations of duplicity, deviance, and madness directed at Wells suggest that the threat of a woman "acting out" was particularly resonant at the beginning of the nineteenth century. Wells's madness can be seen as a type of precursor to depictions of Victorian literary madwomen, whose theatrical outbursts are juxtaposed with the docile and gentle demeanor of proper English women. Wells was unique, but in her thwarting of convention she became unrecognizable: a state that reinforced public perceptions of her "madness" and made fashioning her own celebrity close to impossible.

Epilogue

Fanny Kemble's Inherited Celebrity

FANNY KEMBLE AND SARAH SIDDONS

In 1830, the year before her death, Sarah Siddons posed for a portrait with her niece, the actress Fanny Kemble (figure 18). In this painting by Henry Perronet Briggs, Siddons is seated on a large throne-like chair with Kemble perched lovingly by her side, her hand resting comfortably on her aunt's wrist. Siddons appears feeble—her gaze is unfixed and distracted. She holds a large book in her hand as if she has been leafing through its pages and paused to digest an idea. She wears the costume of an aging aristocrat: a black dress trimmed with lace, a white-frilled cap, and a sumptuous fur mantle draped around her shoulders. Kemble, by contrast, wears a fashionable white dress, which suggestively reveals the creamy pale skin of her neck. Her expression of calm seriousness masks the hint of a smile. Kemble's half of the portrait is framed by the background of blue sky; Siddons is almost engulfed by the red drapery of the backdrop.

In many ways, this portrait represents the passing on of theatrical genius, the dynastic transference of celebrity from Siddons to Kemble.[1] At the time of the painting, Kemble had just made her debut on stage as Juliet to rave reviews.[2] In addition to featuring the relationship between the newly famous Kemble and her legendary aunt, the details of the painting reveal how Siddons significantly changed the position of the actress in British society through her clever self-fashioning strategies. The depiction of Siddons on a "throne" is a reference to her position in Reynolds's and Gainsborough's

FIGURE 18. Henry Perronet Briggs. *Fanny Kemble and Her Aunt, Mrs. Siddons*, c. 1830–31, Boston Athenaeum

portraits. Her costume, accessories, and jewelry indicate wealth and comfort, a status that she achieved through her fame. The book she holds is a reference not only to the lofty Shakespearean heroines that she portrayed, but also to her "literary" education. Siddons had little formal schooling, yet at the time of her death she had created the illusion that she was part of an elite learned class.[3]

Kemble was the direct beneficiary of the star persona that Siddons invented and that Mary Robinson and Mary Wells struggled to achieve. Once Siddons had invented the category of theatrical royalty, Kemble could easily inhabit that role and still make mistakes in her private life.[4] Despite her divorce and her separation from her children, Kemble's position as a theatrical heroine somehow transcended her role as an "ordinary" woman in nineteenth-century society.[5] Like Siddons, Kemble came to represent the embodiment of "true Englishness" through her performances both onstage and offstage. Her close friend, American author Henry James, remarked, "she uttered with her pen as well as her lips the most agreeable, uncontemporary, self-respecting English, as idiomatic as possible and just as little common."[6] By the middle of the nineteenth century, methods for fashioning celebrity used by eighteenth-century actresses were established strategies of self-promotion that began early in an actress's career. Kemble sustained her position as a famous person through a constant production of images, texts, and performances. Stereotypes of actresses as immoral and disreputable persisted into the nineteenth century; however, actresses who served as role models and moved in aristocratic circles had become a clear part of British society.[7]

Kemble was born into a family of actors, but from the outset she was raised to be part of the upper class. She was well-educated and spent her early years dreaming of becoming a writer.[8] She had already drafted an historical novel and two plays when she made her first entrance on the stage. After her triumph as Juliet, her theatrical career became essential to supporting her family. Writing, however, remained in many ways her first love. Over the course of her long life (1809–1893) she published six memoirs (totaling eleven volumes) that chronicled her teenage years, her career on the stage, her marriage and divorce to the American plantation owner Pierce Butler, her later career in England and America, and her old age. While Siddons, Robinson, and Wells published narratives that were carefully scripted memories of their lives and careers, Kemble's memoirs were drawn from her "journals" and "letters"—excerpts of her everyday writings and correspondence. Even though Kemble edited these fragments, by offering the public a glimpse of her "private" thoughts, she created the illusion that she was not engaged in active self-fashioning strategies.[9]

This appearance of "authenticity" was central to Kemble's success as a nineteenth-century female celebrity. In fact, throughout her life she maintained a disdain for the stage. In her memoirs, Kemble attributes her dislike of the theater to the necessity of exposing oneself to an audience:

> I do not think it is the acting itself that is so disagreeable to me, but the public personal exhibition, the violence done (as it seems to me) to womanly dignity and decorum in thus becoming the gaze of every eye and the theme of every tongue. If my audience was reduced to my intimates and associates I should not mind it so much, I think; but I am not quite sure that I would like it then.[10]

Kemble's assertion that "public personal exhibition" is at odds with Victorian ideals of "womanly dignity and decorum" puts her in the position of critiquing herself as a performer. She claims that if she were surrounded by "intimates and associates" (something that she did later in life with her "private" readings of Shakespeare), she would not feel so over exposed.

According to Henry James, Kemble's theatrical talents were part of her charm and originality, but she had never wished to be a "celebrity." In an essay published after Kemble's death, James wrote: "She detested the stage, to which she had been dedicated while she was too young to judge. . . . She had been, in short, a celebrity in the twenties, had attracted the town while the century was still almost as immature as herself."[11] James suggests that Kemble became famous when she was too young to understand the dangers of celebrity. Thus, her public persona was based on an image of her that she did not have a hand in creating. James's attempt to distance Kemble from the active process of self-fashioning indicates that, while celebrity was rooted in nineteenth-century culture, it was important not to appear too anxious to be famous.

THE LOVELY FANNY KEMBLE

The enormous appeal of early portraits of Kemble by Thomas Lawrence and Thomas Sully contributed greatly to Kemble's success in promoting herself as a theatrical heroine. These portraits established Kemble as an exemplar of nineteenth-century beauty and grace.[12] Lawrence's drawing of Kemble as Juliet (lithographed by R. J. Lane), the "most widely produced and imitated portrait" of the actress, portrayed her as an extremely lovely young woman.[13] To most nineteenth-century observers, however, Kemble's dark skin, full chin, and compact figure was not considered conventionally attractive. A friend of Siddons once declared, "Fanny Kemble you are the ugliest and handsomest woman in London!"[14] After sending a copy of the Lawrence drawing to an acquaintance, Kemble wrote:

> I am glad that you got my print safe; it is a very beautiful thing (I mean the drawing), and I am glad to think it is like me, though much flattered. I suppose it is like what those who love me have sometimes seen me, but to the majority of my acquaintance it must appear unwarrantably good looking. The effect of it is much too large for me, but when my mother ventured to suggest this to Lawrence, he said that was a peculiarity of his drawings, and that he thought persons familiar with his style would understand it.[15]

Here, Kemble illustrates that she understands the humility expected of a female celebrity. She is careful to praise the image, while at the same time she distances herself from her own vanity by insisting that it really does not resemble her at all. As she says, the portrait only depicts the way that "those who love her" might choose to see her. Echoing her sentiments on "public personal exhibition," Kemble again participates in the appropriate rhetoric for a proper Victorian lady. Unlike her aunt, who had described in detail her vital contributions to the creation of Reynolds's famous portrait, *Mrs. Siddons as the Tragic Muse* (chapter 1, figure 6), Kemble maintains that her beauty in Lawrence's image is just a pleasing illusion, and that she had no part in crafting this deception.

Despite the fact that Lawrence's representation of Kemble looked nothing like her, his portrait of the actress became a template for nineteenth-century style. Fanny Kemble curls were all the rage. Her dress was the height of fashion for respectable young ladies.[16] Kemble's innocent expression—her "liquid" eyes and bow shaped lips—were typical of the "ideal" characteristics of turn of the century femininity. One nineteenth-century art critic writes of Lawrence's portraits of women: "the seat of sweet, soft, feminine character lies in the outer corner of the eyes, especially the lower eyelid, and the corners of the mouth: this the painter should catch, towards completion, with a few delicate touches."[17] Like eighteenth-century actresses who served as arbiters of style and grace, Kemble's image came to represent the "best" qualities of a young British lady.

FANNY KEMBLE AS "BEATRICE" AND QUEEN VICTORIA AS "HERSELF"

Kemble was not only a model for aristocratic women, but also for the newly crowned Queen Victoria. Thomas Sully, an American artist, painted one of the most recognized portraits of Queen Victoria in her coronation year based on portraits that he created of Kemble.[18]

Like his mentor Thomas Lawrence (who had a long history of intimate acquaintance with the Kemble/Siddons family), Sully was enthralled by Kemble's charms, both onstage and offstage.[19] He painted thirteen portraits of her during his lifetime, most of which were done from memory while he was in Philadelphia and Kemble remained in London. His journals are full of references to Kemble's name. At one point, he describes topics of conversation with friends that revolved around a discussion of "the arts, America and Mrs. Butler (Kemble's married name)."[20] Sully was also connected to Kemble's family—her husband, Pierce Butler, was his cousin. As the child of actors himself, Sully may have considered promoting Kemble a part of raising the status of theatrical families in general.

When Sully arrived in London in 1837, hoping to gain an audience with the Queen, he brought his portrait of Kemble as Beatrice with him as an example of one of his finer works (figure 19).[21] In this painting (an image that Kemble hated because she did not think it resembled her), Sully equates the qualities of Shakespeare's popular heroine with Kemble's own character.[22] According to Sully, Kemble's wit, charm, strength, and sense of humor made her the perfect actress to play such a feisty role. Henry James echoed Sully's impressions of Kemble: "She wrote exactly as she talked observing, asserting, complaining, confiding, crying out and bounding off, always effectually communicating."[23]

Sully's decision to base his portrait of the Queen on his image of Kemble illustrates his belief that the two shared both physical and personal qualities. In his journal, Sully wrote that his daughter, Blanch, who was travelling with him, decided that the Queen resembled Fanny Kemble.[24] She considered Victoria "a good-natured, fat face ugly likeness of Mrs. P. Butler."[25] Even though Kemble and the Queen had vastly different backgrounds, Sully was surprised that Victoria was so like an "ordinary" aristocratic lady. He wrote: "I should be gratified if I were able to give an idea of the sweet tone of voice and gentle manner of Queen Victoria! It was impressive of dignity and mildness, and at the same time I felt quite at my ease, as tho in company with merely a well bred lady."[26] Sully's reference to the Queen as a "well bred aristocrat" reinforces the idea, promoted by King George III

FIGURE 19. Anonymous. *Fanny Kemble, 1809–1893*, from *Harpers's Weekly*, 1893. Print Collection, Miriam and Ira D. Wallach Division of Arts, Prints, and Photographs, The New York Public Library, Astor, Lenox and Tilden Foundations

and Queen Charlotte decades earlier, of the royal family as ordinary and accessible. Comparisons of Kemble and Queen Victoria recall the similarities between Sarah Siddons and Queen Charlotte, and the ways in which they were simultaneously adored by audiences.

In crafting an image of the Queen, Sully had to consider both her royal status and what would appeal to spectators (figure 20). In other words, how could he make the Queen appear attractive and alluring but not sexualized? He made two artistic decisions that worked to convey a sense of majesty and femininity without presenting the Queen as an object of desire. First, he modeled the portrait after an already successful image of Kemble, an established celebrity. Second, he depicted the Queen as she ascended her throne, giving the viewer a glimpse of the Queen's bare back. This technique allowed Sully to portray the Queen's youth and beauty without drawing attention to her breasts or neckline.

It is ironic that the Queen's expression and pose resemble Sully's depiction of Kemble as Beatrice, which was an idealized image of an actress representing a fictional theatrical heroine. The Queen's shiny brown hair, large eyes, and cherubic mouth mirror the conventions of desirable nineteenth-century femininity portrayed by Sully and Lawrence in their depictions of Kemble. The Queen's portrait was extremely popular. *The London Examiner* reported: "It is quite understood to be the prevailing opinion of the court circle that the American artist has succeeded in rendering the best and the most graceful likeness of our youthful Queen."[27] Sully's portrait of Victoria became the most circulated image of the Queen; both in America and in England engravings and prints were copied and distributed everywhere.[28]

The relationship between the portraits of Fanny Kemble and Queen Victoria suggests that the connections among royalty, actresses, and the fashioning of celebrity that began in the eighteenth century continued well into the nineteenth century. The self-fashioning strategies practiced by eighteenth-century actresses were copied by other significant public figures. Actresses were, after all, experts in illusion. By the nineteenth century, even the Queen had to be concerned with marketing and selling her image, and she, too, borrowed from theatrical examples.

PHOTOGRAPHS OF KEMBLE AND THE QUEEN

The year 1837, when Victoria ascended the throne, was also the year that Louis Daguerre invented the photograph.[29] Photography would forever change the impact of portraiture and the options for fashioning celebrity available to actresses, aristocrats, public figures, and for the first time, an emerging middle class. While portraits were expensive (and depended on the skill of the painter or the engraver), the invention of photography put image making in the hands of anyone who could afford a visit to a photography studio. Unlike paintings, photographs could be used as highly effective marketing tools or as devastating evidence of age and decay.

Comparing photographs of Kemble and the Queen to their youthful portraits illustrates the ways in which fashioning celebrity, marketing, and promotion are subject to the forces of time. Both women led very long lives

FIGURE 20. Thomas Sully. *Queen Victoria*, 1838. By kind permission of the Trustees of the Wallace Collection, London

and were photographed in their eighties.[30] These images are poignant and strange. In one such photograph, a grim corpulent Victoria looks away from the camera; in another, Kemble appears slightly deranged in a kerchief and shawl (figures 21 and 22). Unlike the polished and deliberately staged portraits of them as young women, these two images function only as pure documentation. They are simply pictures of two elderly ladies. Still, the jarring

FIGURE 21. *Fanny Kemble in Old Age* (undated). Courtesy of The Lenox Library Association, Kemble Collection

FIGURE 22. *Victoria, Queen of England* (undated). Benjamin R. Tucker Papers, Manuscripts and Archives Division, The New York Public Library, Astor, Lenox, and Tilden Foundations

juxtaposition between the portraits and the photographs reinforces the link between visual images and the fashioning of celebrity demonstrated by eighteenth-century actresses. As women dependent on the approval of audiences for their survival, they developed self-promotion strategies that continuously referenced the visual. Actresses understood, long before the technology of pictorial image making became accessible to all, how identity was tied inextricably to the way that one appeared.

CONCLUSION

The history of the portraits and memoirs of Sarah Siddons, Mary Robinson, Mary Wells, and Fanny Kemble is also the history of the earliest modern female celebrities. For these actresses, creating and manipulating versions of themselves onstage, on canvas, and in print resulted in either effective or misdirected public-relations strategies. Sarah Siddons was a success because she associated herself with models of female worship—woman as queen, woman as mother—already in place in the eighteenth century, roles that specifically de-emphasized Siddons's sexuality. The public display of her body served the purpose of representing true Britishness and sublime femininity. Mary Robinson was able to use her literary talents to present herself as a victim of unfortunate circumstances, while her visual presence (as a fashion model and a notorious public figure) tainted her reputation, excluding her from the celebrity status that Siddons achieved. Mary Wells's beauty, ambition, talent, and bravado resulted in her short-lived theatrical achievements and her eventual demise. Furthermore, Wells's association with madness illustrates the threat she posed to traditional notions of gender in the eighteenth century. Her experience suggests that if a woman operated solely in the public sphere, without any attachment to domestic life, she was destined to become an outcast.

In order to be famous, these actresses had to negotiate and manipulate central paradoxes of femininity that still exist today: they were expected to be domestic and seductive, private and public, ordinary and extraordinary, divine and real, passive and powerful. Whether they embraced or defied these ideas, actresses set the stage for the range of possibilities for female roles. Contemporary actresses continue to use photography, film, and television to shape and frame their personas according to the popular trend and ideals of the moment, a process that is even more complicated by television, film, and most recently, the Internet. Just as in the eighteenth century, when professions became open to talented individuals and were not subject to restrictions based on social status, celebrity continues to be a method of changing classes. Those who achieve fame have access to wealth and prestige, while losing celebrity status can result in poverty and disgrace. Excessive interest in actresses' private lives is still the main focus of contemporary print and media culture, a practice that began in the eighteenth century. Reconciling actresses' private and public personas remains the central focus of most interviews and the central issue of most popular celebrity scandals. Readers continue to be captivated by actresses' memoirs and biographies because these texts promise to provide an inside look into the lives of elusive performers, a window into the "real" world behind their onstage identities.

Perhaps the most lasting element of the emergence of modern celebrity in the eighteenth century is the notion that fame is the celebration of the individual in a media-saturated society. As fashion plates, objects of desire, and subjects of collective fantasy, Siddons, Robinson, Wells, and Kemble were at the center of a world where women were judged by the way that they invented and promoted carefully crafted versions of themselves. Over two hundred years later, such techniques continue to both reinforce and subvert the ways in which female identities are imagined in contemporary culture.

INTRODUCTION

1. Fanny Burney, *Evelina, or The History of a Young Lady's Entrance into the World* (New York: W.W. Norton & Co., 1965), 181.

2. This is the reason why the study does not include chapters on Dorothy Jordon, Mrs. Abington, or Eliza Farren—all popular female celebrities in the late eighteenth century. Although these actresses were the subject of numerous portraits and biographies, they did not write their own memoirs.

3. Kristina Straub's *Sexual Suspects: Eighteenth-Century Players and Sexual Ideology* (Princeton: Princeton University Press, 1992); Elizabeth Howe's *The First English Actresses: Women and Drama, 1660–1700* (Cambridge: Cambridge University Press, 1992); Shearer West's *The Image of the Actor: Verbal and Visual Representation in the Age of Garrick and Kemble* (Boston: St. Martin's Press, 1991); Sandra Richards's *The Rise of the English Actress* (Boston: St. Martin's, 1993); Judith Pascoe's *Romantic Theatricality* (Ithaca, NY: Cornell University Press, 1997); Catherine Burrough's edited collection *Women in British Romantic Theatre: Drama, Performance, and Society, 1790–1840* (Cambridge: Cambridge University Press, 2000); Betsy Bolton's *Women, Nationalism and the Romantic Stage* (Cambridge: Cambridge University Press, 2001); Robyn Asleson's edited volumes, *A Passion for Performance: Sarah Siddons and Her Portraitists* (Los Angeles: The J. Paul Getty Museum, 1999) and *Notorious Muse: The Actress in British Art and Culture, 1776–1812* (New Haven, CT: Yale University Press, 2003); Cheryl Wanko's *Roles of Authority: Thespian Biography and Celebrity in Eighteenth-Century Britain* (Lubbock: Texas Tech University Press, 2003); and Mary Luckhurst and Jane Moody's collection, *Theatre and Celebrity in Britain, 1660–2000* (New York: Palgrave Macmillan, 2005).

4. Felicity Nussbaum, "Actresses and the Economics of Celebrity, 1770–1800," in *Theatre and Celebrity*, ed. Luckhurst and Moody, 152.

5. Nussbaum, "Actresses," 152.

6. Joseph Roach, "Public Intimacy: The Prior History of 'It,'" in *Theatre and Celebrity*, ed. Luckhurst and Moody, 27.

7. Marvin Carlson, *The Haunted Stage* (Ann Arbor: University of Michigan Press, 2001), 3–4.

8. Carlson, *Haunted*, 8.

9. Joseph Roach, *Cities of the Dead: Circum-Atlantic Performance* (New York: Columbia University Press, 1996), 77.

10. Leo Braudy, *The Frenzy of Renown: Fame and Its History* (New York: Vintage Books, 1997), 397, 13. Braudy suggests that fame in the eighteenth century was particularly modern because it concerned ways of "defining oneself, making oneself known, beyond the limitations of class and family" (14). In his study *Illusions of Immortality: A Psychology of Fame and Celebrity* (New York: St. Martin's Press, 2000), David Giles cites the emergence of literary culture, publishing, engraving, portraiture, and the theater as crucial elements in the development of modern celebrity (16–17).

11. Wanko, *Roles of Authority*, 5.

12. As Braudy explains: "Public fame from the time of the American and French revolutions is thus shaped by a world where the image and idea of fame can be reproduced and disseminated in unprecedented quantities" (*The Frenzy of Renown*, 396).

13. Howe, *First English Actresses*, 21.

14. Straub, *Sexual Suspects*, 89.

15. Deborah C. Payne, "Reified Object or Emergent Professional? Retheorizing the Restoration Actress," in *Cultural Readings of Restoration and Eighteenth-Century English Theater*, ed. J. Douglas Canfield and Deborah C. Payne (Athens: University of Georgia Press, 1995), 35. For another excellent reading of the ambiguous position of Restoration actresses, see Cynthia Lowenthal's *Performing Identities on the Restoration Stage* (Carbondale: Southern Illinois University Press, 2003), 111–34.

16. Charles Beecher Hogan, ed., *The London Stage, 1776–1800: A Critical Introduction* (Carbondale: Southern Illinois University Press, 1968), xi.

17. Robyn Asleson, "Introduction," in *Notorious Muse*, ed. Asleson, 1.

18. Gill Perry, *Spectacular Flirtations: Viewing the Actress in British Art and Theatre, 1768–1820* (New Haven, CT: Yale University Press, 2007), 19.

19. Perry, *Spectacular Flirtations*, 19.

20. Eighteenth-century playwrights often wrote roles with specific actors and actresses in mind. This is why many theater historians suggest that eighteenth-century plays have not survived. There were too many inside jokes and references that do not make sense today. See my discussion of Mary Wells and Frederick Reynolds in chapter 3.

21. Quoted in Jonathan Bate, ed., *The Romantics on Shakespeare* (London: Penguin Books, 1992), 112. From Charles Lamb "On the Tragedies of Shakespeare, Considered with Reference to Their Fitness for Stage Representation," in his *Works* (London, 1818). Lamb's idea that it is a "perverse" thing to identify a character with the actor who represents him is interesting, given the fact that he acknowledges that this is a common practice in the late eighteenth century.

22. Lisa Freeman, *Character's Theater: Genre and Identity on the Eighteenth-Century English Stage* (Philadelphia: University of Pennsylvania Press, 2002), 18.

23. For more on the composition of eighteenth-century audiences, see Leo Hughes, *The Drama's Patrons: A Study of the Eighteenth-Century London Audience* (Austin: University of Texas Press, 1971).

24. Charles Beecher Hogan, ed. *The London Stage, 1776–1800: A Critical Introduction* (Carbondale: Southern Illinois University Press, 1968), xiii–clxxiv.

25. According to Felicity Nussbaum in *The Autobiographical Subject: Gender and Ideology in Eighteenth-Century England* (Baltimore, MD: Johns Hopkins University Press, 1989), at the end of the eighteenth century, writing one's memoirs was a usual activity, particularly for notable figures. She explains: "By the latter half of the eighteenth century, a private subject who engaged in constant textual self-scrutiny throughout his or her life is a commonplace. James Boswell, Fanny Burney and Hester Thrale all wrote multiple serial volumes that seemingly account for each and every activity and desire" (201). Siddons's notes to her biographer can be seen then as a way of including herself in this aristocratic trend. Her life was important enough to receive a biography, and she was important enough to contribute the crucial and necessary information to it.

26. For a detailed discussion of Cibber's memoirs, see Kristina Straub's *Sexual Suspects*, 24–69.

27. Straub, *Sexual Suspects*, 24.

28. Wanko, *Roles of Authority*, 8.

29. Two groundbreaking studies on this subject are Nussbaum's *The Autobiographical Subject* and Nancy Armstrong's *Desire and Domestic Fiction: A Political History of the Novel* (New York: Oxford University Press, 1986).

30. Recent studies on women in the Romantic theater have stressed the influence of actresses on several important writers of the period, including Joanna Baillie, Elizabeth Inchbald, and Anna Seward. While Sarah Siddons, in particular, served as a powerful model of female independence and agency, I would argue that actresses' attempts to fashion themselves after literary models was a vexed prospect. For more on actresses and their relationship to Romantic women writers, see Pascoe, *Romantic Theatricality*, and Burroughs, ed., *Women in British Romantic Theatre*.

31. Thomas Postlewait, "Autobiography and Theatre History," in *Interpreting the Theatrical Past*, ed. Postlewait and Bruce A. McConachie (Iowa City: University of Iowa Press, 1989), 268–69.

32. For interdisciplinary analyses of Charlotte Charke's memoirs, see Phillip E. Baruth, ed., *Introducing Charlotte Charke: Actress, Author, Enigma* (Urbana: University of Illinois Press, 1998). For approaches to Robinson's *Memoirs*, see chapter 2.

33. Recently Pickering and Chatto has published the first volume of *Women's Theatrical Memoirs* (Jennie Batchelor, series editor), a collection that contains both memoirs written by actresses and biographies of the actresses written by other authors. Although actresses' memoirs are certainly related to the memoirs written about them, I believe a text authored by an actress herself should be treated as distinct and different from one written about her.

34. Linda Peterson. "Institutionalizing Women's Autobiography: Nineteenth-Century Editors and the Shaping of an Autobiographical Tradition," in *The Culture of Autobiography: Constructions of Self-Representation*, ed. Robert Folkenflik (Stanford, CA: Stanford University Press, 1993), 226.

35. Peterson, "Institutionalizing," 214.

36. Jacky Bratton, *New Readings in Theatre History* (Cambridge: Cambridge University Press, 2003), 131–32.

37. See particularly Anne K. Mellor's analysis of Mary Robinson's *Memoirs* in "Mary Robinson and the Scripts of Female Sexuality," in *Representations of the Self from the*

Renaissance to Romanticism, ed. Patrick Coleman, Jayne Elizabeth Lewis, and Jill Anne Kowalik (Cambridge: Cambridge University Press, 2000), 230–59.

38. For more on Garrick, his portraits, and his own art collection, see Shearer West, *The Image of the Actor: Verbal and Visual Representation in the Age of Garrick and Kemble* (New York: St. Martin's Press, 1991), 29–31 and 40–42. For a discussion of Garrick's relationship to Sir Joshua Reynolds, see Richard Wendorf, *Sir Joshua Reynolds: The Painter in Society* (Cambridge: Harvard University Press, 1998), 129–58.

39. Shearer West explains, "Theatrical portraits were saleable commodities, offering a guaranteed recompense to painters and engravers operating in the highly competitive London market" (*Image of the Actor,* 27).

40. West, *Image of the Actor,* 31.

41. West, *Image of the Actor,* 5.

42. For a detailed discussion of the relationship between eighteenth-century theatrical gesture and the iconography of eighteenth-century theatrical portraiture, see West, *Image of the Actor,* particularly chapters 4 and 5.

43. Quoted in Gill Perry "Women in Disguise: Likeness, the Grand Style and the Conventions of 'Feminine' Portraiture in the Work of Sir Joshua Reynolds," in *Femininity and Masculinity in Eighteenth-Century Art and Culture,* ed. Perry and Michael Rossington (Manchester: Manchester University Press, 1994), 20.

44. Perry "Women in Disguise," 20.

45. Perry "Women in Disguise," 21.

46. Perry uses the examples of Reynolds's portraits of *Lady Sarah Bunbury Sacrificing to the Graces* (1765), *Mrs. Hale as Euphrosyne* (1764–66) (both at the Fitzwilliam Museum, Cambridge); *Lady Blake as Juno Receiving the Girdle from Venus* (1769); *The Montgomery Sisters Adorning a Term of Hymen* (1773) (Tate Gallery); and *Mrs. Masters as Hebe* (1785) (The Iveagh Bequest, Kenwood) to illustrate the popularity of being painted in disguise.

47. Aileen Ribeiro, *The Art of Dress: Fashion in England and France, 1750–1820* (New Haven, CT: Yale University Press, 1995), 183.

48. A critic writes in *The Morning Chronicle* on 23 September 1791: "It is a general fault that all of the performers (at Drury Lane) seem to dress merely according to their own whim" (cited in Charles Beecher Hogan, ed., *The London Stage,* lxix). See also A. M. Nagler, *A Source Book in Theatrical History* (New York: Dover, 1952), 382–91.

49. For more on eighteenth-century theories of acting, particularly Garrick's technique, see Joseph R. Roach, *The Player's Passion: Studies in the Science of Acting* (Ann Arbor: University of Michigan Press, 1993), 58–92.

50. Ribeiro writes: "All kinds of cotton, and especially muslin, were *de rigueur* for fashionable dress; in an age when distinctions between formal and informal dress were increasingly blurred, fine muslin was acceptable on all occasions. In England, raw cotton imports quintupled between 1780–1800, the price falling steeply once the plantation system was established in the American South" (*The Art of Dress,* 110).

51. See the discussion of Queen Charlotte's portraits in chapter 1.

52. For more on the ways in which fashion has been read historically as an indicator of identity, see Anne Hollander's groundbreaking study *Seeing through Clothes* (New York: Viking Press, 1978). For connections among eighteenth-century fashion, portraiture, and image making, see Ribeiro's *The Art of Dress* and Marsha Pointon's *Hanging the Head: Portraiture and Social Formation in Eighteenth-Century England* (New Haven, CT:

Yale University Press, 1993). These studies contend that visual information is crucial to understanding how identities were formulated and perceived in eighteenth-century culture. Pointon also relates the viewing of portraits to the desire to invent biographies of the subjects. She writes: "Paintings of people and, in particular, portraits of individuals known to have lived in the past, appear to invite us to understand them as visual biographies" (141).

53. Perry, *Spectacular Flirtations,* 15–16.

54. Julia Watson and Sidonie Smith, "Introduction: Mapping Women's Self-Representation at Visual/Textual Interfaces, in *Interfaces: Women/Autobiography/Image/Performance,* ed. Smith and Watson (Ann Arbor: University of Michigan Press, 2002), 9–10.

55. Watson and Smith, "Introduction," 11.

56. See Judith Butler's discussion of gender and its relationship to performance in *Gender Trouble: Feminism and the Subversion of Identity* (New York: Routledge, 1990).

57. Quoted in Watson and Smith, "Introduction," 20.

CHAPTER ONE

1. For more on this event see Shearer West, *The Image of the Actor: Verbal and Visual Representation in the Age of Garrick and Kemble* (New York: St. Martin's Press, 1991), 114. West explains that, in the first performance of Garrick's Shakespeare Jubilee in 1785, Sarah Siddons was wheeled in as a part of the opening act, seated in the pose of "The Tragic Muse." Similar to her famous role as Shakespeare's Hermione, Siddons poses as she appears in Reynolds' portrait of her, magically transforming to life as the painting is enacted on the stage.

2. William Hazlitt, *Complete Works of William Hazlitt,* vol. 5 (London: J. M. Dent and Sons, 1930), 312.

3. See Robyn Asleson's edited volumes, *A Passion for Performance: Sarah Siddons and Her Portraits* (Los Angeles: The Paul J. Getty Museum, 1991) and *Notorious Muse: The Actress in British Art and Culture, 1776–1812* (New Haven, CT: Yale University Press, 2003); Shearer West, "The Public and Private Roles of Sarah Siddons," in *A Passion for Performance,* ed. Asleson, and "Siddons, Celebrity, and Regality," in *Theatre and Celebrity in Britain, 1660–2000,* ed. Mary Luckhurst and Jane Moody (New York: Palgrave Macmillan, 2005), 191–213; and Heather McPherson, "Masculinity, Femininity and the Tragic Sublime: Reinventing Lady Macbeth," *Studies in Eighteenth-Century Culture,* vol. 29, ed. Timothy Irwin and Ouinda Mostefai, 299–334 (Baltimore, MD: Johns Hopkins University Press, 2000), and "Picturing Tragedy: *Mrs. Siddons as the Tragic Muse* Revisited," *Eighteenth-Century Studies* 33.3 (2000).

4. See Judith Pascoe, *Romantic Theatricality: Gender, Poetry, and Spectatorship* (Ithaca, NY: Cornell University Press, 1997); Catherine Burroughs, *Closet Stages: Joanna Baillie and the Theater Theory of British Romantic Women Writers* (Philadelphia: University of Pennsylvania Press, 1997); and Laura Rosenthal, "The Sublime, the Beautiful, the Siddons," in *The Clothes That Wear Us,* ed. Jessica Munns and Penny Richards (Newark: University of Delaware Press, 2003).

5. Joseph Roach, *It* (Ann Arbor: University of Michigan, 2007), 153.

6. Román, David, *Performance in America: Contemporary U.S. Culture and the Performing Arts (Durham,* NC: Duke University Press, 2005), 142.

7. Román, *Performance in America*, 158.
8. Román, *Performance in America*, 152.
9. Román, *Performance in America*, 158.
10. Román, *Performance in America*, 145.
11. Cheryl Wanko, *Roles of Authority: Thespian Biography and Celebrity in Eighteenth-Century Britain* (Lubbock: Texas Tech University Press, 2003), 210.
12. Kristina Straub, *Sexual Suspects: Eighteenth-Century Players and Sexual Ideology* (Princeton: Princeton University Press, 1992), 13.
13. West, "Public and Private," 3.
14. West, "Siddons, Celebrity," 206. West goes on to suggest that Siddons's role as a queen had a "healing quality" and that her "fairy tale regality allowed her audiences to retain a fantasy of royal power at a time of monarchical disintegration" (208).
15. Linda Colley, *Britons: Forging the Nation, 1707–1837* (New Haven, CT: Yale University Press, 1992), 206. According to Colley, George III had a portrait of him by Allan Ramsay distributed to "every British embassy and major government office." He also assisted in establishing the Royal Academy of Art in 1768.
16. Colley, *Britons*, 232. See also Christopher Hibbert's *George III* (New York: Basic Books, 1998), particularly pp. 78–79, 304–6, 390–92, which discuss the king's popularity.
17. Colley notes that although Charlotte was not seen as particularly glamorous, she was "just as important as a totem of morality as her husband was" (*Britons*, 268).
18. For more on celebrity and aging in relation to Siddons and Queen Charlotte, see Shearer West's "Siddons, Celebrity."
19. Wayne Koestenbaum, *The Queen's Throat: Opera, Homosexuality, and the Mystery of Desire* (New York: Poseidon Press, 1993), 107–8.
20. Koestenbaum, *The Queen's Throat*, 13.
21. For more on Siddons's biography and performance history, see Roger Manvell's *Sarah Siddons: Portrait of an Actress* (London: Heinemann, 1970) and Asleson, ed., *A Passion for Performance*.
22. For an analysis of portraits of Siddons as Lady Macbeth, see Heather McPherson, "Masculinity, Femininity."
23. This is the date that Siddons's biographer, Roger Manvell, provides in *Sarah Siddons*, 120.
24. Sarah Siddons, *The Reminiscences of Sarah Kemble Siddons, 1773–1785*, ed. William Van Lennep (Cambridge, Widener Library, 1942), foreword. (All subsequent page references to Siddons's memoir will be to this edition.)
25. Siddons, *Reminiscences*, 1–2.
26. The biographies of Siddons are James Boaden's *Memoirs of Mrs. Siddons* (London: Henry Colburn, 1827), Thomas Campbell's *Life of Mrs. Siddons* (London: Edward Moxon, 1834), Percy Fizgerald's *The Kembles* (London: Tinsley Brothers, 1871), Mrs. Clement Parsons's *The Incomparable Siddons* (London: Methuen, 1909), Yvonne French's *Mrs. Siddons: Tragic Actress* (London: Cobden-Sanderson, 1936; rev. ed., Verschoyle, 1954), Naomi Royde-Smith's *The Private Life of Mrs. Siddons* (London: Gollancz, 1933), and Roger Manvell's *Sarah Siddons*. Manvell is the only biographer who looks at the *Reminiscences* as a text itself. (He is the only biographer who post-dates Lennep.)
27. For more about the legacy of Siddons's portrayal of a variety of Shakespearean heroines, see Russ McDonald's *Look to the Lady: Sarah Siddons, Ellen Terry, and Judy Dench on the Shakespearean Stage* (Athens: University of Georgia Press, 2005), 1–50.

28. Beatrice W. Kliman, *Shakespeare in Performance: Macbeth*, 2nd ed. (Manchester: Manchester University Press, 2004), 28.

29. Kliman, *Shakespeare in Performance*, 28.

30. McDonald, *Look to the Lady*, 38.

31. Burroughs, *Closet Stages*, 56.

32. Burroughs, *Closet Stages*, 56.

33. Burroughs, *Closet Stages*, 57.

34. Judith Pascoe, *Romantic Theatricality: Gender, Poetry, and Spectatorship* (Ithaca, NY: Cornell University Press, 1997), 24.

35. Campbell, *Life of Mrs. Siddons*, vol. 2, 10–11.

36. Siddons's reference to "the person of her representative which you have been so long accustomed to contemplate" may refer to the actress Mrs. Pritchard, who was known for her portrayal of Lady Macbeth on the London stage between 1744 and 1768. One of Siddons's new additions to the performance of Lady Macbeth was to break with Mrs. Pritchard's tradition of holding the candle in the sleepwalking scene.

37. Campbell, *Life of Mrs. Siddons*, vol. 2, 18.

38. Campbell, *Life of Mrs. Siddons*, vol. 2, 13–14.

39. Quoted in Phillip H. Highfill, Jr., Kalman A. Burnim, and Edward A. Langhans, *A Biographical Dictionary of Actors, Actresses, Musicians, Dancers, Managers and Other Stage Personnel in London, 1660–1800* (Carbondale: Southern Illinois University Press, 1991), vol. 14, 10.

40. Quoted in Brander Matthews and Lawrence Hutton, ed., *The Kembles and Their Contemporaries* (Boston: L.C. Page and Co., 1886), 35.

41. Aileen Ribeiro, "Costuming the Part: A Discourse on Fashion and Fiction in the Images of Actresses in England, 1776–1812," in *Notorious Muse*, ed. Asleson, 73. According to Ribeiro, this type of gown was also known as a "Levite," a name that came from a costume worn by actresses playing the Jewish priestess character in Racine's *Athalie*.

42. Quoted in William T. Whitley, *Thomas Gainsborough* (London: Smith, Elder, 1915), 370. In a small miniature of Siddons in the National Portrait Gallery, her nose is twice normal size, almost to the point of a caricature. Most likely Siddons's real nose was somewhere in between these representations.

43. Ribeiro, "Costuming the Part," 62. Ribeiro also notes that it would have taken nearly twenty yards of fabric to make this dress.

44. Quoted in Anon., *Gainsborough and Reynolds: Contrasts in Royal Patronage*, exhibition catalogue (London: The Queen's Gallery, Buckingham Palace, 1994), 50.

45. Anon., *Gainsborough and Reynolds*, 50.

46. Colley notes that Queen Charlotte "delighted in having her smiling and abundant maternity commemorated in art, often posing with books on child care in her hands or on her dressing table" (*Britons*, 268).

47. In "'She Was Tragedy Personified': Crafting the Siddons Legend in Art and Life," in *A Passion for Performance*, ed. Asleson, Robyn Asleson argues that Siddons's role as Isabella in Thomas Southerne's play *Isabella* is connected to the late-eighteenth-century cult of sensibility. Asleson adds: "Of the numerous representations of Siddons as Isabella that appeared between 1782 and 1785, several focused on a private interview between the mourning mother and son—one of the most emotionally wrenching scenes in the play" (53). For a reproduction of Hamilton's portrait of Siddons as Isabella, see p. 54.

48. Apparently Siddons's moving performance as Isabella affected her own young son, who played opposite her in several performances. *The Morning Post* of 10 October 1782 reports: "Mrs. Siddons, of Drury Lane Theatre, has a lovely little boy about eight years old. Yesterday in the rehearsal of the 'Fatal Marriage' the boy, observing his mother in the agonies of the dying scene, took the fiction for reality, and burst into a flood of tears, a circumstance which struck the feelings of the company in a singular manner" (quoted in Brander Matthews and Lawrence Hutton, ed., *The Kembles and Their Contemporaries,* 37). Just as Siddons's child was unable to distinguish between his real mother and the part his mother was playing, the boundaries between art and life are similarly complicated by the image in Hamilton's painting.

49. Siddons was not shy about bringing her children on stage with her, a marketing technique that reminded audiences that she was earning a living on stage for her family. Although she was famous for this role, she also became sick of it. In a letter to Viscountess Percival on 24 November 1795, Siddons writes: "I am now acting in a grand Pantomime calld Alexander the Great in which I have a very bad part and a very fine dress. Will go it several nights I suppose: well, anything is better than saying Isabella over and over again until one is so tired" (Sarah Siddons, Collection of Letters, 1785–1796 [manuscripts], Harvard Theatre Collection, Houghton Library, Harvard College, Cambridge, Massachusetts). Traces of Siddons's frustration and exhaustion are not evident in her portraits, which instead suggest that her life on stage mirrors her activities off stage.

50. Siddons, *Reminiscences,* 11
51. Siddons, *Reminiscences,* 11.
52. Siddons, *Reminiscences,* 12.
53. For more on the ways in which Garrick fashioned his celebrity status and created a link between actors and aristocrats, see Shearer West's *The Image of the Actor: Verbal and Visual Representation in the Age of Garrick and Kemble* (New York: St. Martin's Press, 1991), 26–31.
54. Siddons, *Reminiscences,* 12.
55. Siddons, *Reminiscences,* 12.
56. Tita Chico, *Designing Women: The Dressing Room in Eighteenth-Century Literature and Culture* (Lewisburg, PA: Bucknell University Press, 2005), 9.
57. Campbell, *Life of Mrs. Siddons,* vol. 2, 18.
58. Campbell, *Life of Mrs. Siddons,* vol. 2, 19.
59. Campbell, *Life of Mrs. Siddons,* vol. 2, 18.
60. For an excellent chronology of Siddons's performances and events in her life and career, see Asleson, ed., *A Passion for Performance,* xiv–xv.
61. See also West's discussion of Siddons's pregnant and ageing body in "Siddons, Celebrity," 195–96.
62. For more on Siddons acting while pregnant, see Laura Rosenthal's excellent essay, "The Sublime, the Beautiful."
63. Campbell, *Life of Mrs. Siddons,* vol. 2, 21–22.
64. Campbell, *Life of Mrs. Siddons,* vol. 2, 22.
65. Campbell, *Life of Mrs. Siddons,* vol. 2, 22–23.
66. Campbell, *Life of Mrs. Siddons,* vol. 2, 23.
67. Campbell, *Life of Mrs. Siddons,* vol. 2, 27.
68. Campbell, *Life of Mrs. Siddons,* vol. 2, 28.

69. Siddons, *Reminiscences*, 21.
70. Siddons, *Reminiscences*, 22.
71. In a powerful letter to her sister, Esther, written in December 1785, Frances Burney provides a similarly vexed description of "performing" in front of Queen Charlotte entitled "Directions for Coughing, Sneezing, or Moving before the King and Queen." Through a satirical vision of what happens when you have a bodily function that you can't control in front of royalty, Burney illustrates the absurd extent to which subjectivity is based on performance and how those performances have direct impact on the body (*Journals and Letters*, ed. Peter Sabor and Lars E. Troide (London: Penguin, 2001, 230).
72. Siddons, *Reminiscences*, 22.
73. Campbell, *Life of Mrs. Siddons*, vol. 2, 32–33.
74. Campbell, *Life of Mrs. Siddons*, vol. 2, 33.
75. Campbell, *Life of Mrs. Siddons*, vol. 2, 24.
76. Campbell, *Life of Mrs. Siddons*, vol. 2, 24–25.
77. For more on the connections among contemporary theories of acting and performance practices in the eighteenth century, see Joseph Roach's *The Player's Passion: Studies in the Science of Acting* (Ann Arbor: University of Michigan Press, 1993).
78. Campbell, *Life of Mrs. Siddons*, vol. 2, 31.
79. In her letters Siddons often complained of fatigue and depression. In a letter to Miss Wynn on Monday, 8 October 1787, Siddons writes: "I am almost dead of Belvidera, as done in every limb as if I had been severely beaten." And on Sunday, 26 July 1789, she writes: "I am to play Rosalind for them next Wednesday—I hope to be in better spirits then [*sic*] I am this day which has been spent in weeping." (Sarah Siddons, Collection of Letters, 1785–1796).
80. Siddons, *Reminiscences*, 30.
81. Siddons, *Reminiscences*, 31.
82. Siddons also aligns herself here with famous fainting heroines in eighteenth-century novels. Samuel Richardson's heroines Pamela and Clarissa and Frances Burney's Evelina, to name just a few, all have fainting episodes in narrative moments where their bodies are placed in suspect positions.
83. Koestenbaum, *The Queen's Throat*, 108.
84. For reproductions of these portraits see Asleson, ed., *A Passion for Performance*, 11–12.
85. Quoted in Ribeiro, "Costuming the Part," 116.
86. Quoted in Ribeiro, "Costuming the Part," 116.
87. For more on images of Siddons as "herself," see Shearer West's "Public and Private."
88. For a history of the Beechey portrait, see William Roberts, *Sir William Beechey, R.A.* (London: Duckworth, 1907), 45.
89. Siddons, *Reminiscences*, 17–18.
90. Siddons, *Reminiscences*, 17–18.
91. Siddons, *Reminiscences*, 18.
92. Siddons, *Reminiscences*, 18.
93. Quoted in Richard Wendorf, *The Elements of Life: Biography and Portrait-Painting in Stuart and Georgian England* (Oxford: Clarendon Press, 1990), 246.
94. Wendorf, *Elements of Life*, 247.

95. Shelley Bennett and Mark Leonard, with technical studies by Narayan Khandekar, "A Sublime and Masterly Performance: The Making of Sir Joshua Reynolds's *Sarah Siddons as the Tragic Muse*," in *A Passion for Performance*, ed. Asleson, 97–141. See particularly page 115 for details about Siddons's pose.

CHAPTER TWO

1. Much recent scholarly work has been done to establish Mary Robinson as a significant celebrity presence in London in the 1780s and 1790s. See specifically, Judith Pascoe's discussion of Robinson in *Romantic Theatricality: Gender, Poetry, and Spectatorship* (Ithaca, NY: Cornell University Press, 1997) and Claire Brock's analysis of Robinson's journalistic writings in *The Feminization of Fame, 1750–1830* (London: Palgave Macmillan, 2006). Work done specifically on Robinson's portraits has established her participation in her own self-fashioning. See particularly, Elizabeth Fay's excellent article, "Framing Romantic Dress: Mary Robinson, Princess Caroline and the Sex/Text" in *Historicizing Romantic Sexualities*, ed. Richard C. Sha (Romantic Circles Praxis Series, January 2006), http://www.rc.umd.edu/praxis/sexuality/fay/fay.html. Fay compares Robinson's visual strategies for self-fashioning to Queen Caroline's sartorial self-representations. Paula Byrne's recent biography of Robinson has also contributed to critical discussions about Robinson's public life. See her *Perdita: The Literary, Theatrical, and Scandalous Life of Mary Robinson* (New York: Random House, 2006).

2. Anne K. Mellor, "Mary Robinson and the Scripts of Female Sexuality," in *Representations of the Self from the Renaissance to Romanticism*, ed. Patrick Coleman, Jayne Elizabeth Lewis, and Jill Anne Kowalik (Cambridge: Cambridge University Press, 2000), 231.

3. Mellor, "Mary Robinson," 231.

4. See Linda H. Peterson's discussion of Robinson as a Romantic artist in "Becoming an Author: Mary Robinson's *Memoirs* and the Origins of the Woman Artist's Autobiography," in *Re-Visioning Romanticism: British Women Writers, 1776–1837*, ed. Carol Shine-Wilson and Joel Haefner (Philadelphia: University of Pennsylvania Press, 1994), 42–48.

5. Laura Runge, "Mary Robinson's *Memoirs* and the Anti-Adultery Campaign of the Late Eighteenth Century," *Modern Philology* 101.4 (2004): 564.

6. Runge, "Mary Robinson's *Memoirs*," 574.

7. Runge, "Mary Robinson's *Memoirs*," 575.

8. Leo Braudy suggests that fame in the eighteenth century was particularly modern because it concerned ways of "defining oneself, making oneself known, beyond the limitations of class and family" (*The Frenzy of Renown: Fame and Its History* [New York: Vintage Books, 1997], 14). David Giles, in *Illusions of Immortality: A Psychology of Fame and Celebrity* (New York: St. Martin's Press, 2000), cites the emergence of literary culture, publishing, engraving, portraiture, and the theater as crucial elements in the development of modern celebrity (16–17).

9. Anne Close, "Notorious: Mary Robinson and the Gothic," *Gothic Studies* 6.2 (2004): 172.

10. Close, "Notorious," 188.

11. Jeffrey Cox, *Seven Gothic Dramas, 1789–1825* (Athens: Ohio University Press, 1992), 61.

12. Terry Castle, *The Female Thermometer* (Oxford: Oxford University Press, 1995), 125.

13. Catherine Spooner, *Fashioning Gothic Bodies* (Manchester: Manchester University Press, 2004), 7.

14. Spooner, *Fashioning*, 7.

15. Spooner, *Fashioning*, 7.

16. Spooner, *Fashioning*, 110.

17. At the time these portraits were commissioned, Robinson was already a well-known public figure. During this period (1781–84), she may have had affairs with Charles Fox and Prime Minister North, and she met Colonel Banastre Tarleton, who was to be the other significant man in her life. Her career as an actress was all but ruined by the negative publicity over her dealings with the prince, and she turned to writing as her sole occupation. She had published a small volume of poems in 1775, and she would go on to write several novels, volumes of poetry, essays, and a play. For more on the financial details of Robinson's career as an author, see Jan Fergus and Janice Farrar Thaddeus, "Women, Publishers, and Money, 1790–1820," *Studies in Eighteenth-Century Culture* 17 (1987): 191–207.

18. John Ingamells, *Mrs. Robinson and Her Portraits* (London: Wallace Collection Monographs, 1978), 30–34. According to Ingamells, there is no concrete record of specific conversations with the artists. However, Robinson's name appears in Reynolds's sitters diary three times in January 1782, twice in March, and, finally, on 5 April of the same year. Sittings for Reynolds's 1784 portrait of Mrs. Robinson took place between July of 1783 and August of 1784. Mrs. Robinson sat for Romney several times in 1781, from January to April and once in July.

19. Robyn Asleson, "Introduction," in *Notorious Muse: The Actress in British Art and Culture, 1776–1812*, ed. Asleson (New Haven, CT: Yale University Press, 2003), 8.

20. The portraits that I refer to in this essay are all reproduced in Ingamells, *Mrs. Robinson*. Apart from the paintings I discuss, other portraits of Robinson by these artists are as follows: Reynolds: 1) oil on canvas, 76 x 63 cm, 1782, Waddesdon Manor, National Trust; 2) oil on canvas, 89 x 68 cm, sketch for Wallace Collection Portrait, Center for British Art, Yale University. Gainsborough: 1) oil on canvas 76 x 63 cm, sketch for Wallace Collection portrait, Windsor Castle. 2) oil on canvas, 76 x 63 cm, bust-length version of the Wallace Collection portrait, Waddesdon Manor, National Trust. The Romney painting is the only portrait that he completed of Mary Robinson; another portrait painted in 1781 has not been satisfactorily identified. For more information about engravings, sculptures, and miniatures of Robinson, see Ingamells, *Mrs. Robinson*, 37–39.

21. Chris Rojek, *Celebrity* (London: Reakton Books, 2001), 107.

22. For more on eighteenth-century women as consumers, see Ann Bermingham's "Elegant Females and Gentleman Connoisseurs: The Commerce in Culture and Self-Image in Eighteenth-Century England," in *The Consumption of Culture, 1600–1800: Image, Object, Text*, ed. Bermingham and John Brewer (London: Routledge, 1997), 489–509. Bermingham says this about the accomplished woman: "Like the aesthetic object, her very lack of usefulness signaled a value which could only be realized through exchange and consumption" (509).

23. In her excellent book, *The Art of Dress: Fashion in England and France, 1750–1820* (New Haven, CT: Yale University Press, 1995), Aileen Ribeiro discusses a caricature by R. Dighton entitled "A Morning Ramble; or The Milliner's Shop" (c. 1782) in

which the milliners are dressed in outfits similar to the costume that Robinson wears in the Romney portrait. She writes: "Here the milliners are advertisements for their own wares, such as the large lace, gauze and muslin caps and the folded kerchiefs; one woman sews a ruched silk muff which would complement the fashionable rounded headdress" (78).

24. Joshua Reynolds, *Discourses on Art,* ed. Robert R. Warle (New Haven, CT: Yale University Press, 1975), Discourse VII, 140. For more on Reynolds's theories of painting, particularly as they apply to portraits of women, see Gill Perry's "Women in Disguise: Likeness, the Grand Style and the Conventions of 'Feminine' Portraiture in the Work of Sir Joshua Reynolds," in *Femininity and Masculinity in Eighteenth-Century Art and Culture,* ed. Perry and Michael Rossington (Manchester: Manchester University Press, 1994), 18–40. Perry argues that Reynolds uses conventions of eighteenth-century portraiture to "ennoble" his sitters and that he does the same with Mary Robinson, who, unlike his more respectable clients, was in need of ennobling.

25. Ingamells, *Mrs. Robinson,* 31.

26. For more on paintings of actresses that remained in artists' studios, see Asleson, "Introduction," in *Notorious Muse,* ed. Asleson, 9.

27. Quoted in Philip H. Highfill, Jr., Kalman A. Burnim, and Edward A. Langhans, *A Biographical Dictionary of Actors, Actresses, Musicians, Dancers, Managers, and Other Stage Personnel in London, 1660–1800* (Carbondale: Southern Illinois University Press, 1991), vol. 13, 32.

28. Mrs. Laeticia Matilda Hawkins, *Memoirs, Anecdotes, Facts and Opinions* (London, 1824), vol. 2, 24.

29. Quoted in Ingamells, *Mrs. Robinson,* 30.

30. Ingamells, *Mrs. Robinson,* 30.

31. Chris Cullens argues in her essay "The Masquerade of Womanliness," in *Body & Text in the Eighteenth Century,* ed. Veronica Kelly and Dorothea E. Von Mucke (Stanford, CA: Stanford University Press, 1994), that the "transgressive sexual amalgamation of the hermaphroditic central figure" in this print represents a cultural anxiety over the blurring of gender roles, a breakdown in class divisions, and in the separation between public and private spheres (285).

32. Rojek, *Celebrity,* 44.

33. Rojek, *Celebrity,* 44.

34. Robinson's costume, pose, and expression are similar to Gainsborough's portrait of *Mrs. Sheridan* (1785), now in the National Gallery of Art, Washington, D.C. Elizabeth Sheridan was the wife of the actor, dramatist, and politician Richard Brinsley Sheridan. For more on Gainsborough's style, see Nicola Kalinsky, *Gainsborough* (London: Phaidon Press, 1995).

35. In 1818, the Prince of Wales gave the Gainsborough portrait to the Marquess and the Marchioness of Hertford, who were great admirers of Robinson's poetry. After the marchioness's death in 1834, the painting was stored under the anonymous title *Lady with Dog.* Despite the fact that it was exhibited several times over the next decades, the sitter remained unidentified until 1894. For more on Robinson and the Hertford family, see Ingamells, *Mrs. Robinson,* 5.

36. Quoted in Ingamells, *Mrs. Robinson,* 31.

37. Ingamells, *Mrs. Robinson*, 31.

38. Ingamells, *Mrs. Robinson*, 32.

39. Ingamells, *Mrs. Robinson*, 32.

40. Although Robinson's costume here reflects the mood and atmosphere of the portrait, it also reflects the latest fashion of the day, which was to wear white muslin. In *The Art of Dress*, Ribeiro quotes a letter written by Lady Jerningham to her daughter, Charlotte, in 1786, "on the immense popularity of white muslin dresses which, 'are certainly the prettiest at your age, and worn entirely here by people with sashes'" (71).

41. Mary Robinson, *The Memoirs of the Late Mrs. Robinson* (London: R. Phillips, 1801), vol. 1, 39. (Subsequent references will be noted by page number in the text.)

42. The end of Robinson's memoir is told through "letters" supposedly written by Robinson and later pieced together by her daughter, and through commentary by an outside narrator (the "friend" who fills in the extra details). The question of who might have written the end of Robinson's memoir will be discussed later in the chapter.

43. Women's literary memoirs, the Gothic novel, and the domestic novel are genres that emerged in the eighteenth century; the Gothic was popularized by Horace Walpole's *The Castle of Otranto* (1764), and literary memoirs became common with the publication of autobiographies by several seventeenth-century noblewomen, as well as letters and biographical materials from such bluestockings as Elizabeth Montague, Mary Delany, and Elizabeth Carter. For more on women's autobiography in the eighteenth century, see Felicity A. Nussbaum's *The Autobiographical Subject: Gender and Ideology in Eighteenth-Century England* (Baltimore, MD: Johns Hopkins University Press, 1989).

44. Some of Robinson's more popular roles included Viola in *Twelfth Night*, Rosalind in *As You Like It*, Cordelia in *King Lear*, Satira in *Alexander the Great*, and Ophelia in *Hamlet*. For dates of Robinson's performances see Highfill, et al., *A Biographical Dictionary*, vol. 14, 30–47.

45. The ruined castle, Cox suggests, represents an "emblem of the past's influence on the present, the hold that the old world—even in decay—has upon the future" (*Seven Gothic Dramas*, 19).

46. Cox, *Seven Gothic Dramas*, 15.

47. According to Aileen Ribeiro in *The Art of Dress*, the nightgown was a "tight fitting" dress that "began life as an informal garment, but which was stylish everyday wear by the mid-eighteenth century. Depending on the fabric, trimming and accessories, it could be informal (undress) or semi-formal (full dress)" (28). "Lustring" is defined as "lightweight, crisp and very glossy plain woven silk. The lustre was achieved by glazing, stretching and heating the warp before weaving" (Avril Hart and Susan North, *Historical Fashion in Detail: The Seventeenth and Eighteenth Centuries* [London: V&A Publications, 1998], 221).

48. In Frances Burney's *Camilla* (1796), the heroine's younger sister, Eugenia, is disfigured by smallpox. One of the central issues in the novel is the difference between Eugenia's internal beauty, strength, and intelligence and her shocking outward appearance. Eugenia is also an heiress, which makes her social position even more ironic and precarious. For more on the character of Eugenia, see Margaret Doody, *Frances Burney: The Life in the Works* (New Brunswick, NJ: Rutgers University Press, 1988). Doody argues, "In the eyes of many around her, Eugenia has a double deformity—her inferior body and her superior education" (242–43). Given that Robinson was writing her memoirs after she had suffered a miscarriage that left her weak and disabled, she, like Eugenia, is in the position of having an inferior body and a superior mind. See also Claudia L. Johnson's discussion of Eugenia in *Equivocal Beings: Politics, Gender, and Sentimental-*

ity in the 1790s (Chicago: University of Chicago Press, 1995). Johnson explains that it is Eugenia's duty to "prove herself a good daughter by not feeling her distress and thus sparing the sympathetic feelings of the uncle and parents who are responsible for it" (153).

49. Bad marriages, cruel husbands, and mad wives appear often in late-eighteenth-century fiction. In Frances Burney's *Cecilia* (1782), the heroine is advertised as "mad" at the end of the novel by her evil husband. In Burney's *Camilla* (1796), the heroine befriends a tormented woman, Mrs. Berlington, who also hates her husband. In Mary Wollstonecraft's *Maria* (1788), the protagonist is shut up in a madhouse by her diabolical spouse. By recreating the scene of her secret marriage, Robinson sets the stage for her own "madness"—her decision to have an affair with the Prince.

50. The stylish "dishabillé" was an informal gown "often made with lavish fabrics." The dress originated in France and became popular in England in the 1770s with the increase in imported cotton textiles from France and India (Ribeiro, *The Art of Dress*, 70).

51. For more on the significance of disembodied costumes and their relationship to Gothic narratives, see Spooner, *Fashioning Gothic Bodies*, 7–8.

52. In line with many of her bluestocking contemporaries, such as Felicia Hemans, Hannah More, and Anna Laetitia Barbauld, Robinson wrote poetry about the injustices of eighteenth-century life, particularly for women. For more on Robinson's poetic personas, see Judith Pascoe, *Romantic Theatricality: Gender, Poetry and Spectatorship* (Ithaca: Cornell University Press, 1997), 68–95. For a discussion of the importance of Robinson's poetic volume, *Lyrical Tales,* see Stuart Curran, "Mary Robinson's *Lyrical Tales* in Context" in *Re-Visioning Romanticism: British Women Writers, 1776–1837,* ed. Carol Shiner Wilson and Joel Haefner (Philadelphia: University of Pennsylvania Press, 1994), 17–35.

53. The Duchess of Devonshire, who was supposed to be Robinson's great admirer, has a different view of the situation. In her essay "Anecdotes concerning his Royal Highness, the Prince of Wales," she writes: "Mrs. Robinson was a natural daughter of Lord Northington's and had been driven to the stage to support an extravagant husband, who was willing likewise to share the fruits of her ill conduct. . . . The prince was so young that he look'd upon her as a miracle of virtue as well as beauty and imagined that he was the first person she had been attached to" (quoted in Bessborough, ed., *Georgiana: Extracts from the Correspondence of Georgiana, Duchess of Devonshire* (London: John Murray, 1955), 290.

54. Bessborough, ed., *Georgiana*, 49.

55. From Jane Porter's manuscript diary in the Folger Library (M.b. 15), 3 January 1801. On 4 January, Porter reports that she has received Maria Robinson's opinion of her "tribute to Robinson," which she intended for "some monthly magazine." Robinson advises Porter not to publish it because "she fears I may be suspected as the author."

56. This poem appeared in *The Morning Post* on 18 December 1800 (quoted in Ingamells, *Mrs. Robinson*, 26).

CHAPTER THREE

1. Unfortunately, I was unable to secure the rights to publish this portrait. A re-

production of the image can be found in J. T. Herbert Bally, ed., *The Connoisseur: An Illustrated Magazine for Collectors* 17 (January–April, 1907), 76.

2. Philip H. Highfill, Jr., Kalman A. Burnim, and Edward A. Langhans, *A Biographical Dictionary of Actors, Actresses, Musicians, Dancers, Managers, and Other Stage Personnel in London, 1660–1800* (Carbondale: Southern Illinois University Press, 1991), vol. 15, 354. According to the *Biographical Dictionary*, the painting was done for "Mr. Ford Bowes to order." The painting was titled *Mrs. Topham and Her Three Children* in the collection of Rear Admiral Trollope in 1891. It was also owned by J. Pierpont Morgan in 1907. Most recently, it was at Christie's fine art auction house on 24 November 1978, where it sold to a private collector in London.

3. Marcia Pointon, *Hanging the Head: Portraiture and Social Formation in Eighteenth-Century England* (New Haven, CT: Yale University Press, 1993), 160.

4. Compare to Sir Joshua Reynolds's portrait of the Duchess of Devonshire with her daughter, entitled, *Georgiana, Duchess of Devonshire, and Lady Georgiana Cavendish* (1784). It was in fashion in the late eighteenth century for mothers to be directly involved with the care of their children.

5. *Mrs. Wells as Hebe* is now at the Art Galley of Ontario, Canada, and is the bequest of J. J. Vaughan, 1965 (Highfill et al., *A Biographical Dictionary*, vol. 15, 355).

6. Nicholas Penny, ed., *Reynolds,* Royal Academy of Arts catalogue (London: Weidenfeld and Nicholson, 1986), 251. Northcote's mentor, Reynolds, painted several women as Hebe. Art historian Nicholas Penny describes the significance of the Hebe figure in Reynolds's *Miss Mary Meyer in the Character of Hebe*. He writes: "Hebe, who served nectar to Jupiter (represented here in the shape of an eagle) seems to have done nothing improper, so ladies were content to be associated with her, and their husbands and fathers were doubtless gratified by the theme of gracious and decorous service to male needs."

7. Penny, ed., *Reynolds*, 50. Compare to Reynolds's portrait *Mrs. Musters as Hebe* (1785). In this painting, Mrs. Musters's hair is also flowing naturally, but she stands and looks down at the viewer, an effect that gives her a more allegorical/mythological presence than Wells, who is sitting closer to the spectator.

8. Penny, ed., *Reynolds*, 195. In other representations of Hebe, the eagle is portrayed drinking from the cup. In this image, Wells holds the promise of youth away from the eagle. The cup in Northcote's portrait is similar to the cup in Reynolds's painting of the known prostitute Kitty Fisher in the character of Cleopatra. Fisher's delicate removal of the top of the cup is similar to the way that Wells holds the handle of her cup in Northcote's painting.

9. Penny, ed., *Reynolds*, 50. Other paintings of ladies as Hebe include Benjamin West's *Mrs. Worrell as Hebe* (1770) Tate Gallery, London; Romney's *Elizabeth Warren as Hebe* (1776) National Museum of Wales; and Reynolds's *Mrs. Musters as Hebe,* exhibited in 1785, the Iveagh Bequest, Kenwood House GLC. See also Flora Fraser, *Emma Lady Hamilton* (New York: Alfred A. Knopf, 1987). The illustrations following page 246 include Gavin Hamilton's portrait of Emma Hamilton as Hebe. Although there was nothing apparently scandalous about being represented as Hebe, the theme of male gratification, when connected to an actress, also suggests the idea of sexual gratification or prostitution. In Hamilton's painting of Emma Hamilton as Hebe, Hamilton, who was a singer and sometime actress (as well as a notorious mistress), is depicted in a more revealing pose. In this portrait, Hamilton's breast is exposed as she leans down

seductively to allow the eagle (which represents Jupiter and, by extension, male virility) to take a drink from her cup of immortality.

10. Quoted in Highfill et al., *A Biographical Dictionary,* vol. 15, 344.

11. Asleson, "Introduction," in *Notorious Muse,* ed. Asleson, 1.

12. Quoted in Frances Burney, *Journals and Letters,* ed. Peter Sabor and Lars E. Troide (London: Penguin, 2001), 350.

13. Wayne Koestenbaum, *The Queen's Throat: Opera, Homosexuality, and the Mystery of Desire* (New York: Poseidon Press, 1993), 104.

14. Koestenbaum, *The Queen's Throat,* 113. Even though Koestenbaum is using codes of diva behavior to explore resistant strategies for agency within twentieth-century gay culture, his formulation of the diva as a specifically imagined identity "transcends," as he suggests, the boundaries of his argument.

15. Jacky Bratton, *New Readings in Theatre History* (Cambridge: Cambridge University Press, 2003), 106.

16. Highfill et al., *A Biographical Dictionary,* vol. 15, 344.

17. Mary Wells, *Memoirs of the Life of Mrs. Sumbel, Late Wells,* 3 vols. (London: C. Chapple, 1811), vol 1, 1.

18. This may also be a thinly veiled attack on Sarah Siddons, who, as we have seen, was famous for portraying Queens.

19. Wells, *Memoirs,* 3.

20. Since madness has been linked with heredity, it is possible that Wells's madness could be linked to her father's. However, as is the case with Wells, it is difficult to "prove" that her father was mad.

21. Wells, *Memoirs,* 22.

22. Wells, *Memoirs,* vol. 1, 22, 23.

23. Wells, *Memoirs,* vol. 1, 23.

24. Wells, *Memoirs,* vol.1, 22, 24.

25. Wells, *Memoirs,*vol.1, 22, 35.

26. On playbills, Wells was announced as being from the Theatre Royal, Exeter (Highfill et al., *A Biographical Dictionary,* vol. 15, 344).

27. Highfill et al., *A Biographical Dictionary,* vol. 15, 344.

28. Wells, *Memoirs,* vol.1, 39.

29. Highfill et al., *A Biographical Dictionary,* vol. 15, 344.

30. Annabel Jenkins, *I'll Tell You What: The Life of Elizabeth Inchbald* (Lexington: University of Kentucky Press, 2003), 140.

31. Jane Moody, "Stolen Identities: Character, Mimicry and the Invention of Samuel Foote," in *Theatre and Celebrity in Britain, 1660–2000,* ed. Mary Luckhurst and Moody (New York: Palgrave Macmillan, 2005), 71.

32. Moody, "Stolen Identities," 84.

33. Moody, "Stolen Identities," 67.

34. See particularly Sidonie Smith, "The Transgressive Daughter and the Masquerade of Self-Representation" (83–106), and Kristina Straub, "The Guilty Pleasures of Female Theatrical Cross-Dressing and the Autobiography of Charlotte Charke" (107–36), in *Introducing Charlotte Charke: Actress, Author, Enigma,* ed. Phillip Baruth (Urbana: University of Illinois Press, 1998).

35. For more on Charke's relationship with her father, see Jean Marsden, "Charlotte Charke and the Cibbers: Private Life as Public Spectacle," in *Introducing Charlotte Charke,* ed. Baruth, 65–82.

36. Smith, "Transgressive Daughter," 102.
37. Kristina Straub, *Sexual Suspects: Eighteenth-Century Players and Sexual Ideology* (Princeton: Princeton University Press, 1992), 140–41.
38. Wells, *Memoirs*, 26–27. Wells rarely had nice things to say about other actresses. She describes how Mrs. Farren refused to perform with her in *The Suspicious Husband* and criticizes her for not being supportive of younger female actresses (Wells, *Memoirs*, 48–50).
39. Wells, *Memoirs*, vol. 1, 25–26.
40. Highfill et al., *A Biographical Dictionary*, vol. 15, 346. This review is dated 30 October 1784.
41. Robin Asleson, "'She Was Tragedy Personified': Crafting the Siddons Legend in Art and Life," in *A Passion for Performance: Sarah Siddons and Her Portraitists*, ed. Asleson (Los Angeles: J. Paul Getty Museum, 1999), 78.
42. Despite a culture of sensibility in the eighteenth century that emphasized the importance of feelings and sympathies, women were not encouraged to make spectacles out of their emotions. In other words weeping into handkerchiefs and fainting from distress were acceptable forms of emotional performance, while irrational outbursts and temper tantrums were not seen as appropriate for a lady. For more on the culture of sensibility in the late eighteenth century, see Janet Todd's, *Sensibility: An Introduction* (London: Methuen, 1986).
43. For more on actresses with muffs, see my article "The Muff Affair: Fashioning Celebrity in the Portraits of Eighteenth-Century British Actresses," *Fashion Theory: A Journal of Body, Dress & Culture* 13.3 (2009): 279–98.
44. Unfortunately, I was not able to obtain the rights to reproduce this image. The painting can be found in David Mannings and Martin Postle, eds., *Sir Joshua Reynolds: A Complete Catalogue of his Paintings* (New Haven, CT: Yale University Press, 2000), 563.
45. Quoted in Asleson, "Introduction," in *Notorious Muse*, ed. Asleson, 10.
46. Asleson, "Introduction," 10.
47. Wells, *Memoirs*, vol.1, 57.
48. Wells, *Memoirs*, vol.1, 58.
49. The dates in the memoir seem off here—if Wells met Topham in 1785, then it was after two years that she established *The World*, which has its first edition in January of 1787. Wells also gives birth to another child at this time.
50. Wells, *Memoirs*, vol.1, 59. Wells's italics.
51. Wells, *Memoirs*, vol.1, 60. Topham must have mistaken the gender of his child here. Wells never mentions a boy, just her daughters. There is no record of her having any sons.
52. Wells, *Memoirs*, vol.1, 64–65.
53. Wells, *Memoirs*, vol.1, 66. Wells dates this letter 22 October. The italics are hers.
54. Highfill et al., *A Biographical Dictionary*, vol. 15, 346–47.
55. Quoted in Wells, *Memoirs*, vol.1, 90.
56. Definitions of madness dating back to the eighteenth century are described in theatrical terms. *The Oxford English Dictionary* defines a person who is mad as an individual "uncontrolled by reason; passing all rational bounds in demeanor or conduct; extravagant in gaiety; wild." To be "like mad" is to be, "literally in the manner of one who is mad; hence, furiously, with excessive violence or enthusiasm." A theatrical person is defined as someone who "plays a part; representing or exhibiting the manner of

an actor (obs.); that simulates or is simulated; artificial, affected, assumed." A theatrical person can also be an individual who is always associated with theatrics. Another definition listed for theatrical is "having the style of dramatic performance; extravagantly or irrelevantly histrionic; 'stagy'; calculated for display, showy, spectacular." While the first definition implies that there is a conscious choice involved in being theatrical—an actor chooses to play a part—the second definition suggests that theatrical can also refer to a way of being or a personal style. The OED includes an anecdote about Byron that illustrates the slippage between the two definitions. A contemporary of the poet remarked: "How far the character in which he (Byron) exhibited himself was genuine, and how far theatrical, it would probably have puzzled himself to say" (J. A. Simpson and E. S. C. Weiner, eds., vol. 17, 882–83).

57. Sarah Siddons, Letter to Miss Wynn, 26 July 1789, Collection of Letters, 1785–1796 (manuscripts), Harvard Theatre Collection, Houghton Library, Harvard College, Cambridge, Massachusetts. According to Christopher Hibbert in his biography of King George III, the king saw Sarah Siddons, his "favorite actress," perform in Weymouth (*George III* [New York: Basic Books, 1998], 307).

58. The term was derived from the title of Dr. Cheyne's book, but it is also a commentary on the tendency of the English toward depression and melancholy (Ida Macalpine and Richard Hunter, *George III and the Mad-Business* [New York: Pantheon Books, 1969], 287).

59. Quoted in Macalpine and Hunter, *George III*, 288.

60. Quoted in John Fyvie, *Comedy Queens of the Georgian Era* (London: Archibald Constable and Co., 1906), 328.

61. Fanny Burney mentions Wells's strange behavior in Weymouth in a letter to Susanna Phillips discussed at the end of this essay. She does not mention the details of the anecdote.

62. Wells, *Memoirs*, vol. 1, 86.

63. Wells, *Memoirs*, vol. 1, 87.

64. Wells, *Memoirs*, vol. 1, 87. Wells's italics. John Fyvie reports that Wells was being pursued by creditors at this point because of her promises to pay her sister's husband's debts (*Comedy Queens*, 326–27).

65. Wells, *Memoirs*, vol. 1, 87–88.

66. Wells may have been echoing the theatrical desperation of popular tragic heroines, such as Nicholas Rowe's Jane Shore, a role made famous by Sarah Siddons, but also attempted less successfully by Wells herself in 1783.

67. Wells, *Memoirs*, vol. 1, 89.

68. Wells, *Memoirs*, vol. 1, 89; Wells's italics. Precedents for the connections between madness and martyrdom appear in literature of the 1780s. Fanny Burney's heroine in *Cecilia* (1782) is advertised as "mad" by her husband at the end of the novel. In *Camilla* (1796), the heroine befriends a tormented woman, Mrs. Berlington, who also hates her husband. Camilla finds her one night reading a letter in the dark and wearing a white dress, which in the nineteenth century would become the prerequisite outfit for literary madwomen. Mary Wollstonecraft's Maria from *The Wrongs of Woman* (1788) is shut up in a madhouse by her diabolical husband. What is interesting about these heroines in particular is the connections between their rebellious behavior and their "madness." For more on Fanny Burney's novels and the idea of madness, see chapters 4–7 of Margaret Doody's biography, *Frances Burney: The Life in the Works*. While Bur-

ney seemed to be preoccupied with the ways in which accusations of madness are tied to women's oppression in her fiction, her reaction to Wells's alleged madness appears to have been unsympathetic.

69. Wells, *Memoirs*, vol. 1, 90.
70. Edward Topham, "Edward Topham," *Public Characters*, vol. 7 (London, 1804–5), 207.
71. Topham, "Edward Topham," 208.
72. Wells is listed as the actress who originated this role. See Frederick Reynolds, *The Plays of Frederick Reynolds*, ed. Stanley Lindberg. 2 vols. (New York: Garland, 1983). This reference appears on a cast list after the title page in Volume 2.
73. Reynolds, *The Plays*, 7.
74. Reynolds, *The Plays*, 7.
75. Reynolds, *The Plays*, 43.
76. Reynolds, *The Plays*, 45.
77. Frederick Reynolds, *Life and Times of Frederick Reynolds*, 2 vols. (London: Henry Colburn, 1827), vol. 2, 137.
78. Reynolds, *Life and Times*, vol. 2, 151.
79. Reynolds, *Life and Times*, vol. 2, 152–53.
80. Reynolds, *Life and Times*, vol. 2, 138.
81. Reynolds, *Life and Times*, vol. 2, 158.
82. Wells, *Memoirs*, vol. 1, 155–56
83. Wells, *Memoirs*, vol. 1, 155–56.
84. Wells, *Memoirs*, vol. 1, 157.
85. Wells, *Memoirs*, vol. 1, 157–58.
86. Wells, *Memoirs*, vol. 1, 159.
87. According to Highfill et al., *A Biographical Dictionary*, Sumbel was the "former secretary to the ambassador of Morocco." His father, Samuel Sumbel, was a minister of affairs to the sultan of Morocco and previously the ambassador to Denmark in 1751. Samuel Sumbel was sent to jail for embezzlement. He escaped to Gibraltar and died in 1782, "apparently a victim of poisoning" (vol. 15, 350).
88. Highfill et al., *A Biographical Dictionary*, vol. 15, 351.
89. Wells, *Memoirs*, vol. 1, 196.
90. Wells, *Memoirs*, vol. 1, 196.
91. For more on characterizations of exotic heroines in eighteenth-century literature, see Felicity A. Nussbaum's *Torrid Zones: Maternity, Sexuality and Empire in Eighteenth-Century English Narratives* (Baltimore, MD: John's Hopkins University Press, 1995).
92. Wells, *Memoirs*, vol. 1, 196–97.
93. Wells, *Memoirs*, vol. 1, 197.
94. Wells, *Memoirs*, vol. 1, 198
95. Wells, *Memoirs*, vol. 3, 183–84. Wells also includes a retraction from the next day, 17 October, stating that Mr. Sumbel was not in prison for debt but for contempt of court.
96. Wells, *Memoirs*, vol. 3, 184. Wells's italics.
97. For more on theatricality and Jewishness, see Rachel M. Brownstein's study of the actress Rachel Felix (1821–1858), *Tragic Muse: Rachel of the Comédie-Française* (Durham, NC: Duke University Press, 1995). See also James Shapiro's *Shakespeare and the Jews* (New York: Columbia University, 1997).

98. Wells, *Memoirs*, vol. 3, 185. Wells's italics.
99. Wells, *Memoirs*, vol. 1, 219.
100. Wells, *Memoirs*, vol. 1, 202.
101. Wells, *Memoirs*, vol. 1, 202.
102. Wells, *Memoirs*, vol. 1, 203.
103. Wells, *Memoirs*, vol. 1, 210. Wells's italics.
104. Wells is self-consciously referring to her own roles as particularly English heroines—such as Fanny in Elizabeth Inchbald's *Mogul Tale.*
105. Wells, *Memoirs*, vol. 1, 236.
106. Wells, *Memoirs*, vol. 2, 15.
107. Wells, *Memoirs*, vol. 2, 16.
108. Wells, *Memoirs*, vol. 2, 118, 120.
109. Wells, *Memoirs*, vol. 3, 30.
110. Wells, *Memoirs*, vol. 3, 29–30.
111. Burney, *Journals and Letters*, 349.
112. Burney, *Journals and Letters*, 350.
113. Burney, *Journals and Letters*, 350.
114. Burney, *Journals and Letters*, 352.
115. Burney, *Journals and Letters*, 350.
116. Burney, *Journals and Letters*, 352.
117. Wells, *Memoirs*, vol. 3, 32.
118. Wells, *Memoirs*, vol. 3, 35. Wells's italics.
119. Highfill et al., *A Biographical Dictionary*, vol. 15, 353.
120. In her recent biography of Elizabeth Inchbald, *I'll Tell You What: The Life of Elizabeth Inchbald* (Lexington: The University Press of Kentucky, 2003), Annabel Jenkins writes of Wells, "Like Inchbald, she knew everybody, and everybody in the theatre world knew her after the summer of 1781" (141).

EPILOGUE

1. Kemble explains in her memoirs how sad it was to see her aunt grow old and lose her sense of purpose in the world. She writes: "The vapid vacuity of my Aunt Siddons's life, . . . her apparent deadness and indifference to everything, which I attributed (unjustly, perhaps) less to her advanced age and impaired powers than to what I supposed the withering and drying influence of the over stimulated atmosphere . . . in which she had passed her life." Right before Siddons died, Kemble wrote: "What a price she paid for her great celebrity! . . . The cup has been so highly flavored that life is absolutely without savor or sweetness to her now" (quoted in J. C Furnas, *Fanny Kemble: Leading Lady of the Nineteenth-Century Stage* [New York: Dial Press, 1982], 11). The image of Siddons as a disappointed, fading diva left Kemble with a haunting reminder of the transitory nature of fame. Kemble would continue to be productive, writing and publishing up until the end of her life, perhaps to avoid the trauma of aging that so affected her celebrated relative.

2. The journalist and theater critic T. Noon Talfourd wrote of Kemble's first performance: "The illusion that she was Shakespeare's Juliet came so speedily upon us as to suspend the power of specific criticism. . . . [S]he moves with such dignity that it is only

on recollection that we discover that she is not tall" (quoted in Furnas, *Fanny Kemble*, 51).

3. As a young girl, Siddons did attend school in Worcester, where she was known for her theatrical talents. For more on Siddons's early education, see Roger Manvell's *Sarah Siddons: Portrait of an Actress* (London: Heinemann, 1970), 14–15. In her later years, Siddons translated sections of Milton's *Paradise Lost* for her children; however, according to William Van Lennep, the editor of her *Reminiscences,* she could barely spell and punctuate. See Van Lennep's introduction to *The Reminiscences of Sarah Kemble Siddons, 1773–1785* (Cambridge: Widener Library, 1942).

4. For more on Kemble's extraordinary life and career, see Deirdre David's recent biography, *Fanny Kemble: A Performed Life* (Philadelphia: University of Pennsylvania Press, 2007).

5. Kemble had such a sense of herself as a member of the upper class that even at the end of her life she insisted on having several servants in attendance (Furnas, *Fanny Kemble*, 441).

6. Henry James, *Essays in London and Elsewhere* (New York: Harper & Brothers, 1893), 106.

7. For more on professional actresses in the nineteenth century, the star system, and the divide between serious and popular forms of theater, see Tracy C. Davis's *Actresses as Working Women: Their Social Identity in Victorian Culture* (London: Routledge, 1991).

8. For more on Fanny Kemble's education and early literary career, see Furnas, *Fanny Kemble*, 22–46.

9. In Kemble's *Further Records* (New York: Henry Holt, 1891), she writes: "Looking over my letters, and copying portions of them, affords me a certain amount of quiet amusement and occupation daily" (11). The letters that Kemble refers to were written to her close friend, Harriet St. Leger. Kemble's letters to St. Leger make up three volumes of her memoirs: *Record of a Girlhood* (1878), *Records of Later Life* (1881), and *Further Records* (1890). St. Leger's letters to Kemble were destroyed at St. Leger's request. Kemble's other memoirs are *Journal of Frances Anne Kemble* (1835), *A Year of Consolation* (1847), and *Journal of a Residence on a Georgian Plantation in 1838–1839* (1863).

10. Frances Anne Kemble, *Record of a Girlhood*, 3 vols. (London: Richard Bentley and Son, 1878), vol. 1, 69.

11. Kemble, *Record of a Girlhood*, 84.

12. In an age of image reproduction that relied on less expensive printing processes, as well as new forms of transportation such as railways and steamships, it was possible to have a greater influence in both England and America. In fact, Kemble was one of the first actresses to have a successful transatlantic career. For more on Kemble's career in America and specifically on the influence of new technologies on her career, see Faye E. Dudden's *Women in the American Theatre: Actresses and Audiences, 1790–1870* (New Haven, CT: Yale University Press, 1994), 27–55.

13. See Furnas, *Fanny Kemble,* plate 10.

14. Quoted in the introduction to Catherine Clinton, ed., *Fanny Kemble's Journals* (Cambridge: Harvard University Press, 2000), 2.

15. Kemble, *Record of a Girlhood*, vol. 2, 104.

16. For more on idealized femininity in eighteenth- and early-nineteenth-century portraiture, see Marcia Pointon's *Hanging the Head: Portraiture and Social Formation in Eighteenth-Century England* (New Haven, CT: Yale University Press, 1993), 177–93.

17. Pointon, *Hanging the Head*, 204–5.

18. It was also through Sully's social connections to Kemble that he first gained entrée into the Queen's chambers. For more on their relationship, see Carrie Rebora Barratt, *Queen Victoria and Thomas Sully* (Princeton: Princeton University Press, 2000), 35.

19. Lawrence was engaged at different times to Siddons's daughters, Sally and Maria. He was also supposedly in love with Siddons herself. See Manvell, *Sarah Siddons*, 205–57.

20. Barratt, *Queen Victoria*, 35.

21. The *Harper's Weekly* image of Fanny Kemble is a very close imitation of Thomas Sully's portrait of Kemble as Beatrice.

22. Barratt, *Queen Victoria*, 33.

23. James, *Essays in London*, 106.

24. Barratt, *Queen Victoria*, 35.

25. Barratt, *Queen Victoria*, 37.

26. Barratt, *Queen Victoria*, 37.

27. Barratt, *Queen Victoria*, 53.

28. Barratt, *Queen Victoria*, 53.

29. For more on the impact of the invention of photography on portraiture, see David Piper, *The English Face* (London: National Portrait Gallery, 1992), 199.

30. In her book, *Royal Representations: Queen Victoria and British Culture, 1837–1876* (Chicago: University of Chicago Press, 1998), Margaret Homans points out that the invention of photography helped to further ally the royal family with their subjects, and that this identification could be seen through fashion choices. She writes: "The technology of the middle classes brings with it an intensification of the royal family's middle-class appearance. Just as photography supplanted oil painting, so trousers supplant knee breeches and hose as Albert's habitual costume, while Victoria's dress rarely suggests her rank" (44).

Bibliography

Anon. *Gainsborough and Reynolds: Contrasts in Royal Patronage.* Exhibition catalogue. London: The Queen's Gallery, Buckingham Palace, 1994.
Anon. "The Beauties of Mrs. Siddons, or a Review of Her Performance of . . . " In *Letters from a Lady of Distinction to Her Friend in the Country.* London, 1786.
Armstrong, Nancy. *Desire and Domestic Fiction: A Political History of the Novel.* Oxford: Oxford University Press, 1987.
Asleson, Robyn, ed. *Notorious Muse: The Actress in British Art and Culture, 1776–1812.* New Haven, CT: Yale University Press, 2003.
———, ed. *A Passion for Performance: Sarah Siddons and Her Portraits.* Los Angeles: The J. Paul Getty Museum, 1999.
———. "'She Was Tragedy Personified': Crafting the Siddons Legend in Art and Life." In *A Passion for Performance: Sarah Siddons and her Portraitists,* edited by Robyn Asleson. J. Paul Getty Museum: Los Angeles, 1999.
Barratt, Carrie Rebora. *Queen Victoria and Thomas Sully.* Princeton: Princeton University Press, 2000.
Baruth, Phillip E., ed. *Introducing Charlotte Charke: Actress, Author, Enigma.* Urbana: University of Illinois Press, 1998.
Bate, Jonathan, ed. *The Romantics on Shakespeare.* London: Penguin Books, 1992.
Bennett, Shelley, Mark Leonard, and Narayan Khandekar. "A Sublime and Masterly Performance: The Making of Joshua Reynolds's *Sarah Siddons as the Tragic Muse.*" In *A Passion for Performance: Sarah Siddons and Her Portraits,* edited by Robyn Aleson, 97–141. Los Angeles: The J. Paul Getty Museum, 1999.
Bermingham, Ann. "Elegant Females and Gentleman Connoisseurs: The Commerce in Culture and Self-Image in Eighteenth-Century England." In *The Consumption of Culture, 1600–1800: Image, Object, Text,* edited by Bermingham and John Brewer. London: Routledge, 1997.
Bessborough, The Earl of, ed. *Georgiana: Extracts from the Correspondence of Georgiana, the Duchess of Devonshire.* London: John Murray, 1955.

Boaden, James. *Memoirs of Mrs. Siddons, Interspersed with Anecdotes of Authors and Actors.* London: H. Colburn, 1827.
Bolton, Betsy. *Women, Nationalism and the Romantic Stage.* Cambridge: Cambridge University Press, 2001.
Booth, Michael R., John Stokes, and Susan Bassnett. *Three Tragic Actresses: Siddons, Rachel, Ristori.* Cambridge: Cambridge University Press, 1996.
Bratton, Jacky. *New Readings in Theatre History.* Cambridge: Cambridge University Press, 2003.
Braudy, Leo. *The Frenzy of Renown: Fame and Its History.* New York: Vintage Books, 1997.
Breward, Christopher. *The Culture of Fashion.* Manchester: Manchester University Press, 1995.
Brewer, John. *The Pleasures of the Imagination: English Culture in the Eighteenth Century.* Chicago: University of Chicago Press, 1997.
Brock, Claire. *The Feminization of Fame, 1750–1830.* London: Palgave Macmillan, 2006.
Brownstein, Rachel M. *Tragic Muse: Rachel of the Comédie-Française.* Durham, NC: Duke University Press, 1995.
Burney, Frances (Fanny). *Evelina: A Bedford Cultural Edition.* Edited by Kristina Straub. Boston: Bedford Books, 1997.
———. *Evelina: or, The History of a Young Lady's Entrance into the World.* New York: W. W. Norton & Co., 1965.
———. *Journals and Letters.* Edited by Peter Sabor and Lars E. Troide. London: Penguin, 2001.
Burroughs, Catherine B. *Closet Stages: Joanna Baillie and the Theater Theory of British Romantic Women Writers.* Philadelphia: University of Pennsylvania Press, 1997.
Burroughs, Catherine, ed. *Women in British Romantic Theatre: Drama, Performance, and Society, 1790–1840.* Cambridge: Cambridge University Press, 2000.
Butler, Judith. *Gender Trouble: Feminism and the Subversion of Identity.* New York: Routledge, 1990.
Byrne, Paula. *Perdita: The Literary, Theatrical, and Scandalous Life of Mary Robinson.* New York: Random House, 2006.
Campbell, Thomas. *Life of Mrs. Siddons.* London: Edward Moxon, 1834.
Carlson, Marvin. *The Haunted Stage.* Ann Arbor: University of Michigan Press, 2001.
Castle, Terry. *The Female Thermometer: Eighteenth-Century Culture and the Invention of the Uncanny.* New York: Oxford University Press, 1995.
Chico, Tita. *Designing Women: The Dressing Room in Eighteenth-Century Literature and Culture.* Lewisburg, PA: Bucknell University Press, 2005.
Clement-Parsons, Mrs. *The Incomparable Siddons.* London: Methuen, 1909.
Clinton, Catherine. *Fanny Kemble's Civil Wars.* New York: Simon & Schuster, 2000.
———, ed., *Fanny Kemble's Journals.* Cambridge: Harvard University Press, 2000.
Close, Anne. "Notorious: Mary Robinson and the Gothic." *Gothic Studies* 6.2 (2004): 172–91.
Colley, Linda. *Britons: Forging the Nation, 1707–1837.* New Haven, CT: Yale University Press, 1992.
Cox, Jeffrey. *Seven Gothic Dramas, 1789–1825.* Athens: Ohio University Press, 1992.
Cullens, Chris. "The Masquerade of Womanliness." In *Body & Text in the Eighteenth*

Century, edited by Veronica Kelly and Dorothea E. Von Mucke. Stanford, CA: Stanford University Press, 1994.

Curran, Stuart. "Mary Robinson's *Lyrical Tales* in Context." In *Re-visioning Romanticism: British Women Writers, 1776–1837*, edited by Carol Shiner Wilson and Joel Haefner, 17–35. Philadelphia: University of Pennsylvania Press, 1994.

David, Deirdre. *Fanny Kemble: A Performed Life*. Philadelphia: University of Pennsylvania Press, 2007.

Davis, Tracy C. *Actresses as Working Women: Their Social Identity in Victorian Culture*. London: Routledge, 1991.

Doody, Margaret. *Frances Burney: The Life in the Works*. New Brunswick, NJ: Rutgers University Press, 1988.

Dudden, Faye E. *Women in the American Theatre: Actresses and Audiences, 1790–1870*. New Haven, CT: Yale University Press, 1994.

Engel, Laura. "The Muff Affair: Fashioning Celebrity in the Portraits of Eighteenth-Century British Actresses." *Fashion Theory: A Journal of Body, Dress & Culture* 13.3 (2009): 279–98.

Fay, Elizabeth. "Framing Romantic Dress: Mary Robinson, Princess Caroline and the Sex/Text." In *Historicizing Romantic Sexualities*, edited by Richard C. Sha. Romantic Circles Praxis Series, January 2006. http://www.rc.umd.edu/praxis/sexuality/fay/fay.html

Fitzgerald, Percy. *The Kembles*. London, 1871.

Folkenflik, Robert. "Charlotte Charke: Images and Afterimages." In *Introducing Charlotte Charke: Actress, Author, Enigma*, edited by Philip Baruth. Chicago: University of Illinois Press, 1998.

Fraser, Flora. *Emma Lady Hamilton*. New York: Alfred A. Knopf, 1987.

Freeman, Lisa. *Character's Theater: Genre and Identity on the Eighteenth-Century English Stage*. Philadelphia: University of Pennsylvania Press, 2002.

French, Yvonne. *Mrs. Siddons: Tragic Actress*. London: Cobden-Sanderson, 1936. Rev. ed., London: Verschoyle, 1954.

Furnas, J. C. *Fanny Kemble: Leading Lady of the Nineteenth-Century Stage*. New York: Dial Press, 1982.

Fyvie, John. *Comedy Queens of the Georgian Era*. London: Archibald Constable and Co., 1906.

Gallindo, Catherine Gough. *Letter to Mrs. Siddons*. London, 1809.

Giles, David. *Illusions of Immortality: A Psychology of Fame and Celebrity*. New York: St. Martin's Press, 2000.

Hart, Avril, and Susan North. *Historical Fashion in Detail: The Seventeenth and Eighteenth Centuries*. London: V&A Publications, 1998.

Hawkins, Mrs. Laeticia Matilda. *Memoirs, Anecdotes, Facts and Opinions*. London, 1824.

Hazlitt, William. *The Complete Works of William Hazlitt*. Edited by P. P. Howe. 21 vols. London: J. M. Dent and Sons, 1930.

Hibbert, Christopher. *George III*. New York: Basic Books, 1998.

———. *Queen Victoria: A Personal History*. New York: Basic Books, 2000.

Highfill, Philip H., Jr., Kalman A. Burnim, and Edward A. Langhans. *A Biographical Dictionary of Actors, Actresses, Musicians, Dancers, Managers, and Other Stage Personnel in London, 1660–1800*. 16 vols. Carbondale: Southern Illinois University Press, 1991.

Hogan, Charles Beecher, ed. *The London Stage, 1776–1800: A Critical Introduction.* Carbondale: Southern Illinois University Press, 1968.
Hollander, Ann. *Seeing through Clothes.* New York: Viking Press, 1978.
Homans, Margaret. *Royal Representations: Queen Victoria and British Culture, 1837–1876.* Chicago: University of Chicago Press, 1998.
Howe, Elizabeth. *The First English Actresses: Women and Drama, 1660–1700.* Cambridge: Cambridge University Press, 1992.
Hughes, Leo. *The Drama's Patrons: A Study of the Eighteenth-Century London Audience.* Austin: University of Texas Press, 1971.
Ingamells, John. *Mrs. Robinson and Her Portraits.* London: Wallace Collection Monographs, 1978.
James, Henry. *Essays in London and Elsewhere.* New York: Harper & Brothers, 1893.
Jenkins, Annabel. *I'll Tell You What: The Life of Elizabeth Inchbald.* Lexington: University of Kentucky Press, 2003.
Johnson, Claudia L. *Equivocal Beings: Politics, Gender, and Sentimentality in the 1790s.* Chicago: University of Chicago Press, 1995.
Kalinsky, Nicola. *Gainsborough.* London: Phaidon Press, 1995.
Kemble, Frances Anne (Fanny). *Further Records.* New York: Henry Holt, 1891.
———. *Record of a Girlhood.* 3 vols. London: Richard Bentley and Son, 1878.
Kliman, Beatrice W. *Shakespeare in Performance: Macbeth.* 2nd ed. Manchester: Manchester University Press, 2004.
Koestenbaum, Wayne. *The Queen's Throat: Opera, Homosexuality, and the Mystery of Desire.* New York: Poseidon Press, 1993.
Lamb, Charles. "On the Tragedies of Shakespeare, Considered with Reference to Their Fitness for Stage Representation." In Lamb, *Works.* London, 1818.
Lowenthal, Cynthia. *Performing Identities on the Restoration Stage.* Carbondale: Southern Illinois University Press, 2003.
Luckhurst, Mary, and Jane Moody, eds. *Theatre and Celebrity in Britain, 1660–2000.* New York: Palgrave, 2005.
Macalpine, Ida, and Richard Hunter. *George III and the Mad-Business.* New York: Pantheon Books, 1969.
Manvell, Roger. *Sarah Siddons: Portrait of an Actress.* London: Heinemann, 1970.
Marsden, Jean. "Charlotte Charke and the Cibbers: Private Life as Public Spectacle." In *Introducing Charlotte Charke: Actress, Author, Enigma,* edited by Phillip Baruth. Urbana: University of Illinois Press, 1998.
Marshall, Gail. *Actresses on the Victorian Stage: Feminine Performance and the Galatea Myth.* Cambridge: Cambridge University Press, 1998.
Matthews, Brander, and Lawrence Hutton, eds. *The Kembles and Their Contemporaries.* Boston: L. C. Page and Co., 1886.
McDonald, Russ. *Look to the Lady: Sarah Siddons, Ellen Terry, and Judy Dench on the Shakespearean Stage.* Athens: University of Georgia Press, 2005.
McPherson, Heather. "Masculinity, Femininity and the Tragic Sublime: Reinventing Lady Macbeth." In *Studies in Eighteenth-Century Culture,* vol. 29, edited by Timothy Irwin and Ouinda Mostefai, 299–334. Baltimore, MD: Johns Hopkins University Press, 2000.
———. "Picturing Tragedy: Mrs. Siddons as the Tragic Muse Revisited." *Eighteenth-Century Studies* 33.3 (2000): 401–30.

Mellor, Anne K. "Mary Robinson and the Scripts of Female Sexuality." In *Representations of the Self from the Renaissance to Romanticism*, edited by Patrick Coleman, Jayne Elizabeth Lewis, and Jill Anne Kowalik, 230–59. Cambridge: Cambridge University Press, 2000.
———. *Romanticism and Gender*. New York: Routledge, 1993.
Merrill, Lisa. *When Romeo Was a Woman: Charlotte Cushman and Her Circle of Female Spectators*. Ann Arbor: University of Michigan Press, 1999.
Moody, Jane. "Stolen Identities: Character, Mimicry and the Invention of Samuel Foote." In *Theatre and Celebrity in Britain, 1660–2000*, edited by Mary Luckhurst and Moody. New York: Palgrave Macmillan, 2005.
Nagler, A. M. *A Source Book in Theatrical History*. New York: Dover, 1952.
Nokes, David. *Jane Austen: A Life*. New York: Farrar, Straus and Glroux, 1997.
Nussbaum, Felicity. "Actresses and the Economics of Celebrity, 1770–1800." In *Theatre and Celebrity in Britain, 1660–2000*, edited by Mary Luckhurst and Jane Moody. New York: Palgrave Macmillan, 2005.
———. *The Autobiographical Subject: Gender and Ideology in Eighteenth-Century England*. Baltimore, MD: Johns Hopkins University Press, 1989.
———. *Torrid Zones: Maternity, Sexuality, and Empire in Eighteenth-Century Narratives*. Baltimore, MD: Johns Hopkins University Press, 1995.
Pascoe, Judith. *Romantic Theatricality: Gender, Poetry, and Spectatorship*. Ithaca, NY: Cornell University Press, 1997.
Payne, Deborah C. "Reified Object or Emergent Professional? Retheorizing the Restoration Actress." In *Cultural Readings of Restoration and Eighteenth-Century English Theater*, edited by J. Douglas Canfield and Deborah C. Payne. Athens: University of Georgia Press, 1995.
Pearson, Jaqueline. *Women's Reading in Britain, 1750–1835*. Cambridge: Cambridge University Press, 1999.
Penny, Nicholas, ed. *Reynolds*. Royal Academy of Arts catalogue. London: Weidenfeld and Nicholson, 1986.
Perry, Gill. *Spectacular Flirtations: Viewing the Actress in British Art and Theatre, 1768–1820*. New Haven, CT: Yale University Press, 2007.
———. "Women in Disguise: Likeness, the Grand Style and the Conventions of 'Feminine' Portraiture in the Work of Sir Joshua Reynolds." In *Femininity and Masculinity in Eighteenth-Century Art and Culture*, edited by Perry and Michael Rossington. Manchester: Manchester University Press, 1994.
Peterson, Linda H. "Becoming an Author: Mary Robinson's *Memoirs* and the Origins of the Woman Artist's Autobiography." In *Re-Visioning Romanticism: British Women Writers, 1776–1837*, edited by Carol Shine-Wilson and Joel Haefner. Philadelphia: University of Pennsylvania Press, 1994.
———. "Institutionalizing Women's Autobiography: Nineteenth-Century Editors and the Shaping of an Autobiographical Tradition." In *The Culture of Autobiography: Constructions of Self-Representation*, edited by Robert Folkenflik. Stanford, CA: Stanford University Press, 1993.
Piper, David. *The English Face*. London: The National Portrait Gallery, 1992.
Pointon, Marcia. *Hanging the Head: Portraiture and Social Formation in Eighteenth-Century England*. New Haven, CT: Yale University Press, 1993.
Postlewait, Thomas. "Autobiography and Theatre History." In *Interpreting the Theatri-

cal Past, edited by Postlewait and Bruce A. McConachie. Iowa City: University of Iowa Press, 1989.

Reynolds, Frederick. *The Life and Times of Frederick Reynolds.* 2 vols. London: Henry Colburn, 1827.

———. *The Plays of Frederick Reynolds.* Edited by Stanley Lindberg. 2 vols. New York: Garland, 1983.

Reynolds, Joshua. *Discourses on Art.* Edited by Robert R, Warle. New Haven, CT: Yale University Press, 1975.

Ribeiro, Aileen. *The Art of Dress: Fashion in England and France, 1750–1820.* New Haven, CT: Yale University Press, 1995.

———. "Costuming the Part: A Discourse on Fashion and Fiction in the Images of Actresses in England, 1776–1812." In *Notorious Muse: The Actress in British Art and Culture, 1776–1812,* edited by Robyn Asleson. New Haven, CT: Yale University Press, 2003.

Richards, Sandra. *The Rise of the English Actress.* Boston: St. Martin's, 1993.

Roach, Joseph. *Cities of the Dead: Circum-Atlantic Performance.* New York: Columbia University Press, 1996.

———. *It.* Ann Arbor: University of Michigan, 2007.

———. *The Player's Passion: Studies in the Science of Acting.* Ann Arbor: University of Michigan Press, 1993.

———. "Public Intimacy: The Prior History of 'It.'" In *Theatre and Celebrity in Britain, 1660–2000,* edited by Mary Luckhurst and Jane Moody. New York: Palgrave Macmillan, 2005.

Roberts, William. *Sir William Beechey, R.A.* London: Duckworth, 1907.

Robinson, Mary. *The Memoirs of the Late Mrs. Robinson.* 4 vols. London: R. Phillips, 1801.

Rojek, Chris. *Celebrity.* London: Reakton Books, 2001.

Román, David. *Performance in America: Contemporary U.S. Culture and the Performing Arts.* Durham, NC: Duke University Press, 2005.

Rosenthal, Laura. "The Sublime, the Beautiful, the Siddons." In *The Clothes That Wear Us,* edited by Jessica Munns and Penny Richards, 56–79. Newark: University of Delaware Press, 2003.

Royde-Smith, Naomi. *The Private Life of Mrs. Siddons.* London: Gollancz, 1933.

Runge, Laura L. "Mary Robinson's *Memoirs* and the Anti-Adultery Campaign of the Late Eighteenth Century." *Modern Philology* 101.4 (2004): 563–86.

Shapiro, James. *Shakespeare and the Jews.* New York: Columbia University Press, 1997.

Showalter, Elaine. *The Female Malady.* New York: Pantheon Books, 1985.

Siddons, Sarah. Collection of Letters, 1785–1796. Manuscripts. Harvard Theatre Collection. Houghton Library, Harvard College, Cambridge, Massachusetts.

———. *The Reminiscences of Sarah Kemble Siddons, 1773–1785.* Edited by William Van Lennep. Cambridge: Widener Library, 1942.

Simpson, J. A., and E. S. C. Weiner, eds. *The Oxford English Dictionary.* 2nd ed. Oxford: Clarendon Press, 1989.

Small, Helen. *Love's Madness: Medicine, the Novel and Female Insanity, 1800–1865.* Oxford: Clarendon Press, 1996.

Smith, Sidonie. "The Transgressive Daughter and the Masquerade of Self-Representation." In *Introducing Charlotte Charke: Actress, Author, Enigma,* edited by Phillip Baruth. Urbana: University of Illinois Press, 1998.

——— and Julia Watson, eds. *Interfaces: Women/Autobiography/Image/Performance.* Ann Arbor: University of Michigan Press, 2002.
Spooner, Catherine. *Fashioning Gothic Bodies.* Manchester: Manchester University Press, 2004.
Straub, Kristina. "The Guilty Pleasures of Female Theatrical Cross-Dressing and the Autobiography of Charlotte Charke." In *Introducing Charlotte Charke: Actress, Author, Enigma,* edited by Phillip Baruth. Urbana: University of Illinois Press, 1998.
———. *Sexual Suspects: Eighteenth-Century Players and Sexual Ideology.* Princeton: Princeton University Press, 1992.
Thaddeus, Janice Farrar. "Women, Publishers and Money, 1790–1820." *Studies in Eighteenth-Century Culture* 17 (1987): 191–207.
Todd, Janet. *Sensibility: An Introduction.* London: Methuen, 1986.
Topham, Edward. "Edward Topham." In *Public Characters.* Vol. 7. London, 1804–5.
Wanko, Cheryl. *Roles of Authority: Thespian Biography and Celebrity in Eighteenth-Century Britain.* Lubbock: Texas Tech University Press, 2003.
Watson, Julia, and Sidonie Smith, "Introduction: Mapping Women's Self-Representation at Visual/Textual Interfaces." In *Interfaces: Women, Autobiography, Image, Performance,* edited by Smith and Watson. Ann Arbor: University of Michigan Press, 2002.
Wells, Mary. *The Memoirs of Mrs. Sumbel, Late Wells.* 3 vols. London: C. Chapple, 1811.
Wendorf, Richard. *The Elements of Life: Biography and Portrait Painting in Stuart and Georgian England.* Oxford: Clarendon Press, 1990.
———. *Sir Joshua Reynolds: The Painter in Society.* Cambridge: Harvard University Press, 1998.
West, Shearer. *The Image of the Actor: Verbal and Visual Representation in the Age of Garrick and Kemble.* New York: St. Martin's Press, 1991.
———. "The Public and Private Roles of Sarah Siddons." In *A Passion for Performance: Sarah Siddons and Her Portraits,* edited by Robyn Asleson, 1–40. Los Angeles: The J. Paul Getty Museum, 1999.
———. "Siddons, Celebrity, and Regality." In *Theatre and Celebrity in Britain, 1660–2000,* edited by Mary Luckhurst and Jane Moody, 191-213. New York: Palgrave Macmillan, 2005.
Whitley, William T. *Thomas Gainsborough.* London: Smith, Elder, 1915.
Williams, Anne. *Art of Darkness: A Poetics of Gothic.* Chicago: University of Chicago Press, 1995.

Index

actresses, 1, 2, 5, 44; anxieties surrounding, 1, 21, 24, 75, 102; audience expectations of, 4, 5, 7, 9, 11, 12, 14, 20–21, 29; biographies of, 3, 9, 16, 147, 151n33; bodies of, 3, 6, 17, 20, 29; celebration of, 8, 10; class status of, 5, 11, 17, 19, 20, 23, 24, 30, 75, 102; and ghosting, 6–8; legitimacy of, 2, 10, 21; memoirs of, 4, 5, 7, 8, 9, 11, 12, 14–17, 20–21, 25, 33, 147, 151n33; objectification of, 4, 17, 21; personas of, 4, 5, 12, 14, 15, 17, 18, 20, 21–22; portraits of, 2, 4, 5, 7, 8, 9, 10, 11, 12, 14, 17–21, 25; and power, 2, 3, 4, 5, 23, 30; private lives of, 10, 11, 12, 15, 147; in public sphere, 10, 14, 20; reputation of, 1, 7, 9, 12; and self-promotion, 9, 11, 12, 20; sexuality of, 1, 20, 24; and social roles, 10, 14; theatrical roles of, 3, 4, 8, 10–12, 20–21

Agreeable Surprise (O'Keefe and Arnold), 118, 130

"All Alone" (Robinson), 96

Apology for the Life of Colley Cibber (Cibber), 14–15

Arnold, Samuel, 118

Art of Dress, The (Ribeiro), 19, 159n23, 161n40, 161n47

Asleson, Robyn, 11, 27, 65, 102, 155n47

As You Like It (Shakespeare), 116, 161n44

audience, 2, 10, 17, 20–21, 29, 107, 146; expectations of, 4, 5, 7, 10–12, 14, 20–21, 29, 103, 141; and memory, 6–8, 20–21; reaction of, 23, 24, 32, 38, 132

authenticity, 2, 5, 14, 17, 24, 25, 66, 71

Author, The (Foote), 106

autobiography. *See* memoir

Babington, William, 117
Beach, Thomas, 51
Beechey, William, 29, 51–53
Betterton, Thomas, 6
Bolton, Betsy, 3
Bonds of Judgment (Topham), 116
Bratton, Jacky, 16, 103
Braudy, Leo, 8–9, 150n10, 150n12, 158n8
Briggs, Henry Perronet, 135

178

Burney, Frances, 1, 103, 130–32, 151n3, 157n71, 157n82, 161n48, 162n49, 166n61, 166n68
Burroughs, Catherine, 3, 27, 34, 151n30
Butler, Judith, 21

Campbell, Thomas, 13, 14, 28, 32–34
Carlson, Marvin, 6–7
Castle, Terry, 63–64
celebrity, 2, 4, 5, 8, 9, 27–28, 126, 146; and audience, 4, 5, 10, 11, 12, 17, 20, 24, 44; and culture, 3, 6, 8, 65, 102; and fashion, 2, 10, 18–19; fashioning of, 2, 5, 6–8, 10, 14, 15, 17, 19–21, 23–24, 25, 31, 58, 62, 74–75, 96, 101, 122–23; and femininity, 2, 4, 8, 14, 21–22, 31, 58, 96, 102–3, 132; and ghosting, 6, 7; images of, 3, 11; and marketing, 11, 12, 17, 25, 62, 221; and narrative, 60–61, 76; "real" factor of, 5; and social status, 9, 102, 147
Celebrity (Rojek), 65
Character's Theater (Freeman), 12
Charke, Charlotte, 4, 16–17, 106–8
Charlotte, Queen, 20, 22, 29, 30, 31, 36–40, 46, 47–48, 49, 141, 155n46, 157n71
Chico, Tita, 44
Cibber, Colley, 14–15, 107
Close, Anne, 62
Coleridge, Samuel Taylor, 96
Colley, Linda, 29, 154n15, 154n17, 155n46
Covent Garden Theater, 10, 109, 116, 121, 127
Cox, Jeffrey, 63, 85, 161n45
Curry, James, 117

Daguerre, Louis, 142
Darby, William, 81, 83–85
Davies, Thomas, 36
Davis, Bette, 26–27, 28
Designing Women (Chico), 44

Discourses on Art (Reynolds), 18, 160n24
Distressed Mother (Philips), 45
divas, 8, 22, 23, 25, 26, 30–31, 35, 44, 51, 103–4, 164n14, 168n1
"Diversions" (Foote), 107
Downman, John, 110
Drury Lane Theater, 7, 10, 34, 40, 43, 45, 109, 152n48, 156n48

Engel, Laura, 165n43
Evelina (Burney), 1, 157n82

Farren, Elizabeth, 10, 149n2, 165n38
fashion, 1, 2, 17–20, 152n48, 152n50, 152n52
Fashioning Gothic Bodies (Spooner), 64
femininity, 1, 2, 9, 35, 102; cultural constructions of, 2, 8, 10, 13, 22, 23–24, 31, 61, 66, 103, 114, 132, 146; and identity, 8, 21–22, 61, 96; and ideology, 9, 15, 31; illusion of, 5
Fenton, Lavinia, 4
First English Actresses, The (Howe), 3
Foote, Samuel, 107
Fox, Charles, 72, 96, 159n17
Freeman, Lisa, 12

Gainsborough, Thomas, 10, 14, 18, 19, 29, 36–38, 53, 64, 65–66, 71, 72, 76, 110, 135, 160n34
Garrick, David, 7, 17, 19, 40–44, 51, 53, 80, 88, 92, 105
George III (king of England), 4, 24, 29, 72, 101, 117–18, 140
George, Prince of Wales, 7, 13, 22, 23, 59–60, 63, 65–67, 71, 72–74, 76, 78, 81, 84, 85, 87, 89, 91, 94–95, 159n17, 160n35, 162n53
Georgiana, Duchess of Devonshire, 96, 162n53, 163n4
"ghosting," 6–8, 60, 63–64
Godwin, William, 96

180   INDEX

gossip columns, 1, 10
Greenblatt, Stephen, 2

Hamilton, William, 40, 155n47, 156n48
Hanging the Head (Pointon), 98
Harlow, George Henry, 51
Hawkins, Leticia, 71
Haymarket Theatre, 11, 106
Hazlitt, William, 27, 28
Henry IV (Shakespeare), 116
Howe, Elizabeth, 3, 9

identity, 8, 9, 19, 147; and idealized femininity, 2, 11, 49, 102; and memory, 20; and performativity, 20–21, 103, 126; public and private, 15; self-fashioning of, 8, 62, 146
Image of the Actor, The (West), 3
Inchbald, Elizabeth, 106, 134, 151n30
Interfaces (Smith and Watson), 20
Isabella (Southerne), 40

James, Henry, 137, 138, 140
Jane Shore (Rowe), 109
Jenkins, Annabel, 106–7, 168n120
Jordan, Dorothy, 10, 24, 101, 103, 133, 149n2

Kemble, Charles, 24
Kemble, Fanny, 2, 24, 134, 146–47; and audience, 138; and authenticity, 25, 138; as author, 137; body of, 135, 139; and costume, 135; and Henry James, 137, 138, 140; and inherited celebrity, 25, 135–37, 138–39; and marriage, 137; and maternity, 137; memoirs of, 137, 138, 146, 169n9; and Queen Victoria, 25, 140–46, 170n30; photographs of, 25, 142–46; portraits of, 24–25, 135–37, 138–39, 140–42,

146; public image of, 138; and Sarah Siddons, 22, 24–25, 135–37, 139, 168n1; and self-representation, 135, 137, 138; and style, 135, 139; as theatrical diva, 24–25, 135–37, 138–39, 168n2, 169n12; and Thomas Sully, 140–42
King John (Shakespeare), 105
Kliman, Bernice, 33
Koestenbaum, Wayne, 26, 30, 51, 103, 164n14

Lady Macbeth, 7, 12, 13–14, 22, 26, 28–40, 45–53, 58, 93, 155n36
Lady Skipwith, 113
Lamb, Charles, 12, 26, 150n21
Lawrence, Thomas, 10, 18, 25, 138–40, 142, 170n19
Licensing Act of 1737, 10
Life of Lavinia Beswick (Fenton), 4
Life of Mrs. Siddons (Campbell), 14, 32. See also "Remarks on the Character of Lady Macbeth"
Lord Derby, 10
Love in a Village (Bickerstaff), 106
Love Makes a Man (Cibber), 116
Luckhurst, Mary, 3
Lyrical Tales (Robinson), 78

Macbeth (Shakespeare), 50, 53
masquerade, 18, 19, 53, 123
McDonald, Russ, 33
McPherson, Heather, 5, 27
Mellon, Harriet, 10
Mellor, Anne, 61, 151n37
Melpomene, 51, 53, 109
memoir, 1–7, 14–17, 20–21, 151n25; and fashioning celebrity, 3, 11, 15; generic patterns of, 7, 15, 16, 20, 33, 101, 105; and ghosting, 6, 7; and image-making, 12, 15; materiality of, 17
Memoirs of the Late Mrs. Robinson (Robinson), 13, 16, 23, 60, 61, 63, 64, 65, 78, 81–95, 146

Memoirs of the Life of Mrs. Sumbel Late Wells (Wells), 13, 16, 23, 60, 61, 63, 64, 65, 78, 81–95, 146
Merchant of Venice, The (Shakespeare), 116
Merry Wives of Windsor, The (Shakespeare), 116
Moody, Jane, 3, 107
muffs, 36, 67–69, 110–14, 159n23, 165n43
Mysteries of Udolpho, The (Radcliffe), 82

Narrative of the Life of Mrs. Charlotte Charke (Charke), 4, 16–17, 106–8
North, Prime Minister, 72, 159n17
Northcote, James, 14, 38, 99–101, 163n8
Notoriety (Reynolds), 122–23, 128
Nussbaum, Felicity, 5, 151n25, 161n43

O'Keefe, John, 118
"On the Tragedies of Shakespeare" (Lamb), 12

painting. *See* portraiture
Pascoe, Judith, 3, 27, 34, 151n30
Payne, Deborah, 10
Perry, Gill, 3, 11, 19, 20, 152n46, 160n24
Peterson, Linda, 16
Phillips, Thomas, 57
photography, 25, 26, 142–46, 170nn29–30
Piscine, Anthony, 53
Poems (Robinson), 78
Pointon, Marcia, 98
Porter, Jane, 96, 162n55
portraiture, 2, 4, 5, 6, 7, 17, 44, 98; and costume, 17–20; and fashioning celebrity, 11, 17, 19, 66, 152n39; and ghosting, 6, 7; and image-making, 4, 12, 17–18, 20; and theatricality, 17–19
Postlewait, Thomas, 15–16

Prince of Wales. *See* George, Prince of Wales
Provok'd Wife, The (Vanbrugh), 116
Public Characters (Topham), 120–21

Queen's Throat, The (Koestenbaum), 26, 30

Radcliffe, Ann, 83
"Remarks on the Character of Lady Macbeth" (Siddons), 14, 22–23, 26, 28, 29–30, 31–36, 38–40, 45, 46–47, 48–50, 58
Reminiscences of Sarah Kemble Siddons 1773–1785 (Siddons), 22, 26, 28, 29–30, 31–35, 40–44, 46, 47–48, 50, 53–57, 146
Reynolds, Frederick, 99, 122–24, 128
Reynolds, Joshua, 10, 14, 18, 19, 26, 27, 29, 53–57, 65–67, 69, 71, 72, 76, 78–79, 99, 110, 113–14, 135, 139, 160n24
Ribeiro, Aileen, 19, 36, 51, 152n50, 155n41, 159n23, 161n47
Richard III (Shakespeare), 105
Richards, Sandra, 3
Rise of the English Actress, The (Richards), 3
Roach, Joseph, 5–6, 27
Robinson, Mary, 2, 11, 13, 17, 96, 101, 104, 134, 137, 146–47; and audience, 60, 62, 63, 65–66, 67, 69, 71, 72, 76–79, 80, 81–82, 84, 85, 88, 91, 93, 94, 95, 96; and authenticity, 59, 60, 64, 68–69, 71, 72, 78, 79, 80, 87, 95, 104; as author, 59, 60, 61, 62, 66, 78, 80–95, 96, 159n17, 162n52; body of, 60–61, 62, 63, 65–66, 67–69, 72–74, 76–79, 80, 87–89, 91–94, 95, 161n48; and Colonel Banastre Tarleton, 72, 84, 85, 95, 159n17; and domesticity, 60, 63, 66, 85, 91–93, 94; and family, 81–87, 88–91; and fashion, 23, 59, 60–61, 64, 65–71, 72–74,

75, 78, 81, 87–91, 96, 159n23, 161n40, 161n47; and ghosting, 7–8, 63–65, 80, 81–82, 88, 91, 94, 95; Gothic celebrity, 8, 22, 23, 24, 60–61, 62–65, 66, 80, 81–82, 94, 95, 96, 102; as literary heroine, 61, 78–80, 81–94; marriage, 61–62, 69, 72, 81, 88–92, 93, 162n49; *Memoirs of the Late Mrs. Robinson,* 13, 16, 23, 60, 61, 63, 64, 65, 78, 81–95, 146, 161n42; and Meribah Lorrington, 86–87; and motherhood, 91–94, 95, 96; objectification of, 60, 62, 63, 65–66, 67–69, 71, 72–74, 79–80; parodies of, 71, 72–75, 78, 95, 160n31; as Perdita, 59, 64–65, 70, 71, 72, 75–78, 94–95; portraits of, 7, 14, 23, 60, 63, 64–71, 75–80, 88, 146, 159nn17–18, 159n23, 160n35; and the Prince of Wales, 7, 13, 22, 23, 59–60, 63, 65–67, 71, 72–74, 76, 78, 81, 84, 85, 87, 89, 91, 94–95, 162n53; public image of, 3, 7, 13, 14, 63, 71, 72–74, 78, 80, 95–96; and seduction, 5, 22, 23, 60, 63, 67, 71, 80, 81, 89, 93, 104; and self-representation, 22, 23, 59–63, 65–66, 71, 72, 81, 88, 96; and sexuality, 60–62, 63, 68–69, 72–74, 89, 93; and sympathy, 5, 7, 14, 22, 59–60, 61, 62, 63, 65, 66, 74, 76, 80, 81–82, 85, 88, 89, 91, 93–94; and theatricality, 68, 71, 80
Rogers, Samuel, 57
Rojek, Chris, 65, 67, 76
Roles of Authority (Wanko), 3, 9
Román, David, 27–28, 31
Romantic Theatricality (Pascoe), 3
Romney, George, 18, 19, 65, 66–69, 71, 72, 76, 159n16, 159n20
Rosenthal, Laura, 5, 27
Royal Academy, 11, 14, 19, 69, 98, 99
Runge, Laura, 61–62
Russell, John, 98, 99, 101

self-representation, 2, 3, 14, 21, 60–63

sentimentality, 10, 11
Sexual Suspects (Straub), 3, 29
Shakespeare Gallery, 131–32
Shakespeare, William, 10, 12, 32, 59, 66, 76, 92, 110, 128, 129, 137, 138, 140
Sheridan, Richard Brinsley, 50, 92–93, 96, 160n34
Sicilian Lover, The (Robinson), 63
Siddons, Sarah, 2, 3, 11, 13, 17, 21, 25, 59, 69, 80, 96, 101, 104, 107, 108, 116, 117, 118, 123, 124, 132, 133, 134, 137, 139, 146–47; and audiences, 27, 29, 31, 32, 34–35, 38, 40–43, 44, 45, 47, 48, 50, 53, 58, 110; and authenticity, 5, 7, 22–23, 30, 31, 47, 104, 109, 114; and David Garrick, 7, 40–44, 51, 53; and "diva" celebrity, 8, 22–23, 26, 28, 30–31, 35, 44, 51, 103; and domesticity, 22, 34–35, 38–43, 44–46, 50, 51; and ghosting, 7, 26, 28, 31, 35, 44; as Isabella, 40–45, 155n47, 156nn48–49; as Lady Macbeth, 7, 13–14, 22, 26, 28, 29–30, 31–32, 33–36, 38–40, 45–47, 48–50, 51, 53, 58, 93, 155n36; *Life of Mrs. Siddons,* 14, 28, 32–34, 151n25; and maternity, 8, 13, 22, 24, 31, 34–35, 38–43, 44–46, 50, 102; portraits of, 7, 14, 26, 27, 28, 29–30, 32, 33, 36–38, 40, 49, 51–57, 67, 110–15, 135–37, 146, 155nn41–42; public image of, 3, 5, 7, 8, 13, 27, 29–30, 31, 34–35, 36, 50–51, 57, 58; and Queen Charlotte, 22, 29–30, 36–38, 40, 46, 47–48, 49, 141; "Remarks on the Character of Lady Macbeth," 14, 22–23, 26, 28, 29–30, 31–36, 38–40, 45, 46–47, 48–50, 58; *The Reminiscences of Sarah Kemble Siddons,* 13, 22, 26, 28, 29–30, 31–35, 40–44, 46, 47–48, 50, 53–57, 146; and royalty, 8, 22–23, 24, 26, 28, 29–30, 31, 35, 44, 46–48, 49, 51, 53–57, 58,

102, 135–37, 154n14; and self-representation, 22, 26, 28, 31, 32–35, 46–48, 51, 53, 58; "Siddons-effect," 27–28, 31; as subject, 28, 31, 44, 48, 58; successful celebrity of, 13, 14, 22, 26, 27–28, 29, 30, 31, 33, 35, 40, 43–44, 45, 46, 48, 50–51, 57, 58; and Thomas Campbell, 13, 28, 32–34; as "The Tragic Muse," 26, 53–57, 58, 109, 139, 153n1
Smith, Sidonie, 20–21, 108
social codes, 4, 21, 30, 31, 35, 62, 69, 103, 115, 132
Southerne, Thomas, 40
Spectacular Flirtations (Perry), 3
Spooner, Catherine, 64
Straub, Kristina, 3, 9, 15, 29, 108
subjectivity, 3, 8, 15, 17, 20–21, 61, 64, 90–91
Sully, Thomas, 25, 138, 140–42, 170n18
Sumbel, Joseph, 24, 99, 101, 126–30, 167n87

Tarleton, Colonel Banastre, 72, 84, 85, 95, 159n17
textual codes, 2, 25
Theater and Celebrity in Britain, 1660–2000 (Luckhurst and Moody), 3
theatrical codes, 2, 25, 90
theatricality, 2, 3, 5, 24, 53, 66, 68, 71, 80, 97, 102, 104, 124, 125, 127, 130, 167n97
Topham, Edward, 7, 13, 98–99, 102, 115–16, 118–21, 122, 126, 130, 165n49, 165n51
Trip to Scotland (Whitehead), 105
Trotter, Thomas, 117

Vancenza (Robinson), 63
Van Lennep, William, 32, 169n3
Victoria (queen of England), 25, 140–46, 170n18, 170n30
visual codes, 2, 3, 14, 19, 25, 90

Walpole, Horace, 19, 161n43
Walsingham (Robinson), 63
Wanko, Cheryl, 3, 4, 9, 15, 28
Watson, Julia, 20–21
Wells, Mary, 2, 11, 13, 21, 97, 137, 146–47; and audience, 102–3, 105, 107, 110, 122, 124, 126, 128, 131–32, 133; and authenticity, 104, 108–9, 113; body of, 99, 125–26; and Charlotte Charke, 106–8; childhood of, 104–6, 110; and costume, 99, 110–15, 129–30; as Cowslip, 110, 117–18, 129, 130; and Dr. Willis, 24, 101, 119, 123, 124–26; and domesticity, 98, 115, 120, 125–26, 129; and Edward Topham, 7, 13, 98–99, 102, 115–16, 118–22, 126, 130; and Ezra Wells, 106, 127; and fame, 101, 133; and Fanny Burney, 130–32; and Frederick Reynolds, 99, 122–24, 128; and ghosting, 7, 103, 110; imitation and mimicry, 7–8, 23–24, 99, 101, 102, 103–4, 106–9, 113–15, 122–24, 133; and Joseph Sumbel, 24, 99, 101, 126–30, 167n87; and Judaism, 24, 99, 101, 126–30; "The Lady as Hebe," 99–101, 163nn6–9; and Lady Skipwith, 113; and madness, 7, 8, 13, 22, 23, 24, 97, 99, 101, 102, 103, 104, 108, 115–22, 123, 124–26, 131, 132, 133, 134, 164n20, 165n56, 166n58, 166n68; as Marie Antoinette, 123–24, 129; and maternity, 98–101, 105, 113, 115–16, 118, 120–21, 124–26, 129–30; *Memoirs of the Life of Mrs. Sumbel Late Wells*, 23, 99, 101, 104–6, 109, 115, 118–22, 124–30, 133–34, 146; and notoriety, 2, 8, 23–24, 102, 103, 104, 113, 115, 122, 128, 133, 134; personas of, 101, 102, 121, 128; portraits of, 7, 14, 24, 98–101, 110–15, 146; public image of, 3, 7, 13, 14, 121, 126, 128, 131, 133–34; and Sarah Siddons, 7, 23–24,

101, 103, 107, 108–15, 116, 124, 133; and satire, 5, 103, 127; and self-representation, 97, 101–2, 104, 105, 113, 119, 121, 122–23, 128, 133; and sexuality, 99, 101, 105, 109, 113, 127; status as "diva," 103, 104; and subversiveness, 23–24, 103, 109, 118, 124; and theatricality, 5, 24, 97, 101, 102, 103, 104, 106, 107–8, 116, 117–18, 122–26, 127, 130–32, 134, 165n42; theatrical roles, 105–6, 109, 110, 116, 122–24, 128, 130; the Weymouth episode, 117–18; and *The World*, 115–16, 121, 165n49

West, Benjamin, 29, 36, 40
West, Shearer, 3, 5, 18, 27, 29 152 n39, 153n1
Wilkinson, Tate, 107
Willis, Frances, 24, 101, 119, 123, 124–26

Winter's Tale, The (Shakespeare), 59, 76, 94, 116
Wollstonecraft, Mary, 92, 96, 162n49, 166n68
women: anxieties surrounding, 1, 4, 8, 12, 21, 58, 61, 66, 80, 113; and desire, 4, 23, 60, 61; and fame, 3, 4, 5, 58, 132; objectification of, 4; and power, 5, 8, 21, 22–23, 30, 58; in the public sphere, 4, 12, 15, 21, 38, 66, 80, 132; and traditional gender roles, 1, 4, 12, 15, 22
Women in British Romantic Theater (Burroughs), 3
Women, Nationalism, and the Romantic Stage (Bolton), 3
World, The (Wells), 115–16, 121, 165n49
Wrongs of Woman (Wollstonecraft), 92, 96, 162n49, 166n68

www.ingramcontent.com/pod-product-compliance
Lightning Source LLC
Chambersburg PA
CBHW030138240426
43672CB00005B/181